Credits

This book is not sponsored, endorsed by, or otherwise affiliated with any companies or the products featured in this book. This is not an official publication.

• Editor in Chief – Bill Gill, AKA "Pojo"
• Creative Director & Graphic Design – Jon Anderson
• Publisher – Bob Baker
• Contributors – Andy Diehl, David Merrell, Eric Gerson, Douglas J. VanDerveer, Israel Quiroz, Jesse Zeller, Brian Valdez

Copyright © 2002 by Triumph Books

An Enjoyable Job!

This was not one of the toughest assignments I've ever had. I've had jobs pumping gas, being a busboy, working in a machine shop, working in a warehouse, bagging groceries, working as an Engineer after college, etc. (You get the point.) They were all jobs to earn money for living expenses and to support hobbies.

Sometimes though, folks catch a lucky break. And one of their hobbies becomes their job. Case in point: the Pojo's Unofficial Absolute Dragon Ball Z book you are reading right now. This is one of my lucky breaks.

Two years ago I was fortunate enough to be Editor-in-Chief of Pojo's Unofficial Dragon Ball Z. We were complimented by many fans for finally putting out a book that accurately captured the happenings of Dragon Ball, Dragon Ball Z, Dragon Ball GT, the collectible card game, and the video games.

Now, I'm a DBZ-aholic! I love the anime. I watch Cartoon Network daily like most of you guys, even if I've seen the episode 5 times. I have about 5 dozen DBZ DVDs, VHS tapes, and Video CDs from Asia. I love the action figures (though mine don't ever leave their packages). I find the collectible card game fascinating. I honestly stink at it, but it's still fun to post the DBZ CCG Card of the Day on Pojo.com and see how good players think.

Over the last couple years I've got to meet and interview DBZ voice actors from Funimation. I met Grant Irwin from Irwin Toys. I've seen the DBZ Hummer in person. I've made a lot of friends with the people at Score (the folks who make the DBZ Collectible Card Game). My kids and I have had our photos taken with Goku and Vegeta countless times. And Artbox even made us our very own Pojo.com Super Saiyan Goku card to give away to Pojo fans. It's been a blast!

Now, more than two years after our first book, we've been asked to follow-up with a new one. This was not a difficult decision. There's so much stuff to cram in a book! It is hard to know where to start and stop. So I listened to my heart, and listened to Dragon Ball fans, and recruited the most knowledgeable Dragon Ball writers from across North America. And we put together another awesome book.

Inside you'll find Episode Summaries for DBZ and Dragon Ball GT. You'll find Movie Summaries for all the movies. You'll find a Fight Guide that details every fight from the Dragon Ball and DBZ mangas. You'll find a great article on collecting DBZ Toys. You'll find 16 pages exploring the immensely popular Collectible Card Game. You'll find Biographies for over 500 characters, and a whole lot more.

Hopefully, you'll enjoy this book so much, it won't take two years to make a 3rd one. ;-)

Enjoy,

Pojo

Inside This Book

Page 6
The Ultimate Episode Guide for DBZ
A review of every single DBZ episode from the Android Saga through the Buu saga. That's 151 episodes for you to peruse.

Page 18
Ultimate Movie Guide
A review/summary of every single Dragon Ball & Dragon Ball Z movie and TV Special ever made.

Page 26
Ultimate Fight Guide
A guide to all 187 fights that occurred in the Dragon Ball & DBZ Mangas.

Page 38
Dragon Ball GT Episode Guide
64 episodes of Dragon Ball GT took place after Dragon Ball Z. This is where Goku & Vegeta go Super Saiyan 4!

Page 46
Dragon Ball Z Video Game Reviews
We have a look at 2 games for your Game Boy Advance.

Page 48
The World of Dragon Ball Z Collectible Toys
A detailed look at some of the hottest action figures money can buy.

Pojo's Unofficial ABSOLUTE Dragon Ball Z

This book is not sponsored, endorsed by, or otherwise affiliated with any of the companies or products featured in this book. This is not an official publication.

Page 56
Dragon Ball Z Collectible Card Game Beginner's Guide
Want to learn about this hot CCG? Here's the place to start.

Page 60
Dragon Ball Z CCG Top 10 Lists
Our Top 10 from every set and the promo cards.

Page 68
Cheap @$$ Deck
A CCG deck for those on a small budget.

Page 70
Killer Deck
One of the best players in the world has his thoughts on a Killer Deck you can play.

Page 72
Dragon Ball 3D
You've seen a lot of DBZ, but never quite like this.

Page 80
Dragon Ball Character Biographies
From A to Z, you'll find over 500 character bios here.

ENJOY!

The Ultimate Dragon Ball Z Episode Guide

— By Bill Gill and David Merrell

We pick things up with the Imperfect Cell Saga. Why are we starting with the Imperfect Cell Saga? Because we already documented summaries for the earlier sagas in our previous book - Pojo's Unofficial Total Dragon Ball Z – ISBN #: 1572434163. We had episode reviews for the Saiyan Saga, the Namek Saga, the Ginyu Force Saga, the Frieza Saga, the Garlic Jr. Saga, the Trunks Saga, and the Android Saga.

The set up: Trunks has traveled from the future to help the Z Warriors fight the androids. Androids 17 and 18 are wreaking havoc on the world. Goku is recovering from a serious illness, and can't fight for a dozen episodes or so. Cell has stolen Trunks time machine, and has come to modern day earth to absorb Androids 17 and 18 and become the Ultimate Warrior.

Imperfect Cell Saga

125. Seized with Fear
Trunks, Krillin, & Bulma find Trunks' Time Machine covered in moss. The shell of the Cell is nearby. Trunks is really confused now. Why is Cell's shell here? This is not good at all!

126. The Reunion
Piccolo fuses with Kami in hopes of destroying Androids 17, 18 & Cell. Piccolo is like a Super Namek now. On earth, Cell is sucking up entire humans left and right to increase his energy.

127. Borrowed Powers
Piccolo finds Cell. Cell and Piccolo talk and duel a bit. Piccolo wants to know why Cell is killing innocent people. Piccolo senses the Ki of other Z Warriors in Cell. He is confused. How does Cell have the Ki of other Z Warriors?

128. His Name is Cell
Cell catches Piccolo from behind and starts absorbing Piccolo's energy. Piccolo breaks free, but one of his arms is shriveled like a raisin. Piccolo tells Cell he'll quit fighting and be absorbed, if Cell explains his past. Cell accepts. (Cell doesn't know about Piccolo's regenerative powers). Cell tells Piccolo he is made of the cells of the greatest warriors in the universe (Goku, Frieza, Vegeta, etc). Dr. Gero created him. Cell tells Piccolo he will be complete, and the strongest warrior in the universe, once he absorbs 17 and 18. The long explanation gives Piccolo enough time to regenerate his arm. Cell is ticked.

129. Piccolo's Folly
Krillin & Trunks arrive to help Piccolo. Cell needs to absorb Androids 17 & 18 to be strong, and he knows he can't beat this trio. Cell fires off a solar flare, and gets away. Vegeta sees Piccolo and is ticked as the Super Namek appears more powerful than a Super Saiyan.

130. Laboratory Basement
Krillin & Trunks fly off to Dr. Gero's lab to look for clues about Cell. They find plans for Android 17 and take them. They also find Cell's embryo. They destroy the lab and the embryo before they leave.

131. Our Hero Awakens
Cell feasts on an entire city for a snack. Goku finally wakes from his illness, and is ready to fight. Krillin finds Cell about to snack on a mother and child and gets ticked off. Krillin fights the monster so the family can escape. Piccolo and Tien show up to save Krillin from certain death and Cell gets away again.

132. Time Chamber
Vegeta and Goku agree there is a level beyond Super Saiyan. Goku, Gohan, Trunks and Vegeta head for the training place where they can get a year of training in one day. The androids go to Goku's house, only to find he has left. Everyone continues to search for Cell.

133. The Monster is Coming
Piccolo shows up at Goku's house with the androids. Piccolo wants to kill 17 and 18 so that Cell can't absorb their energy and reach full power. Piccolo and 17 start a fun battle. No one wins. Yet!

134. He's Here
Piccolo and 17 battle on. Bulma is

studying 17's plans, trying to figure out a way to disable it. As Piccolo and 17 battle, Cells shows up on a cliff. Uh-oh!

135. Up to Piccolo
Cell approaches Piccolo, 17 and 18. Cell is trying to get 17. As he is about to kill 17, Piccolo punches Cell away. Cell keeps repeating that he is powerful and 17 and 18 need to be part of him so he can be perfect. Piccolo and 17 team-up and start fighting Cell. Piccolo uses his strongest attack on Cell and it doesn't even scratch him. Cell appears to kill Piccolo. Tien watches in horror.

136. Silent Warrior
Cell gets ready to absorb 17. Android 16 determines that even though he is programmed to kill Goku, he can't allow Cell to absorb 17. As Cell catches 17, 16 jumps in the way and starts beating on him. He tells Cell that he is as strong as Cell. 16 rips off Cell's absorbing tail, but Cell regenerates it. 16 realizes he miscalculated and cannot defeat Cell.

137. Say Goodbye #17
Android 16 hits Cell with a barrage of power that blows Cell into a hole on the island. Everyone thinks Cell is dead. We all know better, but Android 17 doesn't. Cell pops out of the ground behind 17 and finally absorbs him! Cell transforms into a more powerful being. Androids 16 and 18 try to run away, but the new Cell is too fast. Cell beats a dent into 16's head. Cell gets ready to absorb 18 to become invincible. Tien jumps into the fray and puts Cell down temporarily.

138. Sacrifice
In order to prevent Cell from reaching his final form, Tien joins the battle. He is able to keep the genetic monster pinned down with his Tri Beam attack while Androids 16 and 18 escape. (This is one of the coolest scenes in DBZ Episode History!) He soon runs out of energy and falls to the ground unconscious. Goku uses Instant Transmission to step in and save Tien from Cell's grasp. To his shock, he finds Piccolo still alive as well. Goku teleports back to the lookout to find that Vegeta and Trunks are emerging from the Hyperbolic Time Chamber...

139. Saiyans Emerge
Vegeta and Trunks have completed their training. Vegeta says he can handle everything now and heads off to do so. Goku and Gohan move into the Hyperbolic Time Chamber to begin their training. Meanwhile, Cell begins destroying islands in an effort to find Android 18.

140. Super Vegeta
Cell continues destroying islands in his search for Android 18. He finally reaches the island she is hiding on, but before he can destroy it, Vegeta arrives. They land on the island and after some boasting, Vegeta powers up. His new power amazes everyone, including Cell. With lightning speed, he lands a punch to Cell's stomach. The battle has begun.

141. Bow to the Prince
The battle between Vegeta and Cell is under way. Vegeta is dominating every aspect of the fight. Cell can't lay a finger on him. He declares himself to be Super Vegeta. In the Hyperbolic Time Chamber, Goku and Gohan continue their training.

142. Hour of Temptation
Cell pulls out all the stops to try to beat Vegeta. He even uses Vegeta's Gallic Gun attack, but nothing works. Vegeta continues to pound on him. In a last ditch effort, Cell tries to convince Vegeta to let him absorb Android 18 so he can provide a bigger challenge.

143. Krillin's Decision
Cell continues to try to persuade Vegeta to let him absorb Android 18. Krillin is also searching for 18 so he can shut her down with the controller Bulma gave him. Once he finds her, he can't bring himself to do it. Meanwhile, Vegeta agrees to let Cell absorb 18. Trunks steps in to block the monster's path. As the episode ends, Cell spots Android 18....

144. The Last Defense
Cell makes his charge for Android 18, but Trunks is there to stop him. Vegeta blasts Trunks out of the way to clear the path for Cell. Trunks will not be denied as he attacks his own father to stop Cell. In the end, Trunks cannot stop the inevitable. Cell absorbs 18 and begins his ultimate transformation.

145. Cell is Complete
Cell's transformation is shaking the entire planet, and he becomes his perfect form. In the Hyperbolic Time Chamber, Gohan becomes a Super Saiyan. Meanwhile, Krillin is crushed by the loss of 18, so he launches an attack on the genetic monster. Cell drops Krillin with one kick, and the Z Fighter is down for the count.

146. Vegeta Must Pay
Trunks is able to revive Krillin with a senzu bean. Meanwhile, Vegeta steps up to collect his prize: a fight with Cell in his perfect form. Vegeta throws a barrage of punches at the monster, but to no avail. He lands a powerful kick directly to Cell's head, but even that has no effect. It appears Vegeta may have bitten off more than he can chew....

147. Trunks Ascends
Vegeta's most powerful kick does nothing to Cell. The powerful Android demonstrates his power by catapulting Vegeta with a single punch. Vegeta is sent flying into the ocean, rising after a few seconds more angry than ever. He powers up and prepares a huge energy attack. He fires the Final Flash attack at Cell and manages to blow off one of Cell's arms. Cell regenerates, and pummels Vegeta until he is no longer a Super Saiyan. Trunks begins to power up, as it looks like he will have to step in.

148. Saving Throw
Trunks powers up to battle Cell, and tells Krillin to get Vegeta out of the area while he fights. The two combatants fight evenly for a time, but then Trunks allows Cell to pound on him while Krillin rescues Vegeta. Once his father is safe and sound, Trunks charges up to his maximum power.

149. Ghost from Tomorrow
Cell and Trunks have flashbacks to their past. The two begin to fight again, and Trunks takes the upper hand. Cell declares that Trunks has surpassed him in strength, but has no chance of winning the fight....

The Cell Games Saga
150. The Cell Games
Trunks and Cell continue their battle, but this time Trunks can't hit the biological Android. After attaining the same form in the Hyperbolic Time Chamber, Goku reveals that his form is too slow to be effective. Trunks also realizes this and powers down. Rather than finish him off, Cell plans to have a tournament in 10 days. Trunks is spared for now, and it looks like the fate of the world is again on Goku's shoulders.

The ULTIMATE: DBZ Episode Guide

151. What is the Tournament?
Krillen and the revived Vegeta arrive at Trunks' position and he tells them about the tournament. Android 16 wants to help, so Krillen takes him to Bulma's for repairs. Once everyone is at Bulma's house, Master Roshi tells him or her about the past tournaments that Goku Company have competed in. Meanwhile, Cell lays the groundwork for his tournament ring.

152. The Doomsday Broadcast
Cell invades a television station and announces to the world that the Cell Games will begin in 9 days. He challenges the greatest fighters in the world to come and fight him. Cell destroys part of the city to show the world his strength and power.

153. Meet Me in the Ring
Vegeta and Trunks head to the Hyperbolic Time Chamber to prepare for another round of training. Goku and Gohan finally emerge, and both are in their Super Saiyan forms. They eat, and Trunks fills them in on what has happened. Vegeta is both amazed and angry that they act so casually as Super Saiyans. Goku uses Instant Transmission to meet Cell for the first time. After talking to Cell, Goku teleports back to the others and says he doesn't need any more training in the Hyperbolic Time Chamber. This shocks Vegeta and Piccolo. Goku says he will prepare in the outside world for the next 9 days.

154. No Worries Here
Goku and Gohan leave the lookout and stop by Korin's place. Goku powers up and asks Korin to compare his and Cell's power. Korin states that Cell is quite a bit stronger, but Goku says he figured that he was stronger. The two Super Saiyans head off to meet up with their family and friends. Vegeta and Company discuss Goku's new power. Angered that Goku has again surpassed him, Vegeta commands Piccolo to get in the Chamber and begin training immediately. Cell heads into space and blasts some rocks to warm up for the tournament.

155. A Girl Named Lime
Gohan travels to a nearby town to get groceries for his mom. He meets a girl named Lime and learns that a local con man has tricked the local people into giving up their supplies. He has built a large dome that he says will protect them from Cell. Gohan has a run in with one of Goku's former enemies, General Tao. When the General realizes Gohan's identity, he runs for his life! Gohan destroys the dome to show that it won't stop Cell. He selects the groceries he came for, and heads home.

156. Memories of Gohan
Chi Chi and Goku have flashbacks about Gohan as he was growing up. Chi Chi remembers how hard it was to come up with a name for him, and Goku remembers the time Gohan blasted his way through a tree. Later in the day, Gohan has a birthday party.

157. A New Guardian
Goku has been relaxing ever since he left the Hyperbolic Time Chamber. Cell manages to put him back on edge when he destroys the Royal Military that is sent to kill him. Knowing that all the damage Cell has caused will need to be fixed, Goku decides its time to revive the Dragon Balls.

158. Dende's Dragon
Goku uses Instant Transmission to teleport to King Kai. He asks for the location of the Nameks so he can find a new Guardian. Goku teleports to Namek, and Dende is chosen to be the new Guardian of Earth. He teleports him back to the lookout, and Dende creates a new dragon. This new dragon is capable of granting two wishes instead of just one. Goku heads out to begin collecting the Dragon Balls.

159. The Puzzle of General Tao
Goku's quest for the Dragon Balls leads him to a fortress of a mob boss. The mobster's bodyguard is none other than General Tao! Remembering how strong Goku is, General Tao proposes that Goku solve three puzzles for the Dragon Balls. The puzzles are little trinkets that Goku must take apart. Goku agrees to this, and while he is working on the puzzles, General Tao and the mobster escape with all the Dragon Balls. Goku eventually solves all the puzzles and teleports to their new location. He collects the Dragon Balls and later finds the last one.

160. The Games Begin
Goku and Gohan meet the others at the lookout. They all head to the tournament. A Z-TV reporter is the first to arrive at the scene, followed by the world champion Hercule, aka Mr. Satan. Vegeta is the next to arrive, and after him Android 16. Finally, when Goku and Company arrive, it looks like the tournament is about to begin. Goku says he'll go first, but Hercule insists that he should go first. This is not a good career move by the champ....

161. Losers Fight First
The Z Fighters decide to let Hercule go first. Before he can begin, two of his students drop in from a helicopter. They convince Hercule to let them take care of Cell. He lets them, but Cell crushes both students without even lifting a finger. Hercule tries to fight the monster. He punches him while Cell stands there. He finally slaps Hercule into a nearby mountain. Goku steps into the ring and the real tournament begins.

162. Goku vs Cell
The battle starts between Goku and Cell. The two fighters move at extraordinary speeds. Only the Z Fighters can keep up with their movements. Hercule describes this as an optical illusion. Goku nearly knocks Cell out of the ring, but Cell says he was just playing a little joke on Goku. They battle some more, and Cell lands a few good hits. The two announce that the warm-up is over. Goku begins to charge up to maximum power...

163. Cell's Bag of Tricks
Goku powers up to his max, and the others are amazed by the energy he is releasing. After he is done, Cell begins to power up. The two appear equal. The fight begins again, but this time Cell is using some new tricks. He first uses Tien's multi-form technique and splits himself into four beings. Goku manages to beat all four of them, and Cell is forced back to normal. Next, Cell uses Frieza's last attack. He then powers up a KameHameHa Wave strong enough to destroy the Earth. Goku lures the blast into space and uses Instant Transmission to get out of its way. Goku has done well in combating Cell's attacks, but the android has enhanced his speed to the point where Goku can't track him. The situation is looking grim for Goku.

164. No More Rules
Cell destroys the ring and decides that the survivor will be declared the winner. The two lock horns again. The energy the two are emitting causes rocks to float off the ground. After Cell gets in a few good shots, Goku flies high into the air and powers up a huge KameHameHa wave. At first everyone thinks Goku is bluffing because the blast will destroy the Earth,

The ULTIMATE: DBZ Episode Guide

but he keeps increasing the power. Even Cell is worried. Goku uses Instant Transmission at the last second and appears right in front of Cell. He fires at point-blank range, and Cell's head is completely blown off. It appears Goku has put the monster down for good, or has he?

165. The Fight is Over

It looked as if Goku had defeated Cell with a KameHameHa wave at point-blank range, but the android returns again by regenerating his head. He and Goku continue fighting. Goku fires a ton of energy blasts at Cell, but he creates an energy shield to block them. Cell claims Goku has used up all his energy. To everyone's shock, Goku agrees with him! He powers down, and tells Cell he surrenders. The situation has gone from bad to worse.

166. Faith in a Boy

Goku has given up. Cell announces that if no one can beat him, he will wreak havoc upon Earth. Goku says there is one more person to fight him, and he declares Gohan to be that person. Everyone is dumbfounded by Goku's decision. After a pep talk from Goku, Gohan steps up to the challenge. Before the fight begins, Goku gives Cell a senzu bean! He says that if he didn't, it wouldn't be a fair fight. Cell and Gohan begin to fight, and Gohan holds his own. Cell kicks it up a notch and begins to pummel Gohan. The young Super Saiyan smiles and wipes the blood from his mouth.

Looks like the fight could be interesting after all....

167. Gohan's Desperate Plea

The battle between Gohan and Cell continues. Cell sends Gohan flying into a mountain of rocks, and everyone things he's dead. Much to their relief, he's still alive. Upon emerging from the rubble, Gohan tries to convince Cell that the fight is useless. He tells the genetic android the past history of his hidden power. His speech has the opposite effect on Cell. He now wants to see Gohan's hidden power for himself. He smacks Gohan around, and eventually Gohan retaliates, giving Cell a bloody lip. Cell is more intrigued than ever. Krillen points out that this plan may backfire and get Gohan killed.

168. Android Explosion

Cell begins to pound on Gohan. He wants to inflict enough pain to push the young warrior over the edge. He puts him in a bear hug and begins to squeeze the life out of him. Piccolo berates Goku for using this strategy, saying that Gohan is not a bloodthirsty warrior. Goku begins to realize he made a mistake. He asks Krillen for a senzu bean. Before Krillen can act, Cell darts to where the Z Fighters are watching and steals the bag of senzu beans. Cell has a new plan to get Gohan angry. Suddenly Android 16 grabs him from behind, holds him in a bear hug, and attempts to self-destruct to destroy Cell. Krillen points out that when Bulma repaired 16, his bomb was taken out. Now defenseless, Cell destroys the nature-loving android. Cell now proceeds with his plan. If he can't make Gohan angry directly, he will do so by hurting his friends. He creates 7 Cell Juniors, tiny replicas of himself. They fly towards the Z Fighters and prepare to attack....

169. Children of Cell Attack

The Cell Juniors are on the attack. At first the Z Fighters are able to hold their own, but soon they falter. They go down one by one, until only Vegeta and Trunks can defend themselves. Meanwhile, Hercule is about to leave to fix his "stomach problem" when the head of Android 16 asks for his help. He asks to be thrown towards Gohan. Android 16 says that as champion of Earth, he should help out. Hercule agrees and carries him towards Gohan and Cell. Once he gets close enough, he hurls the head in their direction. Once there, 16 says that Gohan must let it all go. Cell claims he will do things his way, and crushes the Android's head, putting him out of commission for good. This is the last straw for Gohan. He lets out a thunderous scream. His hidden power has now been awakened. Its time for Cell to pay the piper...

170. The Unleashing

Gohan powers up fully, and Cell thinks he is making the same mistake Trunks did. Cell sends his tiny minions after Gohan, but the young Super Saiyan destroys them all one by one. He steals the senzu beans back from Cell, and gives them to Trunks to pass around. With all the Cell Juniors destroyed, Cell himself is next.

171. The Unstoppable Gohan

Trunks passes around the senzu beans to revive the Z Warriors. Meanwhile, the battle between Gohan and Cell begins. Cell can't get a hit on Gohan. After throwing a barrage of punches and kicks that all miss, Cell announces that he will now use his maximum power. Until now he had been holding back. Cell's powering up causes the entire planet to shake. Upon reaching his maximum power, he lands a punch directly to Gohan's face. To Cell's shock, Gohan is unharmed. Cell is about to attack again when Gohan lands two blows of his own. These two attacks bring Cell to his knees. Gohan may have just beaten Cell with two punches.

172. Cell's Might Breakdown

Cell is very angry that his attack did nothing to Gohan, and he is severely hurt by Gohan's two incredible punches. He tries the Z Fighter's techniques, Destructo Disc and Special Beam Canon, but neither are effective. He then flies into the sky and charges up a full power KameHameHa wave. Cell says he will blow up the Earth! Everyone fears this is the end. Cell fires the wave, but at the last minute Gohan counters with a KameHameHa wave of his own. Gohan's blast sends the attack back at Cell. Cell loses some of his appendages, but he is still alive. The others cry out for Gohan to finish Cell, but he wants to let him suffer. Cell regenerates, and bulks up his body. He attacks again, and Gohan lands a vicious blow to the stomach. Cell proceeds to vomit up Android 18, and he begins to revert back to his second form. The tide has turned on Cell.

173 A Hero's Farewell

Cell, now in his imperfect second stage, tries to attack Gohan, but he is outclassed. Gohan beats on him a little more. Realizing he can't defeat Gohan,

The ULTIMATE: DBZ Episode Guide

Cell puffs up his body into a balloon-like state. He is going to self-destruct and take out the planet. Gohan goes to stop him, but he might blow up if he is touched. Goku decides that he must step in and save the planet. He uses the Instant Transmission technique and transports them to King Kai's planet. It was the only place he could think of at the time. Cell blows up, and kills Goku, King Kai, Bubbles and Gregory. Just when the planet seems safe once and for all, a powerful wind catches everyone off guard. An energy blast comes from nowhere and hits Trunks right in the chest. It seems to be a fatal blow. The culprit is none other than Cell. He is back, and seems to be stronger than ever.

174. Cell Returns

Cell explains how he survived his own self-destruction, and how he returned to his perfect form. Gohan is ready to fight the monster again. Meanwhile, Vegeta sees his lifeless son on the ground and realizes that he has ignored him and treated him bad the entire time he'd been here in the past. Trunks has come back to save them, and Vegeta has ignored him. This enrages the Saiyan prince, and he charges at Cell. He blasts the android with everything he has. It is not enough, and Cell puts Vegeta down with a single backhand. He prepares to finish him off with an energy blast, but Gohan blocks the attack.

He is left with a hurt arm that he cannot move. Gohan will now have to fight Cell with only one arm. Cell isn't going to go easy on him. He begins to charge up a KameHameHa wave...

175. The Horror Won't End

Cell remembers his road to perfection. He now realizes what Dr. Gero meant by "ultimate perfection". Meanwhile, Goku talks to Gohan through King Kai. Gohan is ready to give in, but Goku convinces him to keep fighting. Gohan powers up and readies a KameHameHa wave of his own. The two warriors fire their blasts as the episode ends.

176. Saving the World

The two KameHameHa waves strike each other. At first they seem to be equal, but Cell's wave begins to overpower Gohan's wave. Goku continues to root on Gohan from the Other World. He gets him to unleash all of his power, but even this is not enough. The remaining Z Fighters attack Cell to try and help Gohan, but only get hurt in the process. Vegeta finally steps in and fires an attack at Cell. This is all the momentum Gohan needs. With a ferocious scream, Gohan gives one final push, and his blast overcomes Cell. The monster is finally destroyed. The Earth is safe again.

177. Goku's Noble Decision

Everyone flies to the lookout to summon the dragon. It's time to clean up the mess Cell made. They wish everyone back to life. Trunks is revived. They try and wish Goku back, but the dragon refuses because he has already been revived once. Goku talks to them through King Kai, and says he wants to stay dead because he causes too much trouble for Earth. Everyone remembers their favorite moments with Goku as the episode ends.

178. One More Wish

The Z Fighters still have one more wish. Krillen wishes for Android 18's bomb to be taken out, and that's the end of the wishing for now. Everyone leaves the tower. Gohan has to break the bad news to Chi Chi about Goku. Meanwhile, Trunks heads back to the future.

179. Free the Future

Trunks returns to his time. He hears over the radio that the androids are on the attack. He heads out to fight them. Once he finds them, he powers up to Super Saiyan and quickly destroys them both. Later as he is about to head back into the past to tell everyone the great news, an unwelcome guest arrives. It's Cell in his first form. The two fight for a while, but Cell is clearly no match for Trunks. Cell is about to fire a KameHameHa wave when Trunks destroys him with a massive blast. Dr. Gero's reign of terror is finally over in both timelines.

Saiyaman Saga

180. Warriors of the Dead

Goku and King Kai travel in the Other World to the home of the Grand Kai. They meet West Kai and his student Pikkon. Grand Kai asks Pikkon to take care of some "trouble" in HFIL (If you are a newbie, that's "HELL" with parts E & L moved around for us Americans.) The trouble is Cell. Goku goes along, but is stunned when Pikkon beats Cell and Frieza. The problem is solved and it looks like Goku has a new friend and some new competition.

181. Tournament Begins

The four Kais decide to have a tournament to determine who is the best teacher. Goku's first fight is against Catapee. Catapee tries to defeat Goku by tickling him into submission. Goku is able to blow him away by powering up. Catapee begins a metamorphisis. When South Kai says it will take 1200 years for the change to finish, Grand Kai declares Goku the winner.

182. Water Fight

Goku's next fight is against Arqua. The fighter may look puny, but he gains the advantage by turning the ring into water. Goku blinds Arqua with Solar Flare, then knocks him out of the ring with a KameHameHa wave. Meanwhile, Pikkon battles one of King Kai's students named Olibu. It's a close match at first, but Pikkon comes out on top. This has Goku very excited about the challenge Pikkon represents.

183. Final Round

Goku defeats a dinosaur-looking fighter named Meriaco. Pikkon also defeats his opponent. The final match is set. The fight begins with neither fighter gaining the upper hand. Finally, the two decide to get down to business. Pikkon removes his weighted clothing, and Goku powers up to Super Saiyan.

184. Goku vs. Pikkon

The battle between Pikkon and Goku heats up. After dodging a few of Goku's energy blasts, Pikkon traps Goku with his Hyper Tornado Attack. Goku escapes by using the Super Kaio Ken technique. The two fight a bit more, and Pikkon uses his Thunder Flash attack. Goku is devastated by the attack and Pikkon uses it again. On his third attempt, Goku notices a weakness. He uses Instant Transmission to get out of the way and hits Pikkon with the KameHameHa wave. Pikkon is knocked out of the ring. Goku has not won however, as Grand Kai states that both fighters touched the roof of the building. The roof is the same as the floor, so both fighters lose. He does say that he will train both fighters in 200 years, and this pleases Goku.

185. Gohan Goes to High School

The ULTIMATE: DBZ Episode Guide

Seven years have passed since the fight with Cell, and now Gohan is going to High School. On the way there, he runs into some criminals robbing a bank. He goes Super Saiyan and stops them. The appearance of this "Gold Fighter" has everyone talking. Gohan later has a problem containing his powers in gym class. Hercule Satan's daughter, Videl, suspects Gohan and follows him home. He easily evades her and heads to Bulma's house for a solution to his new problem.

186. I Am Saiyaman

Gohan asks Bulma to make a disguise for him so he can fight crime without anyone knowing his true identity. Gohan likes the costume he gets, but Bulma and Trunks think it's ugly. Gohan comes up with the name "The Great Saiyaman" for his alter ego. Later in school, Videl gets a distress call about a hijacked bus. She runs to the rescue and Gohan is not far behind. Videl handles the hijackers, but the bus goes over the cliff. Fortunately, Saiyaman is there to save the day. In Ginyu Force fashion, Saiyaman strikes a pose for the people before leaving.

187. Gohan's First Date

A girl in Gohan's class sees him changing out of his Saiyaman outfit. She threatens to reveal his secret if he doesn't go on a date with her. While on the date, they spot a building on fire. Gohan changes into Saiyaman and runs to help Videl, who is already trying to stop the fire. They use a water tank to put out the flames. Videl notices when Gohan slips away later, and she confronts him. When Gohan's date sees him talking to Videl, she gets angry and tells Videl his secret. Fortunately for Gohan, the secret is that he wears teddy bear underwear. His date has seen him change in the locker room. The next day she dumps Gohan and tells everyone his secret. Gohan must love school....

188. Rescue Videl

The Red Shark Gang kidnaps the mayor of Hercule City. They do so because they want to fight Hercule. However, Videl is the one they get. Gohan doesn't think she can handle the entire gang, so he follows behind as Saiyaman. He takes care of the rest of the gang while Videl takes down the leader. The mayor is saved, and all is good. Videl thanks Saiyaman for his help, but promises she will unmask him someday.

189. Blackmail

A local baby dinosaur named Chobi is stolen by a circus. Saiyaman rescues Chobi, but he is chased by Videl for stealing from the circus. Chobi's parents turn up in the city looking for their baby, and Videl realizes what Saiyamon is doing is right. The next day in school, Videl notices a scratch on Gohan that Saiyaman received the previous day. She figures out the identity of the Great Saiyaman. She tells him he must compete in the World Martial Arts tournament or she will tell everyone his secret. He must also teach her to fly. Gohan has such a way with women...

190. I'll Fight Too!

Gohan saves a plane from crashing, typical work for Saiyaman. He heads to Bulma's house to rework his costume. He can't wear a helmet in the World Martial Arts tournament. Vegeta decides to enter the tournament so he can beat Gohan. Suddenly they hear another voice saying he'll be in the tournament. It's Goku! He gets to return to the Earth for one day. After hearing the news, Gohan rushes to tell all of their friends. Piccolo, Krillen, and 18 also decide to enter the tournament.

191. The Newest Super Saiyan

Gohan and Goten train for the tournament. During a sparring match, Goten becomes a Super Saiyan. Gohan is shocked, so Goten tells him how he first transformed while sparring with Chi Chi. It turns out Trunks can also become a Super Saiyan. They spar some more and Goten gets upset because Gohan can fly and he can't. Gohan says he will teach him, but before he can do it, he sees Videl flying towards his house. Gohan and Goten rush home only to find Videl and Chi Chi in a screaming contest. Now Gohan has two students....

192. Take Flight Videl

Gohan starts the flying lesson by teaching Videl about a person's energy. Goten can easily tap into his energy because he's already a Super Saiyan, but Videl has a hard time. She eventually gets it. Next, they actually practice flying. Goten picks up the trick pretty quick, but Videl is still behind. She is able to get off the ground and decides that it's enough for one lesson. After a conversation about her cutting her hair short, she storms off. Meanwhile, Goku is training for the tournament in the Other World and Vegeta discovers that Trunks can tun into a Super Saiyan. This comes as quite a shock for the Saiyan prince.

193. Gather for the Tournament

Videl is able to master the art of flying. Afterward, she leaves to train for the tournament. Gohan and Goten also begin their real training. Once the day of the tournament arrives, everyone meets up on the island where it's held. To everyone's delight, Goku shows up. This tournament looks to be very interesting....

194. Camera Shy

Videl meets up with Saiyaman and walks with him into the tournament. This angers Sharpener, a boy from their school. He decides to find out who the Great Saiyaman is once and for all. All his efforts come up short. Next, the Z Fighters have to punch a machine to measure their strength. Despite the fact that they only tap it, they all come up with higher scores than Mr. Satan does. Vegeta is angry about the whole thing so he just punches the machine through the wall. The Z Fighters are now in the tournament, but which of them will come out on top? Only time will tell...

World Tournament Saga

195. The World Tournament

Vegeta has just finished destroying the punching machine in one blow, so everyone heads over to the Junior Tournament. On the way they meet up with Gohan and Videl. Before the fighting begins, they show some "video" taken from the Cell Games. It turns out to be some badly doctored video showing Mr. Satan beating Cell. After the video, the Junior Tournament begins. The fighting is very childish until Trunks steps into the ring for his fight. He fights a kid named Idasa who tried to bully him in the locker room. Trunks puts him down with two hits. The tournament is underway.

196. Trunks vs. Goten

Goten and Trunks breeze through their matches and both make it to the finals. Gohan and Videl are late arriving for the match, since they had to wait for a new punching machine to be installed. Before the fight begins, it is announced that the winner gets to fight Mr. Satan in an exhibition match. The two half Saiyans put on a show for the crowd. It's just your typical Saiyan duel. Looks like Mr. Satan is going to have his hands full.

The ULTIMATE: DBZ Episode Guide

197. The Best of the Boys
It's the final round. Trunks and Goten fire energy blasts at each other, but agree not to use anymore for the remainder of the fight. Trunks grabs Goten in a stranglehold and tries to force him to give up. Goten refuses, and breaks free by going Super Saiyan. They had agreed earlier not to go SSJ in the tournament. Trunks gets angry. He claims he can beat Goten with his left arm. Goten attempts a headbutt, but Trunks dodges and turns Super Saiyan. He throws Goten in the stands and wins the fight. Next up for Trunks is a bout with Mr. Satan!

198. Big Trouble, Little Trunks
Trunks is set for his exhibition bout with Mr. Satan. Knowing the kid will crush him, Mr. Satan tells Trunks they should exchange taps on the cheek. Trunks' tap sends Mr. Satan flying out of the ring. He gets up and waves to the crowd indicating he did it on purpose. After the fight the Z Fighters head over to where the food is being served. Naturally Goku gobbles down everything in sight. As they are heading to get ready for the tournament they bump into two strange characters. Piccolo has a funny feeling about them....

199. Who Will Fight Who?
The Z Fighters walk away from Shin and Kibito (the two strange people from the previous episode) and head to the drawing for the match-ups. Trunks and Goten sneak into the back and trick a fighter named Mighty Mask and steal his costume. The drawing begins and there are some interesting matches in the first round. Krillin is fighting a guy named Pintar, Piccolo is fighting Shin, Videl matches up against Spopovich, Gohan is facing Kibito, and 18 is up against Mr. Satan. But the biggest match of the round, and possibly the tournament, is Goku vs. Vegeta! They will battle in the first round no less! The announcer tells everyone the rules. Piccolo is very stressed out having to fight Shin....

200. Forfeit of Piccolo
Krillin is the first to fight. He makes short work of Pintar. Piccolo and Shin are next. The fight begins, but no one attacks. Piccolo discovers Shin's true identity, but he can't understand what he's doing in the tournament. Shin says he will learn soon enough, shocking Piccolo with the fact that he can read minds. Piccolo forfeits the match. Next up are Videl and Spopovich. When Shin passes Spopovich, he notices something weird about him....

201. A Dark and Secret Power
When Piccolo and Shin get back to the area with the other fighters, Piccolo asks if he is the Grand Kai. He says no, he is the Supreme Kai! This stuns Piccolo. Supreme Kai tells Piccolo to keep his secret. Meanwhile, the fight between Videl and Spopovich is underway. Videl gives it everything she's got, but she can't hurt him. She even kicks his head around, apparently breaking his neck. Spopovich twists his head back around and continues fighting. Goku, Shin, and Kibito notice something strange about this fighter.....

202. Videl is Crushed
The fight between Videl and Spopovich continues. This time, Videl is taking the beating. Spopovich even uses energy waves. He can also fly. Goku recalls that he could not do this last time. Videl is beaten so badly that Gohan almost goes into the ring after Spopovich. Yammu, the other fighter with Spopovich, tells him to finish the match. He does, and Videl is seriously injured. Goku uses Instant Transmission to get to Korin's place so he can get some senzu beans.

203. Identities Revealed

After a quick meal at Korin's, Goku returns with the senzu beans. Gohan brings one to Videl, much to the chagrin of Mr. Satan. Gohan has to quickly return to the ring for his fight with Kibito. Videl takes the bean and is healed instantly. She runs to watch Gohan's match. When Gohan enters the ring, two of his classmates recognize him. Now that his secret is out, he takes off the turban and sunglasses.

204. Energy Drain
Kibito wants Gohan to transform into a Super Saiyan. Gohan not only does it, but he goes to the level beyond Super Saiyan. Supreme Kai informs everyone that Spopovich and Yammu are going to attack Gohan, and that no one can interfere. When the two make their move, Supreme Kai paralyzes Gohan. The two fighters stab Gohan with a device that drains his energy. Once they've got it all they fly out of the ring. Supreme Kai follows after them, along with Goku, Vegeta, Piccolo, and Krillin. Kibito stays behind to heal Gohan. Then he, Gohan, and Videl follow after the Supreme Kai. The Z Fighters are told about Majin Buu, a creature created by the dark magician Bibidi for the sole purpose of destruction. He was sealed up inside of a ball and trapped there when Bibidi was killed. Now his son, Babidi, is trying to unleash this all-powerful monster....

Babadi Saga
205. The Wizard's Curse
The Z Fighters follow Yammu and Spopovich to Babidi's ship. Videl grows tired from flying and heads back to the tournament. Gohan and Kibito catch up with the others, and they reach Babidi's ship. Once there, three figures emerge from the ship: Babidi, Dabura, and PuiPui. Spopovich and Yammu give Babidi the energy they stole from Gohan. As a reward for their service, Babidi has PuiPui kill the two fighters. Dabura discovers the Z Fighters on the cliff above, and Babidi plans to use this situation to his advantage.

206. King of the Demons
Babidi orders Dabura to destroy the weaker Z Fighters and lure the stronger ones into his ship. Dabura flies up to the cliff and destroys Kibito in a single blast. He then spits on Krillin and Piccolo, turning them into stone. After this attack, he heads back into the ship. Supreme Kai explains that the only way to turn them back to normal is to defeat Dabura. They all head into the ship, and on the first level they meet PuiPui. He says they must defeat a warrior at each stage, and he is guarding this one. Vegeta wins a contest of Rock, Paper, Scissors, so he gets to go first.

The ULTIMATE: DBZ Episode Guide

207. Vegeta Attacks
PuiPui and Vegeta square off. PuiPui can't lay a finger on Vegeta, so Babidi uses his magic to change the area to PuiPui's home planet. The gravity is 10x that of Earth's gravity. Vegeta laughs that PuiPui thinks he has the advantage. After dodging a few more attacks, Vegeta finishes him with an energy blast. The door opens, and the group moves on to the next stage.

208. Next Up, Goku
There are only 5 fighters left at the World Martial Arts tournament, so Mr. Satan proposes that they have a battle royal to determine the winner. Meanwhile, its Goku's turn to fight at Babidi's ship. He must fight a big monster named Yakon. Babidi changes the surroundings to Yakon's home planet, the planet of darkness. This doesn't bother Goku, because he can sense Yakon's energy and still avoid him. He turns Super Saiyan, but Yakon absorbs his light energy. Goku decides to give the monster all the energy he can ever want, and more. He fills him so full of light that he explodes. The door opens, and the fighters move to stage 3.

209. Battle Supreme
The battle royal at the World Martial Arts tournament begins. Mighty Mask (a.k.a. Trunks and Goten) and 18 quickly eliminate the other two fighters. All that remain are themselves and Mr. Satan, and they begin to fight each other. Meanwhile, Dabura realizes that the Z Fighters are getting too close to Majin Buu. He decides he needs to be the next one to fight against them. Before he does, he meditates to concentrate his power. This has Babidi very pleased, but the Z Fighters are getting impatient.

210. Eighteen Unmasks

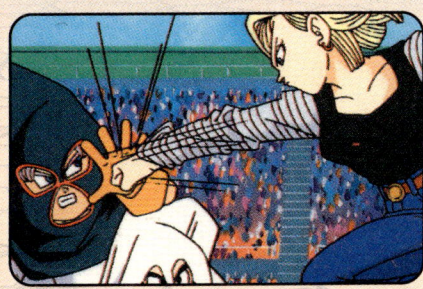

The battle between 18 and Mighty Mask goes back and forth between the fighters. 18 starts to lose, but when she hears her daughter cheer for her, she gets a boost and starts to win. Trunks and Goten turn Super Saiyan, and they regain the advantage. 18 realizes who they are, so she cuts their costume in half. Once their true identity is revealed, they are disqualified. They fly off to find the other Z Fighters. Meanwhile, Dabura's meditation is complete. It's time for him to get his feet wet...

211. Pay to Win

18 moves on to her next opponent in the battle royal: Mr. Satan. She grabs him in a headlock, and offers to throw the match for 20 million zeni. Mr. Satan agrees, and she lets him punch her out of the ring. Meanwhile, Goten and Trunks meet up with Videl, and she tells them everything about Babidi and Buu. They get excited since they weren't around for the other major battles the Z Fighters fought, so they head after the action. Dabura comes into the 3rd stage, and Gohan is ready to fight. They go at it, and Dabura seems to have the early advantage. Gohan turns Super Saiyan, and the real fireworks are set to go off.

212. Heart of a Villain
Gohan starts to beat Dabura. The Demon King powers up, and he regains the advantage. Vegeta gets angry that Gohan can't finish Dabura off quickly. He says he could beat the demon hands down in no time. Dabura notices something, and asks Babidi to bring them back to the ship. He leaves the Z Fighters for a moment to talk with Babidi. He tells the wizard that one of the warriors has a rage in his heart unlike the others. It can be used to their advantage. Three guesses who that fighter is....

213. The Dark Prince Returns
Vegeta is extremely angry that Gohan didn't beat Dabura, and now they have to wait. He is about to blow the ship to pieces, but Supreme Kai and Goku manage to convince him not to do it. Dabura tells Babidi that Vegeta can be used against the Z Fighters to revive Majin Buu. Babidi loves the idea, so he begins to work his magic on Vegeta. Vegeta feels a pain in his head, and Supreme Kai knows what's going on, but he is too late to stop it. When Vegeta lifts his head, he wields the mark of Babidi's henchmen. Babidi transports them back to the World Martial Arts tournament. Once there, Vegeta blasts a section of the bleachers. Hundreds of people are killed. Naturally this infuriates Goku, and it seems the stage is set for an epic battle between the last two members of the Saiyan race...

214. Vegeta's Pride
Vegeta blasts another hole in the bleachers to provoke Goku to fight him. Goku tells Babidi to move them to an uninhabited area, and he will fight Vegeta. Supreme Kai tries to warn Goku, but he is powerless to stop him. Babidi moves the group to the desert. Supreme Kai and Gohan decide to try and stop Babidi before Buu is born. The episode ends as Goku and Vegeta power up to clash one more time....

215. The Long Awaited Fight
Goku and Vegeta go at it in an all-out brawl. They appear to be even in terms of power, and neither fighter can gain the advantage. Gohan and Supreme Kai run into a small patrol of Babidi's troops, but Gohan beats them by powering up. Goten and Trunks are now nearing Babidi's space ship as well.

216. Magic Ball of Buu
Gohan and Supreme Kai reach the final stage of Babidi's ship. Babidi and Dabura are there to greet them. Gohan prepares to fight the Demon King again. As Vegeta and Goku battle, Vegeta reveals that he let Babidi control him so he could gain more power. Just as Gohan and Dabura are about to begin fighting, Babidi discovers that Majin Buu is now at full power. He will be reborn....

Buu Saga

217. Buu is Hatched
Steam is erupting from Majin Buu's egg. Supreme Kai tries to get Gohan to run away. Gohan is determined to stop Buu from being born. He fires a KamaHameHa wave at the egg, but it does nothing. He fires again and again, but still nothing. The egg finally opens, but there is nothing in it! Supreme Kai is relieved, and Gohan is about to fight

The ULTIMATE: DBZ Episode Guide

Dabura. Suddenly they notice that the steam coming from the egg is starting to take form. A fat pink fighter appears before their very eyes. Even Goku and Vegeta stop their fight when they sense a huge power level coming from nowhere....

218. The Losses Begin
Buu has finally been unleashed. He is not the ferocious monster that everyone thought. He seems kind of playful. Dabura quickly becomes angry at his childish antics. His anger disappears when Buu smashes him in the face and throws him into a mountain. Goku and Vegeta agree to stop fighting so they can fight Majin Buu. Before they can leave, Vegeta knocks Goku out and steals the last senzu bean. Babidi orders Buu to kill Gohan and the Supreme Kai. Gohan grabs the Kai and takes off, but Buu quickly catches up. He drops Gohan with a blow to the head. The Supreme Kai is next...

219. The Terror of Mr. Buu
Supreme Kai tries to fight Buu, but gets pummeled. Buu is about to kill him when Gohan knocks Buu out of the way. Buu blasts Gohan with an energy blast. Supreme Kai causes the blast to explode and saves Gohan from being incinerated. Buu is going to kill Supreme Kai, when Dabura saves him! The Demon King throws a spear through Buu, but the pink monster simply pulls it out and regenerates the hole. Meanwhile, Trunks and Goten arrive on the scene. Trunks accidentally breaks the statue of Piccolo. On the battle field, Buu is looking mighty hungry...

220. Meal Time
Dabura throws all the power he has at Buu, but it doesn't faze him. Buu turns Dabura into a cookie and eats him. Krillin returns to normal, and tells Goten and Trunks what's happened. Trunks is horrified about what he did to Piccolo, but he is relieved when the Namek uses his regenerative abilities to resurface. Meanwhile, Vegeta realizes that Goku stole his honor and his pride. He will only regain both by destroying Majin Buu. He destroys Babdidi's ship and appears on the battlefield. After smoking Buu a little, he lands a few punches on the pink blob. The battle of the Majins is under way.

221. The Warrior's Decision
Vegeta pounds on Buu, and appears to hold the advantage. The only problem is he can't do any permanent damage. Buu keeps regenerating. He wraps Vegeta up in a piece of his own blob. Buu proceeds to pound on the Saiyan prince. Trunks can't take watching his father get beat up. He turns Super Saiyan and charges the battlefield with Goten not far behind.

222. Final Atonement
Trunks manages to save Vegeta from the clutches of Majin Buu. Vegeta has only one chance at beating the titan. He decides he must self-destruct in order to take Buu down. He tells Trunks he loves him, and then knocks him and Goten out. Piccolo takes them to safety and Vegeta uses every bit of his energy to self-destruct and take Buu with him.

223. Evil Lives On
Vegeta's lifeless body falls to the ground and turns to dust. Piccolo returns to the battle scene, and to his horror, Majin Buu begins to reform himself. He rushes to Krillin and they high-tail it back to Dende's place. An injured Babidi screams for Buu to heal him, which he does. The two fly off into the horizon.

224. Find the Dragon Balls
Yamchu, Bulma, Chi Chi, and company collect all seven Dragon Balls so they can revive the people Vegeta killed. Meanwhile, Goku wakes up and senses the others at Dende's place, so he teleports to them. Dende heals Goku's wounds, and they must come up with a new plan to combat Majin Buu.

225. Revival
Goku explains that the Z Fighters may be able to beat Buu with the fusion technique. They decide that Goten and Trunks are the best candidates to learn the fusion. Krillin is about to bring everyone else back to the lookout when the sky goes black. Bulma and company have summoned Shenron. Before Goku can get to Bulma, she wishes back all the people Vegeta killed. They are able to save the second wish, but they have to wait 4 months to use it. Goku teleports everyone to the lookout.

226. Global Announcement
Kibito finds and revives the Supreme Kai. They next find Gohan, and Supreme Kai has Kibito teleport him to their home world. Meanwhile, Goku breaks the bad news about Gohan and Vegeta to everyone. They are about to begin teaching the boys the fusion technique when Babidi uses his magic to talk telepathically to every inhabitant of Earth. He wants Goten, Trunks, and Piccolo to show themselves or he will destroy the Earth. To prove he means business, he has Buu turn an entire city's population to candy and eats them.

227. Learn to Fuse
Buu destroys the vacant city where he has eaten all the people. Babidi says the Earth will be destroyed in 5 days if the three don't show themselves. In the Other World, Gohan is revived. Supreme Kai reveals that he wants Gohan to pull and wield the Z Sword. With it, he will be able to defeat Majin Buu. At the lookout, Goku tells Goten and Trunks what happened to Gohan and Vegeta, and they take the news hard. However, they are determined to learn the fusion technique and take Majin Buu down....

228. The Z Sword
Goku begins to teach the boys the fusion technique. Babidi contacts everyone telepathically again, and Trunks and Goten warn him that he is a dead man. Meanwhile, Gohan is able to pull the Z Sword after powering up to Super Saiyan. The sword is very heavy, and Kibito can't even hold it up. The quest to beat Majin Buu has now begun on two fronts.

229. Race to Capsule Corp.
Babidi discovers the location of Trunks' home town. He sets out to destroy Trunks' family and friends in an effort to draw him out. Bulma realizes that the Dragon Radar is in West City. Goku sends Trunks to fetch the radar while he fends off Buu. Goku teleports in front of their path, and a huge confrontation is brewing. Goku mentions taking his power to the next level, but can he surpass an ascended Saiyan?

230. Super Saiyan 3!?
Goku shows Babidi the two different levels of Super Saiyan. He then shocks everyone by powering up to a third level of Super Saiyan. He dubs it Super Saiyan 3. In this form, Goku is an even match for Majin Buu. However, how long can he hold out against the growing power of Majin Buu?....

231. Buu's Mutiny
The battle between Majin Buu and

The ULTIMATE: DBZ Episode Guide

Super Saiyan 3 Goku continues. Trunks finds the radar and heads back to the lookout. Sensing Trunks' energy signal leaving West City, Goku ends his fight with Majin Buu and teleports back to the lookout. Buu isn't done fighting. He now turns his aggression on Babidi, punching the wizard's head off in a single shot. Buu is now free to do as he pleases, but what does that mean for the rest of the world?

232. The Fusion Dance
Buu is now free to roam the Earth. Even though Babidi is gone, he continues to terrify and kill people for fun. Meanwhile, Goku has only 30 minutes left on Earth. Transforming to Super Saiyan 3 used too much of his energy. He quickly teaches the boys the fusion dance. He also teaches it to Piccolo so he can train them when he's gone. In the Other World, Gohan continues to train with the Z Sword.

233. Goku's Time is Up
The boys request that Goku transform into Super Saiyan 3 so they can begin their training. Doing so uses up the last of his time, so Baba comes to take him back. Goku says goodbye to everyone and returns to the Other World. Majin Buu continues his reign of terror. He turns a city full of people into clay and builds a house out of them.

234. Return to Other World
Goku returns to the Other World and senses Gohan's energy. He teleports to the Supreme Kai's planet and meets up with him. Piccolo continues to teach the boys the fusion technique.

235. Out From the Broken Sword
Gohan breaks the Z Sword when Goku throws a hard piece of metal at him. An Old Kai emerges from the sword. He agrees to unleash Gohan's sleeping powers, if Goku will find a woman for him. The ritual will take several hours.

236. Gotenks is Born
Goten and Trunks are finally ready to perform the fusion dance. The first time they try fusion, it's a failure because it produces a fat Gotenks. The second time is also a failure, as it creates a really skinny Gotenks. The third time is just right. The true Gotenks is born. The major flaw of the fusion is revealed however, as Gotenks is extremely cocky. He rushes down to fight Majin Buu and gets pummeled. He returns to the lookout bruised and battered.

237. Unlikely Friendship
Hercule marches off to Buu's house to fight the monster, and after a few of his harebrain ideas fail, he takes a liking to Buu. Meanwhile, Old Kai finishes the first stage to unleashing Gohan's power.

238. I Kill No More
Buu brings back an injured Puppy from one of his "trips" and heals it so it will run away from him. After healing it, the puppy likes him. Buu is happy that he has two friends. Hercule asks Buu if he will stop killing people, and the monster says OK! It appears Hercule really has saved the world. Meanwhile, two snipers travel to Buu's house seeking a thrill. They shoot Buu's puppy. Killing the puppy of a person who has already annihilated two-thirds of the world's population, bad idea.....

The Fusion Saga

239. The Evil of Men
Buu's puppy still lives. Buu heals it, and Mr. Satan beats the stew out of the two snipers. The two had blown up Buu's house, so he rebuilds it to look like the puppy. Later one of the snipers shoots Mr. Satan. Buu heals him, and tells him to take the puppy and run away. Buu's anger takes over, and a new Buu is formed from the steam he emits. This Buu is skinnier, and a lot more evil. It kills the sniper in one blast. Skinny Buu now turns his attention to Majin Buu.

240. Buu Against Buu
Majin Buu battles Skinny Buu, and the Majin Buu appears to be losing. He can't do much against this new Buu. He gets very angry and tries to turn Skinny Buu

into chocolate. Skinny Buu blows the attack back at Majin Buu, and HE is turned into chocolate. Skinny Buu eats Majin Buu and transforms into Super Buu. This new form can sense power levels. He detects the Z Fighters and flies to the lookout....

241. Empty Planet
In an effort to buy the boys more time, Piccolo suggests that Buu finish killing the rest of the people on Earth. This is a bad idea, as Buu kills everyone left in one attack. Videl, being the daughter of Majin Buu's former best friend, is able to convince him to give the boys an hour to prepare. The Z Fighters move Goten and Trunks to the Hyperbolic Time Chamber to train as much as they can. Meanwhile, Gohan's powers are finally coming around....

242. Time Struggle
Chi Chi begins to berate Buu, so he turns her into an egg and squashes her. His patience wears out, and he demands that the boys show themselves. Piccolo takes him to the Hyperbolic Time Chamber, but detours the monster as much as he can. They finally reach the door and go in. Trunks and Goten perform the fusion dance, and Gotenks is ready to fight Buu.

243. Super Moves of Gotenks
Gotenks uses a bunch of silly named attacks that do nothing to Buu. Buu begins to taunt Gotenks, claiming he's not strong at all. Gotenks powers up to Super Saiyan, and after his first attack doesn't work he prepares to use one of his better moves: Super Ghost Kamikaze Attack!

244. Trapped In Forever
The Super Ghost Kamikaze Attack surprises Buu when it explodes on impact. He is able to easily regenerate from the blast. Gotenks next uses several Ghosts against Buu, and he is blown to pieces. He and Piccolo make sure to destroy all of the pieces so Buu can't regenerate. Even with all visible pieces destroyed, Buu still regenerates. Gotenks claims he's beaten, he can do no more. He's really putting on an act so his "victory" will seem much greater. However, Piccolo takes him seriously and goes for his backup plan. He destroys the door to the Time Chamber, trapping them all in it for an eternity.

245. Feeding Frenzy
Buu reaches into the depths of his evil power and is able to create a hole in the

The ULTIMATE: DBZ Episode Guide

dimensions with a scream. He exits the hole and returns to Earth's dimension. With no one to stop him, he devours the remaining Z Fighters. Gotenks shows Piccolo his final technique he was going to use on Buu. He powers up to Super Saiyan 3! He lets out a scream of his own and opens up a portal. When Gotenks learns that Buu killed his parents, he promises that Buu will pay...

246. Gotenks is Awesome
Gotenks and Buu go all out in a ferocious battle that rips the lookout apart. As a Super Saiyan 3, Gotenks has the advantage over Buu. As the two warriors fight on Earth, Gohan continues to power up on the Supreme Kai's planet.

247. Unlucky Break
Gotenks continues his assault on Buu. However, his time runs out, and the fusion wears off. It looks like Trunks and Goten are cooked. There may be some hope, Old Kai has finished awakening Gohan's hidden powers. Kibito brings him to Earth, and Gohan heads to the battlefield in an outfit that looks like his father's.

248. A Whole New Gohan
Gohan arrives on the scene. He confronts Buu head on. Goten convinces Trunks to try to do the fusion again so they can protect his brother. Before they can complete the fusion dance, Gohan unloads a barrage of punches and kicks on Buu. He totally dominates the monster in a way no one has yet. The battle looks like it's won...

249. Search for Survivors
Gohan continues to maul Buu. Buu self-destructs to try and beat Gohan, but the plan fails. When he regenerates, he goes into hiding. Gohan and company decide to look for survivors. They find Dende and Mr. Satan. Dende tells them how Mr. Popo saved him from certain death when Buu escaped the Time Chamber. Buu reappears, but now he wants to continue his fight with Gotenks. It appears Buu has a plan....

250. Majin Buu Transforms
Trunks and Goten do the fusion again and prepare to fight Buu. Before they can act, Buu absorbs both Gotenks and Piccolo. He transforms into an even more powerful form. Having both the power of Gotenks and the wisdom of Piccolo, he is now more dangerous than ever. Gohan prepares to battle a powered up Buu once more.

251. The Old Kai's Weapon
Buu has become too powerful for Gohan. He is dominating the fight. The Old Kai decides to give his life to Goku, so he can return to Earth and fight. He also gives Goku his earrings. If he and Gohan wear one each they will fuse together. Supreme Kai and Kibito fuse this way. However, the Old Kai reveals, the fusion is permanent. Meanwhile, Babu and King Yemma allow Vegeta to return to Earth...

252. Ready to Fuse?
Buu is about to finish off Gohan when Tien arrives and saves him. Tien is obviously no match for Buu. Goku arrives just in time and splits Buu in half with an energy disk. He throws the earring to Gohan so they can fuse, but Gohan drops it. While he searches for it, Buu attacks Goku. He turns Super Saiyan and tries to hold him off, but it isn't going well. All of a sudden, Gotenks fusion wears off and Buu loses a lot of power. Gohan finds the earring, but Goku tells him not to worry about it. Gohan can beat Buu himself now. A piece of Buu is still on the ground, and it swallows Gohan. Upon returning to its owner, Buu transforms again. He is now more powerful than ever, and Goku's fusion partner is gone....

253. Union of Rivals
Goku searches desperately for someone to fuse with. Mr. Satan appears to be the only viable option. He's about to throw him the earring when he senses a familiar power level. He teleports to it, and its Vegeta! Goku tries to convince Vegeta to fuse with him, but he refuses. Buu tracks them down, and they both battle the monster. They are no match for him, and Vegeta finally agrees to fuse. He puts on the earring, and Vegetto is born.

254. Meet Vegetto
Vegetto shows off his thunderous might by pummeling Buu. He appears to be superior to Buu in his base form. Buu charges up a huge ball of energy and hurls it right at Vegetto. The fused Saiyan catches the ball and kicks it into space. He then flies up at Buu, and powers up to Super Saiyan. Business is about to pick up.

255. Rip in the Universe
Vegetto continues to dominate Buu completely. Buu gets so angry that his power begins to tear holes in the physical universe. Vegetto has a hard time getting through his energy, but eventually does and socks Buu in the jaw. Vegetto better be careful, for even though he is strong, Buu is still lethal....

256. Vegetto....Downsized
Buu cannot beat Vegetto. He finally resorts to one of his most powerful techniques. He turns Vegetto into candy. Coffee flavored candy to be exact. Meanwhile, Bulma, Videl, Chi Chi, and Dabura (yes, that Dabura) search for Gohan in the Other World.

257. The Incredible Fighting Candy
Vegetto shocks Buu when he attacks him as candy. It turns out he has retained all of his power. Now he's actually more dangerous because he's too small for Buu to fight. He beats the tar out of Buu until he is forced to return him to human form. Vegetto now decides to give Buu ten seconds to do what he wants before he is destroyed. Buu takes this opportunity to absorb the fused Saiyan. The tide has turned yet again, as there is now no one to fight Buu....

258. The Innards of Buu
Vegetto uses an energy barrier to protect himself inside of Buu. He was intentionally absorbed so he can rescue the others. Once he lets the barrier down, Vegetto defuses. Vegeta destroys the earring, so Vegetto is gone for good. The two Saiyans explore Buu's stomach and are attacked by giant worm-like creatures. So that's why Buu eats so much. He has worms!

259. Mind Trap
Goku and Vegeta make the journey to Buu's head. Once there they battle Buu's memories of Gotenks, Gohan, and Piccolo. Buu visits a nearby town and eye balls all of the cakes and sweets. His thoughts turn to food, so Gotenks, Piccolo, and Gohan disappear. Vegeta and Goku find the cocoons they are trapped inside.

260. Visions of Deadly
Vegeta and Goku disconnect the cocoons from Buu, and he reverts to his

The ULTIMATE: DBZ Episode Guide

weaker form. (The one that fought Gotenks) Realizing that he's losing power, he sends a vision of himself to fight Goku and Vegeta. No matter what they try they can't defeat this vision. Every time he's seemingly destroyed, he returns again. Buu's slime is about to swallow Vegeta as the episode ends.

Kid Buu Saga

261. Evil Kid Buu
Goku saves Vegeta from Buu, but he is now in danger himself. Vegeta repays the favor by cutting Fat Buu's cocoon free. Buu begins to transform again, and the two Saiyans take this opportunity to escape. Buu reverts back to his original form: a tiny but powerful new version commonly known as Kid Buu. Supreme Kai explains that this is his most evil form. Kid Buu proves this by immediately firing a large energy ball at the Earth. Goku grabs Hercule, Dende, and Buu's puppy and teleports to the Supreme Kai's planet. The Supreme Kai himself teleports Vegeta to safety. Vegeta berates Goku for not rescuing the others instead.

262. End of Earth
Kid Buu has destroyed the Earth. Goku and Vegeta escape with Hercule and Dende to the Supreme Kai's planet. Their safety is short-lived as Kid Buu senses their location and uses his newly learned Instant Transmission technique to appear on that planet....

263. True Saiyans Fight Alone
Kid Buu has appeared on Supreme Kai's planet. It's up to Goku and Vegeta to defeat this menace to the universe once and for all.

264. Battle for the Universe Begins
Goku tells all of the others except Vegeta to leave the planet, and they do it. By using a game of rock, scissors, paper, Goku gets to fight first. He charges up to Super Saiyan 2 and battles Kid Buu. They fight evenly for awhile. Goku finally powers up to Super Saiyan 3 and prepares to finish Kid Buu off...

265. Vegeta's Respect
Goku fights Kid Buu at Super Saiyan 3, but can't destroy the tiny monster. He just keeps regenerating. Goku's power begins to drain, and he returns to normal form. Vegeta steps in and fights Kid Buu in his base form, but gets slapped around. Just when Kid Buu is about to kill Vegeta, Goku steps in and bats him away. He then powers back up to Super Saiyan 3. Vegeta flashes back to his first battle with Goku. He realizes that his love for his planet, friends, and family are what makes him so strong. Vegeta admits that Goku is #1. Unfortunately, he may wind up #2 to Kid Buu as they continue their brawl....

266. Minute of Desperation

Goku is getting weak again. He can't disintegrate Kid Buu, because he regenerates very fast. Goku is hoping to power up to his max while Buu is down, but his regeneration is just too fast. Vegeta steps in to give Goku the time he needs. Even at Super Saiyan 2, Vegeta is no match for Kid Buu. Vegeta is pummeled for the entire minute and blasted back to his base form. The minute isn't long enough as Goku needs more time. Vegeta gets back up and powers up again to Super Saiyan 2! Kid Buu pounds him again, and grabs him by the throat. Vegeta's time may be up....

267. Old Buu Emerges
Kid Buu is about to deliver a death blow to Vegeta. Suddenly, Mr. Satan attacks Kid Buu! It turns out he has some courage after all. One punch from Kid Buu has Mr. Satan in a lot of pain. Kid Buu is about to kill Mr. Satan when he stops dead in his tracks. He spits up Fat Buu, who appears to be dead. Kid Buu moves to attack Mr. Satan, when Fat Buu awakens and stops him. The two go at it, but Kid Buu has a slight advantage. Goku realizes he is losing power rather than gaining it and powers down. Fat Buu can't last forever. The Z Fighters are running out of options.

268. Earth Reborn
Vegeta comes up with a plan to destroy Buu forever. He has Dende go to Namek and wish for the Earth to be revived. All of the people killed by Buu are brought back to life.

269. Call to Action
The next part of Vegeta's plan is for Goku to gather energy for a huge Spirit Bomb. He gathers energy from all over, but people on Earth won't give him their energy...

270. People of Earth Unite
The people of Earth will not give Goku their energy. Kid Buu sees the Spirit Bomb and tries to attack it. Vegeta intercepts, but can't last long. Mr. Satan finally steps in and says he needs the energy to fight Buu. Being a world hero, the people give their energy to Mr. Satan. The Spirit Bomb reaches maximum power and is ready for deployment.

271. Spirit Bomb Triumphant
Goku hurls the Spirit Bomb at Kid Buu, but the tiny terror catches it and pushes it back at Goku. The two are in a tug of war with the Spirit Bomb. Goku is very weak from the fight and begins to lose ground. Vegeta uses a wish from Porunga to give Goku his power back. Goku powers up fully and sends the energy ball flying towards Kid Buu. Before being destroyed, Goku hopes to be reincarnated as a good person, so he will know who's stronger. The energy ball obliterates Kid Buu, and the nightmare is finally over.

272. Celebrations with Majin Buu
Everyone returns to Earth, including Majin Buu. Goku meets a guy on the street who will pay 10,000 zeni to anyone who can beat him. Buu beats him and buys ice cream with the money. Next Buu visits a jewelry store with Bulma, and the same guy tries to rob it. Buu beats the guy and the cops arrest the criminal.

273. He's Always Late
Goku is late for one of the Z Team's infamous parties.

274. Granddaughter Pan
Ten years have passed since Kid Buu's defeat. Gohan's daughter, Pan, is introduced. Goku and Company enter the World Martial Arts tournament. Goku has Majin Buu magically rearrange the ordering so he can fight Uubu, the reincarnation of Kid Buu.

275. Buu's Reincarnation
The tournament begins, and we are introduced to Ubuu. Goku wishes for Kid Buu to be reincarnated, and Uubu is the product of that wish.

276. Goku's Next Journey
Goku battles Uubu. It happens to be Uubu's first fight, but he is impressive. Goku decides to leave and train Uubu. Yet another adventure begins for Goku...

Ultimate Movie Guide

— BY: ERIC R. GERSON

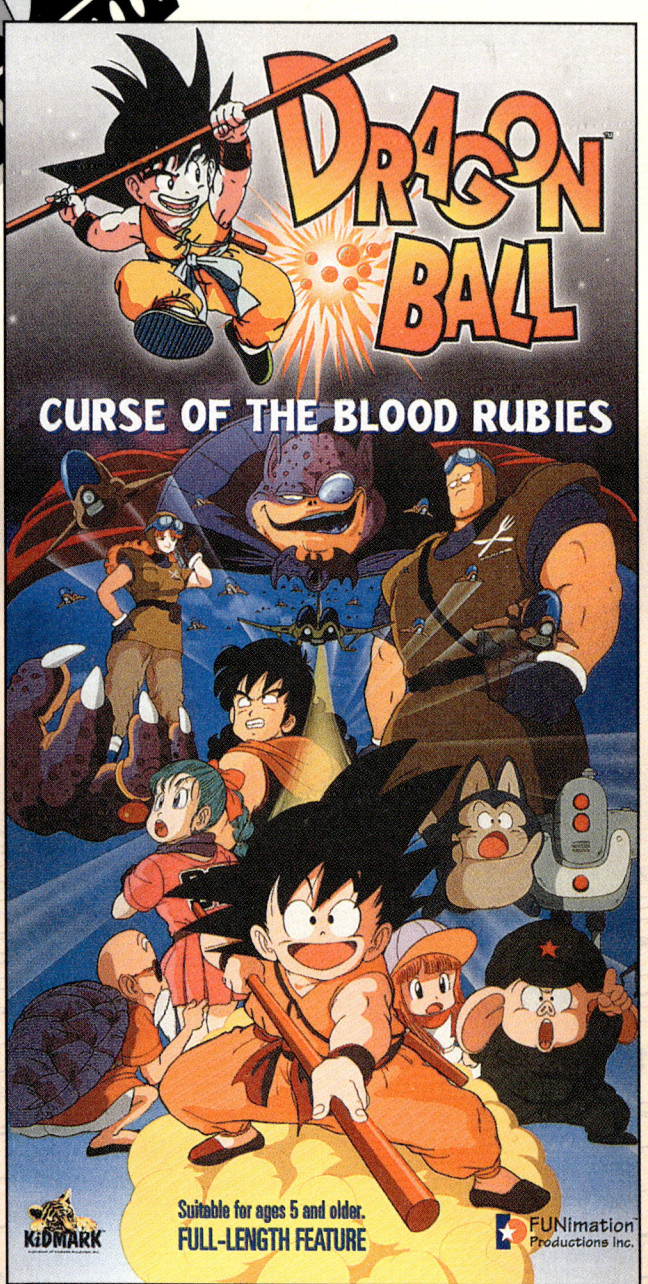

DB Movie 1
English title: Curse of the Blood Rubies
Japanese title: The Legend of Shenron

The retelling of Goku meeting Bulma, Yamcha, and Oolong. This movie summarizes the beginning of the Dragon Ball series. Basically, they all go out looking for Dragon Balls for various reasons, but a monster with an insatiable hunger is looking for the Dragon Balls as well.

This movie has great humor and an original storyline, though boring at times.

DB Movie 2
English title: Sleeping Princess in Devil's Castle
Japanese title: The Princess in Devil's Castle

Once he learns who Roshi is, Goku seeks him out to receive his training. Once he arrives, Krillin also shows up seeking Roshi's training. To earn the right to train, Roshi sends the two boys out on a quest to a castle called "Devil's Hand" where a sleeping princess resides. Whoever brings the princess back to Roshi will receive training. However, there is more in the castle than just a princess.

Though lacking the humor that most Dragon Ball series and movies contain, this movie is extremely entertaining. It also tells how the friendship of Goku and Krillin began.

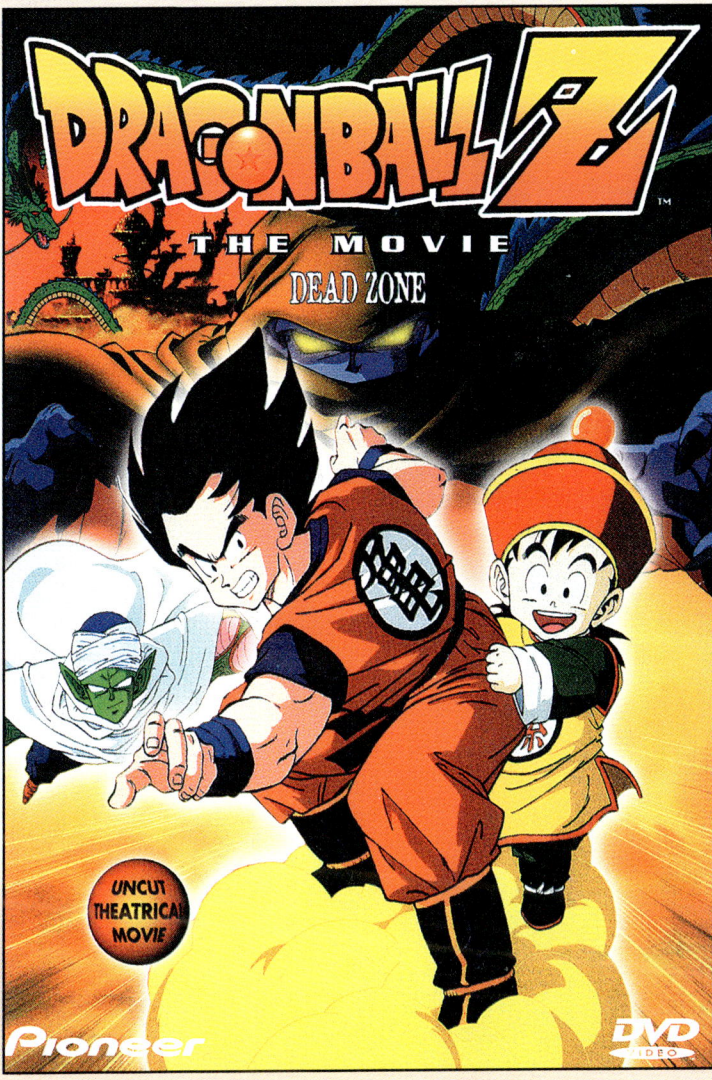

DB Movie 3
English title: Mystical Adventure
Japanese title: Mystical Adventure

The movie is set after Goku and Krillin have completed their training under Master Roshi. Both join the Tenkaichi Budoukai to test their new skills. The young Emperor Chaozu is sponsoring the Budoukai. Unfortunately, Chaozu's wife is kidnapped and Chaozu's evil advisor suggests that the only way to get her back is to find the Dragon Balls. While Goku and Krillin are competing, Bulma also is searching for the Dragon Balls.

This movie presents more action than the previous two and has great fight scenes. The music and story could have been better, but neither lower the quality of the movie.

DB 10th Anniversary Special
Japanese title: The Way to Become the Strongest

Another retelling of Goku's first meeting with Bulma, Oolong, and Yamcha. It continues the story to the point where Goku fights and destroys the Red Ribbon Army.

With the animation of the GT artists, this movie is incredibly drawn when compared to the original Dragon Ball series. The music and story are great, and the action is above the norm for Dragon Ball, but not at the standard for DBZ.

DBZ Movie 1
English title: Dead Zone
Japanese title: Return my Gohan

To gain immortality, Garlic Jr. collects the Dragon Balls. Once done, he hopes to take over Kami's spot as the God of Earth. However, he makes the mistake of kidnapping Gohan who has a Dragon Ball on his hat. To get back his son, Goku journeys to Garlic Jr.'s place along with Krillin and Piccolo. Now that he's immortal, no one seems strong enough to defeat Garlic, until Gohan gets angry.

Despite below average music and parts of the story that don't make sense (such as Garlic Jr.'s minions trying to

The ULTIMATE: DBZ Movie Guide

kill Piccolo although they are sent to collect the Dragon Balls), this movie is decent. There are humorous scenes and the fight sequences aren't too bad.

DBZ Movie 2
English title: The World's Strongest
Japanese title: The World's Strongest Man

Using Shenron to free his master, Dr. Kochin destroys the icy jail that Dr. Wheelo was imprisoned in years ago. Wanting to have the strongest body, Wheelo goes after Roshi thinking that he is still the strongest man on Earth. We he learns that Goku is now the strongest, Wheelo has a new target.

With an easy-to-follow plot that works well with the music and animation, this movie is a definite for any Dragon Ball fan to see. However, after seeing the movie, you won't watch it again for some time. It does not one contain any amazing scenes that you will want to see over and over.

DBZ Movie 3
English title: Tree of Might
Japanese title: Ultimate Decisive Battle for Earth

Needing the Earth to grow the "Shinseiju" (Tree of Might in the dub), Taurus (who looks just like Goku, but is of no relation) and his men plant the seed and hope to harvest its fruit. The fruit of the Shinseiju gives the individual eating it a giant power up. Taurus also has his eye on Gohan, who is the strongest Saiyan, due to his amazing potential if fed the fruit. With his minions, Taurus defeats all of the Z Senshi, including Goku; but Goku has a few surprises for him.

Despite the horrid ending, the movie is excellent. Both the dub and Japanese versions are done extremely well in music, story, and animation.

DBZ Movie 4
English title: Lord Slug
Japanese title: Super Saiyajin Goku

To regain his youth, Slug comes to Earth to gather the Dragon Balls. Once his wish is granted, Slug attempts to destroy the Earth by blocking the sun and turning it into a frozen wasteland. When he fights Goku, he shows his true power and form. Just when all seems lost, Piccolo and Gohan help Goku win.

The ULTIMATE: DBZ Movie Guide

DBZ Movie 6
English title: The Return of Cooler
Japanese title: Clash! 10,000,000,000 Power Warriors

With the new planet Namek being eaten by a Giant Ghetti Star, the Z Senshi fly to the rescue in a Capsule Corp. spaceship. The entire Namekian race is enslaved by large robots. Goku, Gohan, Piccolo, Krillin, Yajirobe, Roshi, and Oolong try to help and learn that Cooler is the mastermind behind the plot. He is now a metallic robot, and is exacting revenge from the people who lived on the planet where his brother was killed. Cooler also wants another chance to kill Goku, since Goku killed his brother. With the help of Vegeta, Cooler is destroyed. But, from the Ghetti Star comes hundreds of Metal Coolers.

With animation from the Frieza Saga, I was surprised that Metal Cooler's appearance and the Super Saiyan transformations were so well drawn. They look great. The fight scenes are exciting but could have been longer. The story can get boring at times, but is still worth seeing.

DBZ Movie 7
Japanese title: Utmost Limits of Battle! The Three Super Saiyajin

Creating three new androids from his hate of Goku, Dr. Gero's computer sends the androids out to complete Gero's plan of killing Goku. The first two, 14 and 15, attack Goku while he is shopping with Chi Chi and Gohan. Not wanting to destroy the city, Goku and Trunks leave for an uninhabited arctic area. The fight seems fairly well-matched, until Android 13 shows up to fight with the other androids. However, once Vegeta and Piccolo turn up to help as well, the Z warriors seem to have the edge. All seems well, until 13 shows off his Super form, making the battle a little tougher for our heroes.

This is one of my favorite movies, the animation is great, the music is perfect, and the story (though not as original as some others) is still cool. This is also a movie you can watch over and over and not become bored with it.

This is the absolute worst of all of the Dragon Ball films. The music, fighting, story, and characters are far below standard. I would only recommend seeing this movie if you want to be able to say you've seen the complete Dragon Ball series.

DBZ Movie 5
English title: Cooler's Revenge
Japanese title: The Best of Strongest versus Strongest

To avenge his dead brother, Cooler comes to Earth to kill the Super Saiyan. With his Tokusentai, Cooler defeats Goku, Gohan, Krillin, and Piccolo. But the fear of death to all life on Earth causes Goku to transform, and even Cooler's final form won't be enough to win.

The story gets a bit boring at times, but the movie takes a different approach to the Frieza saga, showing Frieza's brother and the anger he felt over Frieza's death. His reaction is surprising since Frieza didn't care for anything. Cooler's final form is also very cool.

DBZ Movie 8
Japanese title: Burnout!! Fierce fight, Violent Fight, Super exciting fight

Paragus comes to Earth to get Vegeta to return with him to what Paragus claims is a Planet New Vegeta. However, Paragus and the planet are not what they seem. Paragus' son Brolly is the legendary Super Saiyan, born with a power level of 10,000. Because

The ULTIMATE: DBZ Movie Guide

With an original story, great animation, and beautiful music that fits each scene, this movie is a must see for any Dragon Ball fan.

🟠🟠🟠🟠🟠🟠🟠

Goku is the only one who has ever made Brolly cry (which occurred when they were infants), Brolly loses control and tries to kill everyone. After an amazing battle when everyone seems beaten, it turns out that Goku isn't as weak as Brolly thought.

Though this movie gets boring at times, mainly since it is the longest of the DBZ Movies, the animation is good and the music is great. It also explains more about the Super Saiyan and the Saiyan race.

🟠🟠🟠🟠🟠

DBZ Movie 9
Japanese title: The Galaxy is in Danger!! The Super Awesome Guy!

Having another Tenkaichi Budoukai funded by Mr. Money for his son's birthday, Mr. Satan invites everyone of Earth to compete on an island. The Z Senshi all go, even Goku, who was dead until Lord Kaio wishes for him to compete. After the elimination rounds, the winners go to the final round on another island. Mr. Satan's students are supposed to be dressed up like aliens to be the competitors for the warriors. However, Bojack and his men, who were at one time imprisoned in a star by the Kaios, take over the tournament and fight the Z Senshi. After all seems lost, Goku's words of encouragement give Gohan the power he needs to stand up to Bojack and his men.

DBZ Movie 10
Japanese title: Dangerous Partners! Super Warriors Never Rest

While searching for the Dragon Balls, Goten, Trunks, and Videl encounter Brolly who crash-landed on Earth after being defeated in DBZ Movie 8. The three don't do very fighting against Brolly until Gohan arrives to lend assistance. Despite the years between the fight on New Vegeta and the present fight, even Gohan's Super Saiyan 2 form isn't strong enough to compete against Brolly. The warriors seemed doomed until the Dragon Balls perform a miracle.

Though the majority of this movie can be boring at times, the humor and ending fight make it worth seeing.

🟠🟠🟠🟠🟠🟠

22 Pojo's Unofficial ABSOLUTE Dragon Ball Z

The ULTIMATE: DBZ Movie Guide

DBZ Movie 11
Japanese title: Crushing Super Warrior! I am the winner

Challenged by Jaga Bada, Mr. Satan goes to Jaga's island along with Android 18, who wants her money for throwing the Budoukai. Trunks and Goten tag along seeking adventure. While at Jaga's place, the Bio Warriors challenge Mr. Satan. Because she wants the whole incident over quickly so she can get her money, 18 decides to fight the Bio Warriors instead of Hercule Satan. Goten and Trunks join in the fight for the fun of it. After this initial battle is over, Goten and Trunks discover a cloning vessel that has grown a clone of Brolly. After breaking free, Brolly tries to fight Trunks and Goten, but is engulfed with acid. The warriors think that the acid has killed Brolly, but they are proved wrong when he appears as a hideously deformed monster. After another fight, they again believe that Brolly has been defeated. Unfortunately, Brolly resurfaces as a gigantic monster. Not even Goten, Trunks, and Krillin can defeat Brolly now, but he meets his match in the seawater.

Next to DBZ Movie 4, this is the worst of the Z Movies. The story is boring and Brolly looks stupid. The fight scenes are not too bad, but the only thing that saves this movie is its humor.

DBZ Movie 12
Japanese title: The Rebirth of Fusion! Goku and Vegeta!

When the evil cleansing machine in Hades overloads and blows up, a young demon possessed by all the evil within the machine is created. He grows into a large and powerful demon named Janemba. With all the evil released, Lord Enma (King Yamma) is imprisoned in his castle and is powerless to do anything about the demon. Goku and Pikkon are called upon to deal with the problem and attempt to free Enma. When they learn that the only way to do this is by destroying Janemba, Goku flies into Hell to face him. After transforming into Super Saiyan 3, Goku defeats the large yellow demon and believes he has won. Unfortunately, the demon changes into a smaller, red, and more powerful demon. His power is so great that even Super Saiyan 3 Goku can't fight against him. Once joined by Vegeta, they attempt to fight Janemba together, but learn that the only way to win this fight is through fusion.

Because this movie uses computer graphics for some of the animation, it is amazing to watch. The story, music, humor, fighting, and, of course, animation are great. This is a must see for everyone.

DBZ Movie 13
Japanese title: Dragon Fist Explosion!! If Goku can't do it, who can?

After encountering a strange old man named Hoi with an oracle, Gohan and Videl bring it to Capsule Corporation for examination. They find that the oracle is not of Earth, and the Z Warriors set out to find the

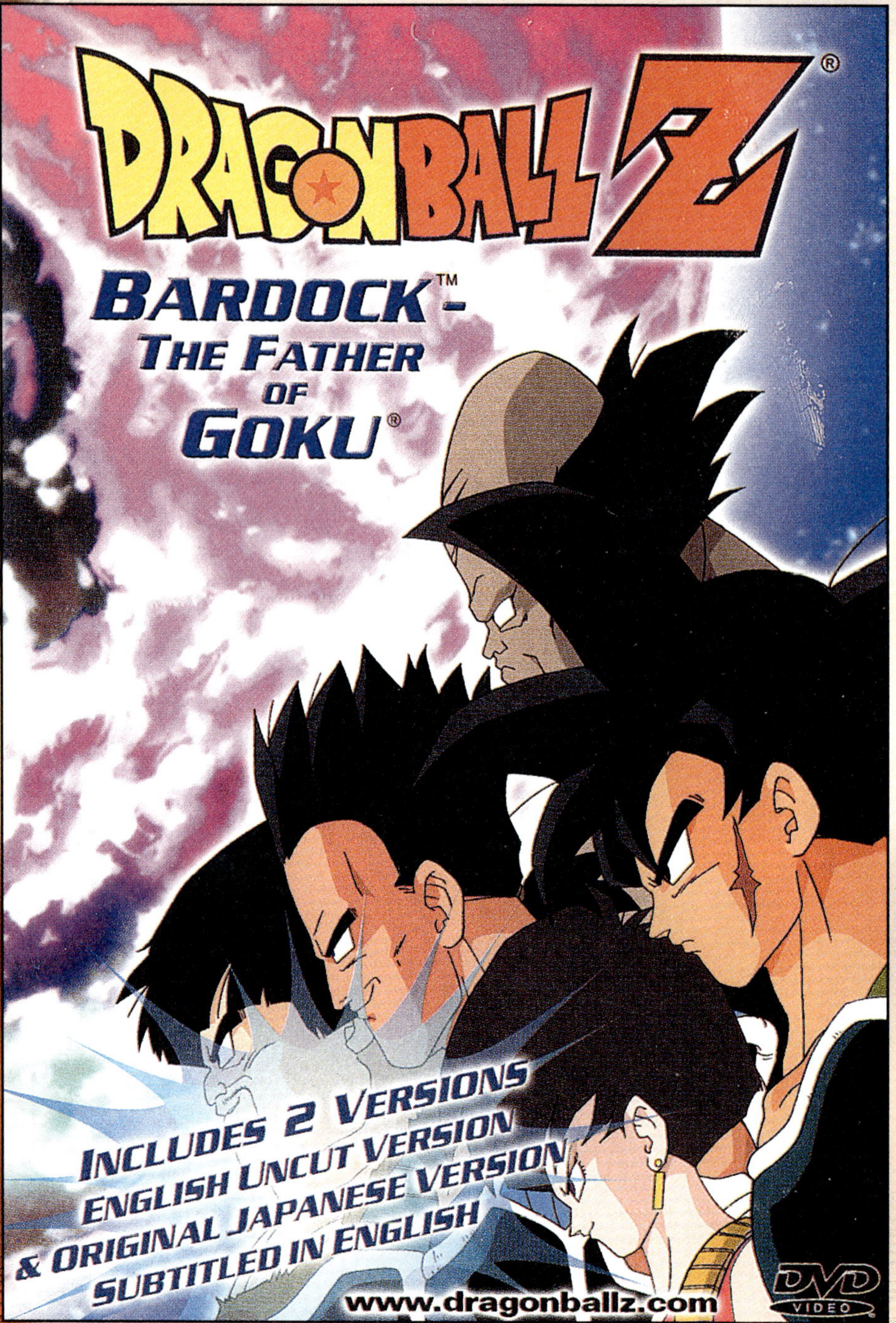

The ULTIMATE: DBZ Movie Guide

DBZ Television Special 1
English title: Bardock: Father of Goku
Japanese title: A Final Solitary Battle! The Z Warrior Son Goku's Father Challenges Furiza

After destroying the entire Kanassan race, Bardock (Goku's father) and his men relax and discuss various topics. The last surviving Kanassan surprises Bardock and hits him in the back of the neck, bestowing upon him the ability to see the future. Bardock sees his planet and people being killed by Frieza, and thinks that his son will also be killed. Bardock attempts to gather the Saiyans to kill the tyrant. When he is mocked and not believed, he flies into space to face Frieza himself.

The story is much deeper and emotional than any other Dragon Ball movie and it should be watched before all the others. Given that the DVD has now been released in the States, all fans should pick up a copy and watch and appreciate this movie's perfection.

DBZ Television Special 2
English title: The History of Trunks
Japanese title: Defiance in the face of despair!! The remaining Super Warriors – Gohan and Trunks

Dragon Balls and summon Shenron to open it. Once done, a strange and mysterious man named Tapion emerges from the oracle playing his ocarina. Tapion is terrified upon being released, since he has a secret that can destroy the galaxy.

With an original story, great music, and enhanced animation, this movie is almost perfect. You'll find yourself singing the themes in your head for days, and wanting to watch the movie as much as possible.

With Goku dead from a viral heart disease, the Z Warriors are faced with defeating Dr. Gero's androids on their own. The battles end and only Gohan has survived. After years of fighting, the Earth has been ravaged and destroyed by the androids. Angered by the destruction, Trunks asks Gohan to train him to help with the android fight. During a battle with the androids, Gohan and Trunks are both severely beaten, and Gohan gives Trunks the last senzu to save the teenager's life. The fight leaves Gohan with only one arm. When the

The ULTIMATE: DBZ Movie Guide

DBGT Television Special
Japanese title: Goku's Supplement! Proof of Courage is the Four Star Dragon Ball

One hundred years have passed since the end of Dragon Ball GT, and the only character still alive from the series is Pan. She is ill, so Pan's grandson, Goku Jr., sets out to find the four-star Dragon Ball to ask Shenron to save her. Unfortunately, Goku Jr. is very cowardly and unaware of his true power, unlike his Great Grandfather Goku. While on his journey, Goku Jr. is joined by Pahku, the bully that picks on him at school. Together, they set out for Goku's old house on Mount Paozu where the four-star ball resides.

This movie has great humor and the story is well done, despite the fact that all of the characters from the three Dragon Ball series are not present (with the exception of Pan). There is also great emotion when Goku Jr. encounters his Great Grandfather.

DBZ OVA Special
Japanese title: Plan to destroy the Saiyajin

While gathering firewood, Goku and Gohan notice the trees and forest area around them are dying. Mr. Popo floats down and explains that a gas called Destron is destroying all life on Earth (including human). Everything will be dead in 72 hours. The two join up with Vegeta, Trunks, and Piccolo, and they all set out to destroy the Destron-emitting machines. They manage to destroy all of the machines but one. The final machine has a protective shield that even Goku's energy attacks can't penetrate. To save the Earth, Goku, Gohan, Trunks, Vegeta, and Piccolo set out for the Dark Planet to face Dr. Raichii.

I enjoyed watching this movie. However, the music wasn't up to DBZ standards. I was very disappointed. The story itself was entertaining, and there were surprises that I wasn't expecting. If it were longer, the plot holes could have been resolved.

androids attack the Western Capital, Gohan dies. When he finds Gohan's body, Trunks is so angry he transforms. Years later, Bulma completes the time machine and wants Trunks to travel back in time. However, Trunks wants one more shot at the androids.

This movie is great and shows what the future will be if Goku dies. The music and story are amazing and Trunks' first Super Saiyan transformation makes it a must see.

The Ultimate Fight Guide

— By Andy Diehl

There's no shortage of fight power in the Dragon Ball and Dragon Ball Z mangas (comic books). In fact, there were 187 fights that occurred in these mangas. If you are like many DBZ fans, you're having trouble remembering who fought who, and when. With that in mind, we've assembled the Ultimate Fight Guide.

Now, remember that the manga doesn't cover Dragon Ball GT, so this fight guide excludes that animated series. Nor does the guide contain the fights that only occurred in the anime – such as the Garlic Jr. Series. All set? Try to keep up with us.

1. Goku vs. The giant fish
This was Goku's first fight. While fishing with his tail, a giant fish bit it. Goku kicked the fish and killed it.

2. Goku vs. The Pterodactyl
A giant talking dinosaur kidnapps Bulma and was flies away. Goku hops on Bulma's motorcycle and flies over a hill. Goku jumps for the dino, but can not reach it. He then hits and kills the dinosaur with his Nyobi.

3. Goku vs. Bear Thief
On the way to bringing Master Roshi's turtle to him, Goku, Bulma, and the turtle run into a gigantic bear dressed like a warrior. The Bear threatens to eat the turtle so Goku and the Bear fight. Goku uses Janken, which is a paper, rock, scissors move and defeats the bear with rock (a punch).

4. Goku vs. Oolong
It was not really much of a battle. Oolong tries to scare Goku, but he has to keep running away because he can only transform for a limited time. Oolong ends up trailing along with Bulma and Goku

5. Goku vs. Yamcha
Goku meets Bulma in the desert. They fight awhile and it's fairly even. Yamcha runs away when Bulma walks over to where they are fighting.

6. Goku vs. Yamcha
Yamcha and Puar are chasing Goku, Bulma, and Oolong in the desert. Yamcha demands the Dragon Balls and when Goku refuses, the two begin to taunt each other. Finally when the fight begins, Yamcha loses a tooth and runs away.

7. Chi Chi vs. T-Rex
Chi Chi is away from home when a giant T-Rex begins to chase her. She takes a giant blade from her helmet and flings it at the Dinosaur. It cuts off his head.

8. Yamcha vs. Chi Chi
After killing the dinosaur, Chi Chi attacks Yamcha with her blade. The blade misses Yamcha. Yamcha defeats Chi Chi without any effort.

9. Goku vs. one of Boss Rabbit's henchmen

Goku runs into one of Boss Rabbit's gun-toting thugs and easily disposes of him.

10. Goku vs. Boss Rabbit

Goku cannot touch Boss Rabbit or he will be turned into a carrot. Instead, he decides to beat Boss Rabbit with his Nyobi. When Boss Rabbit is defeated, he tells Goku the secret word to turn Bulma back into a human.

11. Yamcha, Bulma, Puar, and Oolong vs. Ooroza Goku

Goku sees the full moon and transforms. This frees the others from Lord Pilaf's castle. However, they have to turn Goku back into his normal form. Puar turns into a giant pair of scissors and cuts of Goku's tail

12. Goku vs. Seikan

On Goku and Krillin's quest to find a woman for Master Roshi, Goku saves Lunch from Seikan.

13. Krillin vs. Sabertooth

Krillin defeats a sabertooth with ease. He runs into the sabertooth during his training under Master Roshi.

14. Goku vs. Krillin

During training, Goku and Krillin must find a specific rock for Master Roshi. Goku finds it first, but Krillin steals it and runs away. Krillin turns to face off against Goku. Goku wins the fight, but Krillin tricks Goku into believing that he got rid of the rock.

15. Goku vs. Lunch

Goku wakes up Lunch by mistake. She has a short temper and starts shooting at Goku. He kicks her to stop her.

16. Goku vs. Oootoko

Goku's first match in the World Martial Arts Tournament. Goku easily pushes Oootoko out of the ring, but no one can believe that a mere boy pushed a monster like Oootoko out of the ring.

17. Krillin vs. Magic Oorin Temple Monk

Krillin faces off against one of the monks from the temple. The monks used to pick on Krillin. Despite Krillin's fear, he defeats his opponent in one kick.

18. Goku vs. Bokusa

This is Goku's second match in the World Martial Arts Tournament. Goku easily advances.

19. Krillin vs. Ken Pou Ka

Ken Pou Ka is modeled after Bruce Lee. He looks and talks like him. It's not a bad match, but Ken Pou Ka isn't much of an opponent for Krillin.

20. Goku vs. Bokusa

This was not much of a fight. Goku picks up Bokusa and throws him out of the ring to advance to the next round.

21. Krillin vs. Bear Man

This is Krillin's last match before the championship rounds. Bear Man punches at Krillin, but Krillin dodges the punch and counters with a kick. Bear Man quits.

22. Krillin vs. Bacterium

Krillin is tested by this dirtball. Bacterium has never taken a shower and he smells. At one point, Bacterium puts his hands in his shorts, rubs between his legs, and gives Krillin a whiff. Bacterium sits and jumps on Krillin. After Krillin is reminded by Goku that he does not have a nose, Krillin beats Bacterium

23. Yamcha vs. Jackie Chun (Master Roshi)

Even though Yamcha does most of the attacking, it is an easy victory for Jackie Chun. Yamcha kicks and punches him, but Jackie dodges all of the attacks. Finally, Yamcha tries his Wolf Fang Technique, but Jackie just jumps over him. Jackie uses a blast of wind that knocks Yamcha out of the ring and he wins.

24. Lanfan vs. Namu

Lanfan is no match for Namu, but Namu has trouble hitting a girl. When Lanfan removes her shirt, Namu is shocked, but remembers that he is there to get water for his town. He closes his eyes and in one blow knocks her out.

25. Goku vs. Giran

This was a fight that Goku almost lost. Giran spit two purple rings on Goku, and Goku could not break

The ULTIMATE: Fight Guide

out. When Giran throughs Goku out of the ring, Goku calls Nimbus to bring him back to the ring. After it is agreed that Nimbus is not allowed, Goku brakes free of the rings and kicks a hole in a wall. When Giran sees Goku's strength, he gives up.

26. Krillin vs. Jackie Chun

Krillin is losing to Jackie Chun in the match. Jackie Chun is actually Master Roshi. Krillin eventually pulls out a pair of woman's underwear to distract the old man. Krillin is then able to knock him out of the ring. Jackie Chun uses a Kame Hama Ha to propel himself back into the ring. After more fighting, Krillin charges at Jackie Chun and is knocked out of the ring.

27. Goku vs. Namu

Namu is outmatched, but he does not fall for Goku's fake image technique and whirlwind attack. In the end, Namu loses because Goku outmatches him in speed and power.

28. Goku vs. Jackie Chun

At the beginning of this fight, the two opponents try to outdo each other. Goku wins the Kame Hame Ha match by a slight margin. Jackie Chun tries a double fake image technique, so Goku does a triple fake image technique. Jackie Chun uses his Drunken Style Attack where he wanders the ring acting drunk. Goku realizes what Chun is doing and uses his mad dog attack, where he just attacks wildly. The fight lasts into the night and Goku sees the full moon. He turns into his Monkey Form. Jackie Chun is forced to blow up the moon. When the fighting resumes, the two engage in hand-to-hand combat. Both try to kick each other, but because of his longer legs, Jackie Chun connects more solidly with Goku. Goku is knocked out and Jackie Chun wins the World Martial Arts Tournament

29. Goku vs. Red Ribbon Army Combatant Pair

Under Captain Silver's command, two men are looking for the Dragon Balls at the same time as Goku. Goku gets a Dragon Ball and the two men shoot at him

30. Goku vs. Captain Silver

The two men radio Silver to tell him about Goku. Silver shoots Goku's cloud, destroying it. Silver steals the Dragon Ball and Dragon Radar from Goku. Goku steals it back and easily defeats Silver.

31. Goku vs. Red Ribbon Army's Combatant Pair

Goku defeats the two men who are looking for the Dragon Balls. He learns that the Jingle Village's Head Master has been captured by Red Ribbon.

32. Goku vs. Red Ribbon Army Countless Warriors

Goku defeats all of the Red Ribbon men on the second floor of Muscle Tower.

33. Goku vs. Red Ribbon Army's 4th person

Goku defeats all of the Red Ribbon Army men on the fourth floor of Muscle Tower. Once again, he triumphs very easily.

34. Goku vs. Sergeant Metallic

Goku uses a Kame Hame Ha to knock off the robot's head. Before Metallic can attack again, his batteries run down.

35. Goku vs. Murasaki

This match covers a lot of ground and is fairly even-handed. In the end, Murasaki makes five copies of himself, but Goku is still able to defeat Murasaki and the copies. Murasaki then escapes to release Android #8.

36. Goku vs. Bunyon

When Goku and Bunyon are fighting, they don't seem to be having an impact on each other. In frustration, Goku punches a hole in the wall and jumps into Android 8's coat. Goku also punches a hole in Bunyon, destroying the monster.

37. Goku vs. General White

This is not much of a fight. White is defeated by Android 8 and Goku, even after he takes a hostage.

38. Goku vs. Street Fighter

A man on the street makes an offer of 100,000 zeni (the money used in the DB world) to anyone who can defeat him. Goku accepts the deal, but when the man sees Goku put a hole in a wall, he surrenders and pays Goku.

39. Goku vs. Robbers

Goku encounters robbers on the street. He easily takes care of one of the robbers. The other robber gives up and tells Goku to get the police.

40. Goku vs. Red Ribbon

Goku beats up a few guys who are shooting at Bulma.

41. Master Roshi and Lunch vs. Red Ribbons B Team

A group of Red Ribbon Army soldiers go to Kame House to get the Dragon Balls. Master Roshi beats all of the soldiers except for one. The final soldier is taken care of by Lunch.

42. Goku vs. Robot Pirate

Goku doesn't have any trouble with

The ULTIMATE: Fight Guide

the Robot. After a short fight, Goku wins the battle with a Janken Punch.

43. Goku vs. Octopus
Goku uses a Kame Hame Ha to destroy a large Octopus who wants to eat him.

44. Blue Shogun vs. Krillin
Krillin has the power to defeat Blue, but Blue uses a hypnosis technique to paralyze Krillin. Blue beats Krillin to near death.

45. Blue Shogun vs. Goku
Goku shows up to save Krillin. Blue uses the paralyze technique on Goku, but it's broken when Blue is frightened by a mouse. Goku uses Janken to knock Blue against a wall. Goku, Krillin, and Bulma are able to escape from the cave.

46. Blue Shogun vs. Snow
Blue Shogun has the Dragon Balls and the Dragon Radar when Snow is told to attack Blue. She very quickly beats Blue and the Dragon Balls are recovered.

47. Bora vs. Red Ribbon Army's 7th man
Colonel Yellow and his men are trying to get a Dragon Ball from Bora. They fire at him, but the bullets do nothing. In an effort to protect his land, Bora destroys the army, but Yellow escapes.

48. Goku vs. Colonel Yellow
Goku smashes Yellow's plane, killing him in the process.

49. Blue Shogun vs. Tao Pai Pai
Commander Red meets the great Tao Pai Pai but doesn't believe it's him. To prove it, he wants Tao Pai Pai to battle Blue. However, Blue can attack in any fashion, but Tao Pai Pai can only use his tongue. Blue attacks and Tao Pai Pai uses his tongue to poke a hole in Blue's temple, killing him.

50. Bora vs. Tao Pai Pai
Bora attacks Tao Pai Pai and Tap Pai Pai spears him through the chest.

51. Tao Pai Pai vs. Goku
Goku uses Kame Hame Ha on Tao Pai Pai, but it doesn't hurt him. Tao Pai Pai attacks with Dodon and it looks like Goku is killed.

52. Tao Pai Pai vs. Goku
After training at Korin Tower for three days, Goku becomes faster and more powerful than Tao Pai Pai. Goku easily defeats him.. When Tao Pai Pai throws a bomb at Goku, Goku kicks it back killing him.

53. Goku vs. Red Ribbon Army's Countless Warriors
In an attempt to find the remaining Dragon Balls, Goku attacks Red Ribbon Headquarters. Some of the warriors are defeated and some run away.

54. Goku vs. Advisor Black
Black shoots Commander Red, so he becomes the leader of Red Ribbon. He uses a Battle Jacket (a self-manned robot) to fight Goku. He is successful, but he celebrates too much and acts stupid. Goku is able to go through the Battle Jacket causing Black and the robot to explode.

55. Krillin vs. Dracula Man
Krillin is knocked out of the ring and loses.

56. Upa and Puar vs. Dracula Man
Upa and Puar are next to fight Dracula Man. Upa eats garlic and Puar shape shifts, and by doing so, they defeat Dracula Man.

57. Yamcha vs. Invisible Man
Yamcha has to fight the Invisible Man and he doesn't fare too well. Krillin devises a plan. He pulls down Bulma's tank top, which causes Master Roshi to have a major nosebleed. The blood covers the Invisible Man, and Yamcha is able to fight him. The Invisible Man surrenders.

58. Yamcha vs. Little Mummy
Yamcha fights the Mummy and can't do any damage against his speed or power. Yamcha gives up to avoid being killed.

59. Goku vs. Little Mummy
The Mummy gets in a few blows on

The ULTIMATE: Fight Guide

Goku. Goku defeats the Mummy with one punch.

60. Goku vs. Akkuman
Even though Akkuman can fly, Goku is still too fast for him. Akkuman uses his special attack which causes evil in someone's heart to expand and explode. However, Goku has a pure heart and is not affected. Goku gets serious and defeats the Devil Man.

61. Goku vs. Unknown Ghost (Grandpa Gohan)
Goku has no trouble with the Ghost until it grabs his tail. After finding Goku's one weakness, the Ghost beats up Goku. As the Ghost tries to kill Goku, Goku's tail falls off and he gets angry. The Ghost decides to give up and reveals he is actually Goku's dead grandfather, Gohan.

62. Goku vs. Mei
Goku is able to fight Pilaf, Shuu, and Mei and their Mecha suits to gain the last Dragon Ball.

63. Yamcha vs. Mohichan
Yamcha wins his match with a knock out in the World Martial Arts Tournament.

64. Krillin vs. Oootoko
Krillin defeats the very large Oootoko.

65. Tien vs. Sumo Wrestler
No one realizes how strong Tien is, but he surprises everyone when he wins his match.

66. Goku vs. King Chop
Chop is a strong opponent and the fear is that Goku will lose. Goku hasn't changed much in the three years he has been gone. Goku wins.

67. Jackie Chun vs. Bear Man
Jackie Chun wins this match and then apologizes to Bear Man for being hard on him.

68. Tien vs. Yamcha
The match begins as a draw. At one point, Yamcha uses the Kame Hame Ha, but Tien deflects it back at him. Yamcha jumps up to avoid the attack and Tien appears and knocks him out. Tien is declared the winner.

69. Jackie Chun vs. Man-wolf
Man-wolf is mad at Jackie Chun for destroying the moon. He wants to kill him. During the match, Man-wolf pulls a knife. The fight continues, even though this is against the rules. Jackie Chun convinces Man-wolf to act like a dog, and when he throws a bone, Man-wolf chases it and is disqualified.

70. Krillin vs. Chiaotzu
Krillin is faster than Chiaotzu expected and Krillin knocks him out of the ring. However, Chiaotzu can float so he is fine. Chiaotzu powers up to use Dodon and Krillin powers up to use a Kame Hame Ha. Krillin fires his blast and jumps out of the way of Dodon. Chiaotzu paralyzes Krillin's heart prepares to kill him. In an effort to break his concentration, Krillin asks Chiaotzu a math problem. Krillin has to ask him twice, but it works. He knocks out Chiaotzu.

71. Goku vs. Panputto
Panputto is a multi-world champion, but Goku defeats him with little effort.

72. Tien vs. Jackie Chun
In this match, Jackie Chun purposely loses. He steps out of the ring, so Tien will face Goku.

73. Goku vs. Krillin
Although battling each other, these two friends promise to try their hardest to win. During the fight, they both agree they are having fun. We also learn that Goku's tail is no longer his weakness. Once Goku gets serious and appears in front of Krillin, the boy is so surprised that he is knocked out of the ring.

74. Goku vs. Tien
This is the championship match in the World Martial Arts Tournament. Both opponents are equals, but Tien tries to kill Goku. Tien uses a Kikoho. The fighters survive, but the ring is destroyed. The rule is the first person to hit the ground loses. Goku hits first, so Tien wins the title.

75. Master Roshi vs. Tsurusennin
Master Roshi and Tsurusennin were both trained by Mutaito-sama. However, Master Roshi is good and Tsurusennin is evil. We also learn that when they were younger, Mutaito died trying to seal Piccolo in the Denshi Jar.

76. Tanbarin vs. Goku
Goku finds Tanbarin, but he is still weak from fighting in the tournament. Tanbarin is the one who killed Krillin. Tanbarin destroys Nimbus. Tanbarin smashes Goku down to the Earth and leaves him for dead. He also takes Goku's Dragon Ball.

77. Goku vs. Yajirobe
Goku eats Yajirobe's fish and Yajirobe is not happy. He throws a boulder at Goku and Goku thinks he is the monster that killed Krillin because he has a Dragon Ball. Goku later realizes that it's a different Dragon Ball and apologizes.

78. Yajirobe vs. Cymbol
Cymbol shows up when Goku and Yajirobe are talking. Cymbol wants to kill Yajirobe for his Dragon Ball and Yajirobe wants to eat Cymbol for breakfast. After much discussing and little fighting, Yajirobe uses his sword to slice Cymbol in half.

The ULTIMATE: Fight Guide

79. Tanbarin vs. Giran
Piccolo Daimo orders that all of the World Martial Arts Tournament participants from the last ten years be killed. Tanbarin kills Giran.

80. Tanbarin vs. Goku
Goku defeats Tanbarin. He uses his one pattern to confuse him, and then shoots him. When Tanbarin tries to escape, Goku uses a Kame Hame Ha to kill him.

81. Goku vs. Piccolo Daimo
Piccolo Daimo shows up to see who has killed his children. When Yajirobe hears the name Piccolo, he gives Goku his Dragon Ball and runs away. Piccolo Daimo is only half of his original power because of his age. He still defeats Goku, but Piccolo is surprised at Goku's great power. He leaves thinking that he has killed Goku. Yajirobe has been hiding behind a tree and returns to find out Goku is alive.

82. Master Roshi vs. Piccolo Daimo
Master Roshi fights Piccolo to gain his Dragon Balls. He uses the Mafuuba attack to try to seal Piccolo in the Denshi Jar. However, Master Roshi's aim is off and the attack drains all of his life energy, killing him.

83. Piccolo Daimo vs. Guard
A guard objects to Piccolo taking over and he is killed.

84. Tien vs. Drum
Piccolo spits out a new child to fight Tien. Neither is winning, but then the new child, Drum, blindsides Tien and is ordered to rip his heart out. As Drum is about to kill Tien, Goku shows up to save the day.

85. Goku vs. Drum
Goku defeats Drum. Piccolo can't believe that this is the same Goku that he fought.

86. Goku vs. Piccolo Daimo
Piccolo and Goku fight. At the outset, Goku is beating Piccolo. Piccolo is amazed at his power and Tien can't even follow the two. Goku tells Piccolo to fight at full power. The fight continues and it is clear that Piccolo is winning. He uses Tien as a hostage to assure that Goku will not attack him. Finally, Goku uses a different form of the Kame Hame Ha and defeats Piccolo with one punch. Goku is able to use the power of the Choushin water from Korin Tower in his attack.

87. Goku vs. Mr. PoPo
In order to meet Kami, Goku must fight Popo. Goku does not pass the test, because he does not move like the lightning. However, he is permitted to see Kami.

88. Goku vs. King Chop
As the fight begins, Goku follows behind Chop without anyone seeing him. When Chop turns around, Goku knocks him out.

89. Tao Pai Pai vs. Chiaotzu
Chiaotzu fights Tao Pai Pai in the World Martial Arts Tournament and is killed. He is the only Z warrior not to win his first round.

90. Shien (Kami's Human form) vs. Yajirobe
Shien rushes Yajirobe and knocks him out.

91. Tao Pai Pai vs. Tien
During his fight with Tien, Tao Pai Pai pulls out a blade and is disqualified. However, he continues to fight. Tao Pai Pai is no match for Tien and he is knocked out.

92. Goku vs. Chi Chi
Goku does not remember Chi Chi. The only way she will reveal her identity is if Goku defeats her. Goku uses wind power to knock the girl out of the ring.

93. Krillin vs. Ma Junior (Piccolo)
Krillin is defeated by Piccolo in this fight, but shows that he has learned a new move. Krillin is now able to levitate.

94. Shien (Kami's Human form) vs. Yamcha
Shien defeats Yamcha. During the match, Shien gives Yamcha tips on his fighting. Goku realizes Shien's identity and Yajirobe reveals that he also knows.

95. Goku vs. Tien
The match begins and both fighters are even. Goku asks Tien for a break to take off some clothes. Goku takes off his shirt and shoes, which amount to more than 200 pounds of clothes. Goku begins to win. Tien splits into four different people, but Goku is able to defeat all four.

96. Shien (Kami's human form) vs. Ma Junior (Piccolo)
Shien tries to perform Mafuuba on Piccolo, but Shien is in a weak host body. When Ma Junior strikes back with a Mafuuba, Kami is taken from his human body. Before Kami is knocked unconscious, he warns Goku that fighting Piccolo is not the same as fighting Piccolo Daimo.

97. Goku vs. Ma Junior (Piccolo)
This is the championship fight of the World Martial Arts Tournament, but the fate of the world is at stake. The fight swings back and forth between the two opponents. Goku uses his Chou Kamehameha, but it does not work. After a long fight, Piccolo uses

The ULTIMATE: Fight Guide

his strongest move but Goku has learned how to fly. He flies at Piccolo knocking him out of the ring and winning the World Martial Arts Tournament. Piccolo flies off and the group celebrates.

98. Radditz vs. Goku

This is the first appearance of Radditz on Earth. He tells Goku that Goku must kill one hundred people or Radditz will kill Gohan.

99. Radditz vs. Piccolo and Goku

This battle qualifies as the first major fight in DBZ. Radditz has no problem fighting Goku and Piccolo. In the midst of the fighting, Gohan's true power is revealed. Radditz is eventually defeated when Goku holds Radditz still so Piccolo can use his Special Beam Cannon. This kills both Radditz and Goku. Afterward, Piccolo takes Gohan to be trained.

100. Gohan vs, T-Rex

Gohan has fun with a T-Rex. At first they fight, but later Gohan cuts off the dinosaur's tail and eats it.

101. Tien vs. Saibaman

Tien is the first to fight one of Nappa's Saibamen. He easily defeats it.

102. Yamcha vs. Saibaman

Yamcha fights a Saibaman and appears to be winning. However, when Yamcha is caught off guard, the Saibaman self-destructs and kills him.

103. Krillin vs. Saibamen

Krillin is upset because he is going to fight the Saibamen instead of Yamcha. Krillin forms an amazing energy blast that kills all of the Saibamen in one shot.

104. Piccolo vs. Saibaman

One Saibaman is still alive and jumps for Gohan. Piccolo uses his mouth blast to kill it.

105. Tien vs. Nappa

No matter how hard Tien fights, he is no match for Nappa. Tien gets his hand cut off. In a last ditch effort, Tien forms one last energy blast. Tien might have killed him, but Nappa saw it coming.

106. Piccolo vs. Nappa

Like the others, Piccolo is no match for Nappa. Piccolo is killed when he jumps in front of a blast aimed for Gohan.

107. Nappa vs. Goku

Goku shows up when Krillin and Gohan are the only fighters still alive. Goku makes a fool out of Nappa and breaks his back. Vegeta then kills Nappa.

108. Vegeta vs. Goku

This match-up is considered the second great fight in DBZ. Goku is not able to kill Vegeta. Yajarobie helps by cutting off Vegeta's tail while he is transformed.

Krillin and Gohan also help. Krillin could've killed Vegeta with Yajarobie's sword, but Goku tells Krillin to let him go.

109. Gohan and Krillin vs. Two of Frieza's weak henchman

When Gohan and Krillin arrive on Namek, they are sensed by one of the scouters. Two of Frieza's weak henchmen are sent. Instead of having a fight, Gohan and Krillin kill the two men

110. Vegeta vs. Kuwi

Kuwi follows Vegeta to Namek. Kuwi thinks his power level is stronger than Vegeta's. In one blast, Vegeta kills Kuwi.

111. Zarbon vs. Nameks

When the Namek Elders will not show Frieza the Dragon Ball, Zarbon is ordered to show the Nameks his power. In the process, two Nameks and one of Frieza's henchman are killed.

112. Frieza Henchman vs. Three Nameks

The three Nameks attack and kill all of Frieza's henchman.

113. Dodoria vs. Three Nameks

Although the three Nameks defeat the henchman, they are no match for Dodoria. Dodoria defeats all three. In an effort to show no mercy, Dodoria punches a hole in one of the Nameks.

114. Vegeta vs. Dodoria

This wasn't much of a fight. Dodoria pleads with Vegeta to let him go and promises to tell Vegeta the truth. Dodoria tells Vegeta it was Frieza who blew up Planet Vegeta. Vegeta still kills Dodoria

115. Zarbon vs. Vegeta

At first, Zarbon isn't strong enough to defeat Vegeta until he

The ULTIMATE: Fight Guide

transformed. Once transformed, he beat Vegeta and blasts him into a lake. Later Zarbon retrievs Vegeta and brings him back to Frieza's ship.

116. Zarbon vs. Vegeta
At their second meeting, Vegeta is much stronger than Zarbon. Even after Zarbon transforms, Vegeta punches into his chest and blasts him from inside, killing him.

117. Krillin and Gohan vs. Guldo
Together Krillin and Gohan are much stronger than Guldo. Guldo is able to live though the battle because he can freeze time. Finally, Guldo freezes Krillin and Gohan, takes a tree, and is going to stab them. Vegeta arrives and cuts off Guldo's head.

118. Vegeta vs. Recoome
As usual, Vegeta tries his hardest, but he is no match for Recoome. Recoome knocks Vegeta around for a while, and just when he is going for the kill, Krillin and Gohan interfere.

119. Goku vs. Recoome
It is hard to call this a fight. Goku and Recoome only stand in front of each other. Recoome charges up for his Recoome Boom, but before he can use it, Goku speeds forward and punches Recoome in the stomach.

Goku takes Recoome out of the battle and Vegeta later kills him.

120. Goku vs. Burter and Jeice
Once again, it's not much of a fight. Goku maintains control the whole time. The two Ginyu members can't believe Goku's speed. Even when they use their final attack, Goku is still too fast. Goku takes out Burter but Jeice flies away. Vegeta later kills Burter.

121. Goku vs. Ginyu
At the beginning of this fight, Ginyu does not realize Goku's immense strength. Ginyu's power level is around 120,000 and Goku powers up to over 180,000. At one point, Jeice appears and grabs Goku, giving Ginyu a chance to beat Goku. However, Ginyu refuses to fight unfairly. Ginyu eventually uses his body switch technique to change bodies with Goku.

122. Frieza vs. Nail
Nail's job is to distract Frieza and he does a great job of it. Frieza beats Nail to within an inch of his life. When Frieza finds out what is going on, he speeds away leaving Nail to die.

123. Ginyu (In Goku's body) vs. Gohan and Krillin
Ginyu has trouble using Goku's body. Gohan and Krillin are initially reluctant to attack Goku's body, but they overcome their concern and defeat Ginyu. Ginyu tries to switch bodies with Vegeta, but when a frog is thrown in the way, Ginyu enters the frog's body.

124. Vegeta vs. Jeice
Jeice is no match for Vegeta. Vegeta gets revenge by killing Jeice. During this fight, Vegeta declares himself a Super Saiyan.

125. Gohan vs. Frieza (Second form)
The Z warriors are trying to pass time until Goku is ready to fight. Gohan starts by knocking Frieza to the ground. Frieza fights off Gohan.

126. Goku vs. Frieza
This is a very long fight, but it has several highlights. Frieza is forced to transform into his fourth form. He kills Dende and Vegeta. Piccolo distracts Frieza while Goku forms a giant Spirit Bomb and fires it at Frieza. The Z warriors celebrate. Frieza is still alive and appears on a mountain. He shoots a beam through Piccolo, and nearly kills him. The beam is aimed for Goku but Piccolo jumps in the way. Frieza attacks, causing Krillin to explode. Goku turns SSJ and orders Gohan to leave with Bulma and Piccolo. Frieza is cut in half by a disc he fires at Goku. Goku gives Frieza energy so he can escape the explosion. Frieza turns on Goku and Goku puts Frieza out of commission.

127. Trunks vs. King Cold's henchmen
The henchmen are weak and forced to fight Trunks. Trunks has a field day and kills them.

128. Trunks vs. Frieza bot
Trunks cuts Frieza into a million pieces and blows him up

129. Trunks vs. King Cold
King Cold thinks the only reason Trunks beat his son is because of his sword.
The King gets Trunks' sword from him, but Trunks still sends him into the afterlife.

130. Dr. Gero vs. Yamcha
Yamcha is the first of the Z warriors to meet up with the androids. Dr

The ULTIMATE: Fight Guide

Gero puts his hand through Yamcha's chest and absorbs all of his energy.

131. Android 19 vs. SSJ Goku

When the fight begins, Goku is in perfect condition. He is untouchable and able to dodge Android 19's attacks. Goku begins to feel the effects of his heart disease. After getting severely beaten, he fires a Kame Hame Ha, but it's absorbed by Android 19. Android 19 begins to toy with Goku and Android 20 (who is Dr. Gero) won't let the others intervene. Goku is finally saved when Vegeta appears and kicks Android 19 out of the way.

132. Android 19 vs. SSJ Vegeta

This fight immediately follows Goku's battle with Android 19. Vegeta watched Goku and 19 fight, so he knows a technique to overcome 19's ability to suck energy from his hands. Vegeta asks, "Do androids feel pain?," before he rips off the android's arms and defeats him.

133. Piccolo vs. Dr. Gero

Piccolo is grabbed by Gero and Gero covers Piccolo's mouth (so Piccolo can't yell) and sucks all of his energy. When Piccolo is on the verge of death, he uses telepathy to call Gohan and Gohan knocks Gero off of him. Piccolo is given a senzu and tells Gero that he only let him absorb a little bit of his energy. Piccolo chops Gero's arm off, so he can't absorb more energy. Bulma arrives and when everyone is distracted, Dr. Gero runs away.

134. Dr. Gero vs. Android 17

Android 17 kicks Dr. Gero's head off and steps on it.

135. Android 18 vs. SSJ Vegeta

This fight starts on a freeway and finishes up on a sandy hill. Vegeta says he won't hold back because Android 18 is a girl, but she proves to be a tough opponent. In the end, 18 brakes Vegeta's arm in one swift kick and easily wins.

136. Imperfect Cell vs. Piccolo

Imperfect Cell attacks and surprises Piccolo with a Kame Hame Ha. He destroys Piccolo's arm and begins to suck his energy. However, Piccolo regenerates a new arm and declares he can still defeat Cell. Krillin and Trunks arrive. Cell uses a Solar Flare to escape, and he races off in search of the androids.

137. Piccolo vs. Android 17

This is recognized by most fans as one of the coolest fights in DBZ. It is an all-out slugfest between two evenly-matched characters. At one point, Piccolo is under Android 17, but both are up in the air. Piccolo fires nearly 100 ki blasts, but they all miss. Android 17 is suspicious. When he looks up, he realizes that he is surrounded by hundreds of Ki blasts. They all engage toward 17 at once. Android 17 uses a shield to block the attack. The fight ends in a draw when Cell shows up.

138. Imperfect Cell vs. Android 17

Imperfect Cell arrives to absorb Android 17 and he does it. Piccolo warns Android 17 that he is no match for Cell, but 17 does not listen.

139. Imperfect Cell vs. Android 16

This is Android 16's first battle. In an effort to protect Android 18, 16 has to fight. Android 16 proves to be the strongest of the three androids, but he's still defeated by Cell.

140. Cell vs. Vegeta

Vegeta arrives from the Room of Spirit and Time. He wants to show his pride in this fight. Vegeta is able to hold his own against Cell and the two appear equals. Vegeta wants more of a fight, so he allows Cell to absorb Android 18. In doing so, Cell becomes perfect.

141. Cell vs. Krillin

Krillin attacks Cell, but causes Cell no damage. Krillin realizes he is no match for Cell. Cell defeats him.

142. SSJ Vegeta vs. Cell

Vegeta realizes his mistake in this fight. By allowing Cell to become Perfect, Vegeta can't inflict pain upon him. No matter how hard he tries, he can't defeat Cell.

143. Cell vs. SSJ Trunks

Trunks explodes with energy in this battle and surprises both Vegeta and Cell. At first Cell is worried, but as the battle continues, it becomes apparent that not even Trunks can hurt Cell.

144. Cell vs. Mr. Satan

Mr. Satan attempts to fight Cell. Cell smacks him and Mr. Satan is sent flying from the ring.

145. SSJ Gohan vs. Android 17 and 18

This battle takes place in an alternate time period. It's fought in Trunks' time. In this battle, Gohan fights the two androids with one arm. Gohan appears to be winning, but is soon defeated. The androids use several Ki blasts to finish him off. The sight of Gohan dying causes Trunks to go Super Saiyan.

146. SSJ Goku vs. Cell

This is the first equal opponent for Perfect Cell. The two exchange

The ULTIMATE: Fight Guide

blows evenly and the match is too close to call. In the middle of the fight, Goku gives up and says that Gohan will fight in his place.

147. Cell vs. Gohan

Gohan does poorly and is brought to the brink of death. Goku keeps telling Gohan to "get mad", so Cell tries to make Gohan mad by creating "Cell Juniors" to beat up on the Z warriors. Android 16 jumps in and tries to do a self-destruct on Cell. Cell laughs and blows 16 into pieces. More fighting occurs and Gohan is beaten even worse. The head of the shattered 16 asks Mr. Satan to throw him near Gohan. Mr. Satan regretfully agrees. When 16 is near Gohan, he tells him that it is OK to fight for something you believe. He encourages Gohan to fight with all of his power. Just as he finishes speaking, Cell steps on 16 and destroys him. Gohan becomes enraged at this and everything that has been happening and it causes him to go SSJ2. Gohan kills all of the Cell Juniors and easily destroys Cell. Cell is dying, but Gohan wants to toy with him. Goku tells Gohan to "finish him", but Gohan is so enraged that he wants to torture Cell. Goku is shocked at Gohan's actions. Cell spits out Android 18 and returns to his imperfect body. In desperation, Cell uses his self-destruct and plans to blow up the world. Gohan is upset because he realizes he should have killed Cell when he had the chance, but now he can't be stopped. Suddenly, Goku says good-bye to everyone and uses instant teleportation to teleport Cell to King Kaio's place. When Gohan realizes what Goku is doing, he mourns his death. Krillin helps him up and they walk away.

148. Cell vs. SSJ2 Gohan

Cell destroys Android 16, driving Gohan over the edge. Gohan goes Super Saiyan 2. He battles Cell to a draw. In the end, they agree a Kame Hame Ha battle will decide who wins. Gohan gains the power of all the Z warriors in firing his Kame Hame Ha and is able to kill Cell.

149. Trunks vs. Android 17 and 18

After Cell is defeated in the alternate time, Trunks returns to his time. Trunks kills Androids 17 and 18.

150. Trunks vs. Cell

After killing 17 and 18, Trunks kills Cell before he has a chance to start absorbing people.

151. Gohan vs. The Burglars

Gohan runs into some robbers. In an effort to disguise himself, he goes SSJ. He stops the robbers.

152. Great Saiyaman and Videl vs. A Pair of Burglars

Gohan has a disguise and he and Videl run into more burglars. They also are stopped.

153. Idasa vs. Trunks

This is Chibi Trunks' first match in the Children's World Martial Arts Tournament. Idasa is no match for Trunks.

154. Imamo vs. Koryu

It is not much of a fight. Imamo wins when Koryu cries instead of fighting.

155. Goten vs. Ikose

After Trunks takes care of Ikose's brother Idasa, Goten defeats Ikose.

156. Chibi Trunks vs. Goten

This is a great match that takes place in the World Martial Arts Tournaments Youth Division. After defeating everyone, the only kids left are Goten and Trunks. They agree not to use their Super Saiyan and Ki attacks. During the fight, Trunks puts Goten in a squeeze hold and tells him to give up or he may die. Goten goes SSJ and flies out. Trunks is upset because he broke the rule, but Goten says it was an accident. Trunks tells Goten he can beat him with one arm, and then cheats by going SSJ and uses two arms to knock Goten out of the ring. Goten loses and calls Trunks a cheater. Trunks says it was an accident just like when Goten went SSJ. Trunks tells Goten he can have any three of his toys and Goten is happy again.

157. Chibi Trunks vs. Mr. Satan

Mr. Satan fears for his life when he hears that he has to fight Trunks, the winner of the Youth Division. As usual, Mr. Satan thinks of a plan to get out of the fight. He tells Trunks

The ULTIMATE: Fight Guide

that before they fight, they must tap each other lightly on the cheek. His plan is to act hurt when he gets hit and pretend he "let Trunks win". When the match starts, Satan tells Trunks to tap him on the cheek. The crowd is amazed that he is giving Trunks a free hit. Trunks does what Satan tells him, but the tap sends Satan flying into a brick wall. Satan slowly gets to his feet and pretends like he acted being hurt. The crowd believes him, and they begin to chant his name. Trunks also thinks Satan was being nice and let him win. When Satan returns to his locker room, we see that the punch did hurt him.

158. Krillin vs. Punta
This is Krillin's first match in the 25th World Martial Arts Tournament. Krillin wins this match without breaking a sweat.

159. Ma Junior (Piccolo) vs. Shin (Kaioshin)
Shin uses magic to paralyze Piccolo. Since Piccolo can't move, he gives up.

160. Spopovich vs. Videl
Spopovich beats Videl into submission. However, something doesn't seem right about Spopovich. He is stronger than usual and also has a strange "M" on his forehead.

161. Yamu and Spopovich vs. Gohan
Kibito and Kaioshin set up Gohan in this fight. They paralyze him and allow Yamu and Spopovich to suck out his power. They do this so they can track Yamu and Spopovich to their headquarters.

162. Pui Pui vs. Vegeta
Vegeta tells Kaioshin and Gohan that he wants to fight alone. The fight occurs in Babidi's Spaceship. Pui Pui is surprised that Vegeta wants to fight by himself. Vegeta is taking care of Pui Pui without a problem, when Babidi changes the gravity to 10x. This is the same gravity level as Pui Pui's home planet. He does not realize that Vegeta is used to this gravity and Vegeta defeats Pui Pui.

163. Yakon vs. Goku
Goku fights Yakon after Pui Pui is defeated. They fight in a pitch-black room. Goku uses his ki to light up the room. He doesn't know Yakon swallows energy so he can gain energy. Goku decides to power up and Yakon absorbs so much energy that he explodes.

164. Android 18 vs. Mr. Satan
Android 18 and Satan are the final two contestants in the World Martial Arts Tournament, since everyone else has left. Mr. Satan knows he has no chance of beating 18, so he offers her money to throw the match. Android 18 agrees and Mr. Satan wins with a Super Satan Punch.

165. Gohan vs. Dabura
Gohan fights Dabura on the next level of Babidi's spaceship. Dabura can turn people into stone by hitting them with his spit. Gohan is having trouble in this match. Vegeta draws the attention of Babidi by continuously mocking Gohan. Dabura leaves the fight to inform Babidi that Vegeta has evil in him and that he should be turned into a Majin.

166. Majin Vegeta vs. Goku
Vegeta wants to get more power, so he lets himself get possessed by Babidi. Once he does this, Vegeta, Goku, and the others are teleported to the Tenkachi Budokai Arena. Vegeta blows up the stands to provoke Goku. Goku realizes what Vegeta is doing and that he let himself be possessed. Goku is outraged and agrees to a fight with Vegeta. Kaio Shin tells Goku it's just Babi Dee's way to gain energy for Majin Buu. Vegeta and Goku go to an empty location and start to fight. In the middle of the fight, Goku senses Majin Buu and tells Vegeta they should stop fighting and find out what is happening. Vegeta agrees, so Goku lets his guard down because he thinks the fight is over. When Goku reaches for the last senzu (he is taking it to prepare for the Majin-Buu fight), Vegeta hits Goku and knocks him out. He takes the senzu and flies off.

167. Fat Buu vs. Dabura
Dabura knows that Buu has been released. Dabura fights Buu. Dabura is defeated, but he does not die.

168. Gohan and Kaioushin vs. Fat Buu
Gohan and Kaioushin are no match for Fat Buu. After the fight, Gohan appears to be dead and Kaioushin is close to dead.

169. Fat Buu vs. Dabura
In this fight, Dabura is turned into food and eaten by Fat Buu.

170. Fat Buu vs. Majin Vegeta
This is Majin Vegeta's last fight. Vegeta starts out knocking Buu all over the place. It looks like Buu has no chance to win. However, Buu fully recovers and Vegeta wonders if Buu

The ULTIMATE: Fight Guide

is immortal because he can't be damaged. When Vegeta is near death, Chibi Trunks and Goten fly in and kick Majin Buu away. Vegeta is mortally wounded but realizes the only way to kill Buu is to ensure that all of his flesh is blown up, so that he can't regenerate. Vegeta hugs Trunks and tells him to take care of his mother. Piccolo watches from the air and understands what Vegeta is going to do. Vegeta knocks out Trunks and Goten and tells Piccolo to take them home. Vegeta asks Piccolo if he will be able to see Goku when he dies, but Piccolo tells him that he will not go to heaven and will be sent to hell for killing so many innocent people. Vegeta tells Piccolo to hurry up and get away. Piccolo, Trunks, Goten, and Krillin fly off. Majin Buu approaches and Vegeta prepares to blow himself up to kill Buu. Piccolo flies off knowing that Vegeta is finally fighting for someone other than himself. Vegeta explodes and it wipes out everything…. Or does it?

171. Piccolo vs. Babidi
Babidi uses magic in his battle with Piccolo, which only adds to Piccolo's frustration. Piccolo attacks Babidi. Babidi's shield offers no protection, and he is chopped in half.

172. SSJ3 Goku vs. Fat Buu
This is the first time that Goku goes Super Saiyan 3 in battle. Goku has 24 hours on Earth and he uses the time to fight Buu. Goku tries to buy time from Chibi Trunks so that he can find the Dragon Balls. It is clear that Goku can defeat Buu. Once Trunks finds all of the Dragon Balls, Goku runs out of time and must leave.

173. Satan vs. Bad Guys
Two men go on a killing spree and kill Buu's dog Bee and shoot Mr. Satan. Buu heals them. However, with all of his anger inside, Buu explodes forming Thin Buu.

174. Bad Guy vs. Thin Buu
Thin Buu blows the bad guy to pieces with a Ki blast.

175. Fat Buu vs. Thin Buu
Thin Buu is much more powerful than Fat Buu. Fat Buu can't defeat Thin Buu, so he's absorbed into Thin Buu. Together they form Super Buu.

176. Super Buu vs. Bad Guy's Assistant
Thin Buu liquifies and shoots down the assistant's throat. Once inside, he expands and blows up the assistant.

177. Gotenks vs. Super Buu
Gotenks is excited to fight and doesn't listen when Piccolo warns him about Super Buu. Gotenks fights Super Buu and loses badly. Gotenks retreats.

178. Gohan vs. Super Buu
With the power of Piccolo, Goten, and Trunks in him, Buu is very strong. Despite Buu's strength, Gohan is still winning the fight. However, with pieces of himself lying around, Buu uses them to absorb Gohan.

179. Vegetto vs. Super Buu
Super Buu is now made up of Piccolo, Gohan, Trunks, and Gohan. Only Vegetto is powerful enough to defeat Buu. Vegetto is cocky and cares only about showing off and not fighting Buu. This allows Buu to swallow Vegetto, but while inside Buu, the fusion between Vegeta and Goku wears off.

180. SSJ3 Goku vs. Majin Buu
Buu is now pure evil and in his most deadly form, Kid Buu. This is a great fight, but Goku needs to take a break to recharge.

181. Vegeta vs. Majin Buu
Vegeta is fighting Buu so Goku can recharge his ki. Goku is taking a long time and Vegeta is no match for Buu. It is this fight where Vegeta goes from being a bad guy to a good guy.

182. Majin Buu vs. Fat Buu
Majin Buu spits out Fat Buu while fighting Vegeta. Fat Buu takes Vegeta's place and even though he does not hurt Majin Buu, Goku has more time to recharge.

183. Majin Buu vs. Vegeta
Vegeta is trying to delay time so Goku can form a Spirit Bomb. Vegeta uses the Dragon Balls to wish everyone back to Earth. With his wish, Vegeta is returned to a living state. On Earth, a powerful Spirit Bomb is formed.

184. Majin Buu vs. Goku
With the help of Satan, Goku is able to get energy from all the people on Earth for his Spirit Bomb. Goku uses the Spirit Bomb to destroy Majin Buu. Goku wishes Majin Buu could be brought back as a good person.

185. Vegeta vs. Noshiku
Noshiku calls Vegeta an old man. Without even turning around, Vegeta punches him across the arena.

186. Pan vs. Mou Kekko
Mou Kekko is huge and looks like he could kill Pan. After a punch and a kick, Pan knocks him out of the ring.

187. Goku vs. Ubuu
This fight is during the World Martial Arts Tournament. Ubuu is very nervous, but once Goku attacks, he starts to fight back. Goku realizes this kid's great power and asks him if he would like to go and train with Goku.

Dragon Ball GT
Episode Guide

— BY ANDY DIEHL

Dragon Ball GT was on the air in Japan from February 1996 through November 1997. Akira Toryiyama, who created Dragon Ball and Dragon Ball Z, did not oversee Dragon Ball GT. Critics felt this hurt the storyline and character development in the series. Dragon Ball GT has not aired yet in the United States. It is expected to air sometime in 2004. Many people can't wait for this series to be dubbed into English because they want to see Vegeta & Goku turn Super Saiyan 4! However, that's about all anyone really knows about this series. We'll try to provide you with some additional insights.

Dragon Ball GT picks up 10 years after Dragon Ball Z ended. Gohan and Trunks are adults living in the big city. Gohan is married to Videl, and they have a daughter named Pan.

The Dragon Balls in GT are Black Star Dragon Balls. They look much like Earth's Dragon Balls, except for a dark black star. Their power is greater than the Earth's Dragon Balls. These Dragon Balls were created before Kami & Piccolo split up, so their power is thought to be twice as great. The summoned dragon is now larger and red. If the black star Dragon Balls are not found, Earth will become a pile of dust, so the search becomes the focal point of the story.

Episode 1
The mysterious Dragon Balls appear!! Goku becomes a child!?

While training at Kami's Lookout, Goku is turned into a kid. Pilaf makes this wish using the Black Star Dragon Balls. Goku and gang have one year to search the universe for the Dragon Balls before the Earth is blown up.

Episode 2
I am the Leader! Pan Flies into Space!!

Goku is kidnapped by a couple of kidnappers who think that he is part of the Briefs family. Goku finally gets away from them and goes to the space ship. When liftoff time approaches, it's Pan and not Goten who goes into space with Goku and Trunks.

Episode 3
The Ultimate Moneygrubbers!! Imegga, Planet of Merchants

Trunks lands on Planet Imega to get repair parts for the ship. While on the planet, the Z gang learns the residents are extremely greedy. At the end of the episode, a robot swallows the Dragon Radar and Trunks' space ship is towed away.

Episode 4
Wanted!! Goku is a criminal!?

Goku and gang sneak into Don Kia's Castle to get back their space ship. Even though the guards become aware of their presence, the gang still escapes with the space ship. Goku, Trunks, and Pan are now wanted criminals on Imega.

Episode 5
See, the Strong Guy!! The Bodyguard Rejjik

Thanks to an older couple, the Z travelers learn that Don Kia is evil. After hearing this, they allow themselves to be arrested so that they may fight Don Kia. After Goku defeats Rejjik, Don Kia is forced to give up and Imega is now a free planet.

Episode 6
It hurts, eh!? Goku the Dentist

Goku and Gang land on the planet Momasu. Everything on the planet is super-sized. After saving Pan from a beehive, the Z warriors must get the next Dragon Ball. The group finds the Dragon Ball lodged in the tooth of a giant, but they manage to get it.

Episode 7
Beloved Honey!? The Betro-thed is Trunks

The next planet is Planet Kerubo in which a monster named Zuunama is plaguing the planet. Zuunama is able to create earthquakes. In order to get the Dragon Ball of the planet, the Z warriors must defeat the beast. Trunks takes the place of Reenu as the monster's bride.

Episode 8
Goku also Thunders!! The Whiskers' Power is at Full

Back at Zuunana's house, Trunks is able to get the monster drunk and he passes out. The Z warriors then cut off his earthquake causing whiskers. We learn that he never could create earthquakes, but only detects them. The Z warriors get the Dragon Ball for keeping their promise, but at the end of the episode, an alien steals the Dragon Ball.

Episode 9
Damn!! Goku Leaps into the Trap Planet!?

Trunks and gang chase the aliens onto Planet Bihe, which is inhabited by giant worms. Once there, it is almost impossible to escape. After tricking the Z warriors into going to Bihe, the aliens return to their planet. The aliens are then told to get the other Dragon Ball that is on the Z warrior's ship.

Episode 10
Dance Attack!? Bonpappa!!

After defeating the worms, the Paras put the Z warriors under a spell which makes them dance. However, the worms come back and the spell is broken. The Z warriors are able to defeat the Paras. While Pan is on the Paras ship looking for the Dragon Ball, it takes off and goes back to the Planet Rudo.

Episode 11
The Curse of Rudo!? Pan turns into a Doll

Once on Planet Rudo, Pan attempts to get the Dragon Ball. In the process, she is turned into a doll by M2. Trunks and Goku show up and they defeat a lion and M2. M2's whip then takes its true form of Muchi, the real priest of Rudo.

Episode 12
The Oracle of God is REALLY Troublesome!! Soldier Rudo

Dragon Ball GT - Episode Guide

Muchi is a demon with the power to control the Earth. Goku and Trunks are being beaten by Muchi, until Goku goes SSJ and surprises Muchi. Trunks then goes SSJ and the battle is even. Meanwhile, Doru-Takki turns all of Rudo's followers into dolls. He plans to use their energy to awaken Rudo. At the end of the episode, Rudo is finally awakened.

Episode 13
This is Father and Son? The Riddle of Scientist Myuu

Trunks and Goku begin to fight Rudo and the two Saiyans are winning the fight. When Doru-Takki will not give Pan to Dr. Myuu, Dr. Myuu turns Doru-Takki into a doll. Dr. Myuu then sacrifices Doru-Takki and Pan to Rudo. Rudo is now set for his final stage.

Episode 14
Can We Get the Rhythm Down Perfectly!? Capture Rudo!!

Goku and Trunks are still fighting full-strength Rudo. Pan is inside of Rudo and she awakens all the other people who were sacrificed. Pan and Goku must both attack Rudo's heart at the same time, but they cannot hear one another. Pan talks to Goku telepathically through the Para Brothers and, after many tries, Goku and Pan defeat Rudo and everyone is returned to normal.

Episode 15
I Can't Take Anymore!! Pan Runs Away!?

While on Planet Rudeze, Pan gets mad at Trunks and Goku and runs away. While walking, Pan runs out of water and collapses. Gill comes to her rescue. Pan awakens to find that Gill has saved her, has found water, and has also found the 5 star Dragon Ball.

Episode 16
Machine Planet M2... Gill the Backstabber!?

Gill convinces the Z warriors to land on Planet M2, his home planet. It is a trap. Gill is greeted by Shogun Rirudo and is told he has done a good job of luring the humans to the planet. At the end of the episode, the Z warriors meet up with a group of strong robots who call themselves "M2's Commandos." After a short fight, the robots capture Trunks and Goku and take them away.

Episode 17
Waiting for Pan!! The Tactical Strike to Rescue Goku!!

Pan disguises herself as a robot and sneaks into the tower where Goku and Trunks are held hostage. Through a series of events, Pan finds out about Dr. Myuu and also where Goku and Trunks are being kept. While Goku and Trunks are being examined, Rirudo and the Ener Cannon Shin Go are watching the Z warriors' previous fights. On her way to rescue Goku and Trunks, Pan runs into the smallest of the Ener Cannon robots and defeats him. Pan arrives to save Goku and Trunks and in the process, they are able to break free.

Episode 18
Hey, Some Data is Missing!! Goku's Ultimate True Determination

Goku tells Pan and Trunks to escape. The Ener Cannon Robots combine to form the Mega Cannon. After letting the Mega Cannon fight, Goku declares that he knows the extent of its power and then defeats the Mega Cannon. Goku is then faced with a much stronger force, the powerful Shogun Rirudo.

Episode 19
Set Out and Attack!! The Mighty Mutant Rirudo

Rirudo shows up and, after some talking, turns Trunks into a metal tablet and he is transported away. Pan goes to get Trunks, while Goku and Rirudo fight. After fighting for a short time, Goku goes to Super Saiyan and Rirudo also takes on his final form. The fight continues.

Episode 20
Surprise!! Goku's Attacked By a Metal Storm

Goku is beginning to defeat Rirudo, when Goku demands Rirudo go to full strength. Rirudo's new form is able to control the whole planet. Meanwhile, Pan is still trying to find Trunks. Pan is able to recover one of the Dragon Balls, and Goku and Rirudo continue to fight.

Episode 21
What is this!! Goku is Turned to Metal!?

The fight continues throughout the city, but because of Pan, Rirudo is

Dragon Ball GT - Episode Guide

able to encase both Pan and Goku in metal tablets. On Myuu's planet, the operating begins. At the last minute, Gill shows up and frees Trunks, Goku, and Pan. Apparently, this has been the plan the whole time, so Gill is not a traitor.

Episode 22
Violent Ambition!! Birth of the Evil 'Bebi'

The Z gang are shown a secret room on Myuu's where Bebi is being maintained. Trunks says that he has shut down Bebi because he is so powerful. Myuu gets mad and attempts to save Bebi. Finally, Bebi awakens, but all three of the Z warriors fire and kill Bebi. Myuu takes Bebi's remains and escapes, but Bebi takes over Myuu's body, bursting out and killing Myuu.

Episode 23
A Hidden Crisis!? A Space wrecked and Mysterious Boy

The three Z travelers find the one star Dragon Ball on a destroyed ship. While on the ship, Pan finds a boy who is barely alive. The travelers land on a nearby planet so the boy may be treated. While in the emergency room, the boy causes a large explosion and everyone rushes to see what happened.

Episode 24
Bebi's Counterattack!! Target the Saiyan!!

They learn that Bebi has taken over the boy's body and is now looking to obtain the power of the three Saiyan. In order to find a way out of the hospital, Bebi takes over the body of a doctor. Bebi eventually enters Trunks' body through a wound, but he is not strong enough to take over Trunks. Bebi escapes and the three Saiyan continue their search for the Dragon Balls.

Episode 25
Oh no!! Bebi Has Appeared on Earth

Back on Earth, Goten is on a date. At the same time, Bebi is destroying everything in his path in an attempt to find the Saiyan. While all of this is happening, Goku finds the seven star Dragon Ball and now only two Dragon Balls remain to be found. Mr. Satan shows up to fight Bebi, but when he sees Goten, he has Goten fight for him. Goten and Bebi's true forms are now ready to do battle.

Episode 26
Gohan and Goten... The Worst Brotherly Spat!?

Goten isn't having much of a problem, but through his carelessness, Bebi is able to enter and take over his body. Meanwhile, Goku recovers yet another Dragon Ball and now only one remains. Back on Earth, Gohan and Goten begin to fight. Gohan realizes that something has taken over Goten. While Gohan is powering up, Bebi then enters Gohan's body and goes to look for Vegeta.

Episode 27
Ambition Achieved!? Vegeta Possessed.

Goten is at Capsule Corp being treated and Bebi is looking to fight Vegeta. Bebi finds Vegeta and the two talk before fighting. We learn that Bebi is one of the Tsufuru-jin race. We also learn that Bebi leaves an egg in every body he takes over. During the fight, Goten shows up and attacks Vegeta. Bebi eventually takes over Vegeta's body. In the meantime, Goku has found the final Dragon Ball.

Episode 28
Goku Returns... "All of Earth is My Enemy!?"

Trunks, Goku, and Pan return to Earth and give the Dragon Balls to Dende, but now Dende has been possessed by Bebi. Gill and Trunks go to Capsule Corp but no one meets them. Pan and Goku go back to the countryside and Videl and Chi Chi are there acting like zombies. The egg in Trunks is activated. Back in the countryside, Goten and Gohan attack Goku and Pan.

Dragon Ball GT - Episode Guide

Episode 29
This is Really Bad!? Supper Saiyan 3 Fails!!

Goku realizes that Bebi controls everyone. Super Saiyan 3 Goku begins to fight Vegeta. However, Vegeta has no problem fighting him and Goku has to power down because he cannot handle SSJ3 for long. The fight goes on longer than expected and Goku is no longer able to move. Vegeta goes into Perfect Bebi form and uses a Death Ball to blast Goku. Everyone thinks Goku is dead.

Episode 30
Goku Has Passed On!? "I'm Dead."

Bebi Vegeta takes his throne and wishes for a planet like his old planet to be placed next to Earth. Meanwhile, Goku is playing a game with Suguro to decide whether he is dead or not. We learn from Dai Kaioshin that Goku cannot be rescued.

Episode 31
What the...!? The Sky of Suguro-ku Studio is Collapsing

We discover Suguro and his son are cheaters and they cause the Suguro-ku to fall apart. In the chaos, Goku saves them. As Goku escapes, Kibito shows up and teleports Goku to Dai Kaioshin's. Dai Kaioshin trains Goku. Pan, Satan, and Buu sneak onto Planet Plant, but Pan is caught and about to be killed when Ubuu intervenes.

Episode 32
Goku Returns!! Angry Fighter Ubuu

Ubuu begins to fight Bebi and holds his own. Back at Dai Kaioshin's, Dai Kaioshin plans to pull out Goku's tail with a pair of pliers so Goku will have more power. Ubuu cannot move and Vegeta-Bebi is about to use his Death Ball when Buu jumps in the way and takes the blast. Buu and Ubuu merge, and Ultimate Ubuu continues to fight Vegeta Bebi.

Episode 33
Eat This, Bebi! New Ubuu's Killing Light Ray!!

Vegeta Bebi and Ultimate Ubuu start fighting and Ubuu easily handles Vegeta Bebi. Meanwhile, Goku has his tail pulled out. Ubuu fires a blast at Bebi, but when it's returned, Ubuu is turned into chocolate and eaten. Goku shows up, but can't seem to hurt Bebi. After looking at Earth, Goku changes into a Golden Oozaru Monkey.

Episode 34
The Transformation Fails!? Giant Ape Goku's Rampage!

Golden Oozaru Goku destroys Vegeta Bebi and Planet Plant and enjoys it. Goku sees the Earth and tries to reach it. Pan tries to remind Goku of his real identity. During all of this, Goku goes Super Saiyan 4.

Episode 35
Final Strength! Goku Becomes Super Saiyan 4!!

SSJ4 Goku goes off to fight Vegeta Bebi, but Vegeta Bebi is no match for SSJ4 Goku. As Goku is about to kill Bebi, Bulma uses a machine to turn Vegeta Bebi into a Golden Oozaru and the tables are turned.

Episode 36
Immortal Monster!? Atrocious Giant Monkey Bebi!!

The fight continues and we learn that Vegeta turned into a giant monkey, but Bebi is still in control. Bebi destroys some cities on Earth, which makes Goku mad. In an attempt to stop him, Goku takes one of the blasts and looks like he's dead.

Episode 37
Bebi and Goku -- Double KO!!

Bebi and Goku continue to fight and they knock each other out. Kibito goes to Dende's Lookout to get the Chou-sui water, which will cleanse the evil of Bebi from everyone. As Kibito brings Gohan and Trunks back to normal, Vegeta Bebi and Goku begin to fight again, but Goku has no more power left.

Episode 38
From Everyone's Power... The Revival of Super Saiyan 4

Vegeta Bebi is now just playing with Goku. Trunks tries to interfere, but can't do much. Goku asks his

Dragon Ball GT - Episode Guide

friends to give him their energy. From inside Vegeta Bebi, Ubuu is causing Bebi a massive stomachache and this gives the Z warriors enough time to re-energize Goku. Goku now feels he can win.

Episode 39
This is How it Ends! At Last, Bebi's Extinction.

The Z fighters feel they have a chance and the fight continues. After some taunting from Goku, Bebi fires off a huge Death Ball, but Goku manages to block it. Goku fires off a Kame Hame Ha, which puts Bebi down for the count. Bebi escapes from Vegeta's body and tries to escape from the planet. Goku uses a Kame Hame Ha to destroy Bebi. The gang uses Chou Sui water to return everyone to normal.

Episode 40
Everyone Escape!! 5 Seconds Before Earth Explodes

All of the Z members work to move everyone to Planet Plant before Earth explodes. When it is finally time for the Earth to blow up, Piccolo tells Gohan that he has grown up very well and that he will die with the Earth. The Earth explodes and, a little later with the Dragon Balls, the Earth is restored.

Episode 41
Tenkaichi Budoukai. Who Will Be Satan's Successor?

Goku must fight in the Children's Tenkaichi Budoukai because of his height. Mr. Satan announces that whoever wins the Tenkaichi Budoukai, will take his place as leader. In the final round, Ubuu loses to Mr. Satan on purpose and the Z gang members are thrilled.

Episode 42
Die, Goku!! The Revived Strong Enemies Escape From Hell

In Hell, Dr. Myuu and Dr. Gero become partners and create a new Android 17. Together they create a hole in the sky that links Earth and Hell. This will be used to merge the two 17s. All of the old enemies are coming to Earth, and the only way to stop them is for Goku to go to Hell to fight Android 17. When Goku enters though the hole, 17 leaves and the hole closes.

Episode 43
Hell's Devil Fighters!! The Revival of Cell and Frieza

The fighting in Hell begins and Goku fights Frieza and Cell. After a lot of taunting, Goku easily finishes the two, but in Hell you cannot die. On Earth, Vegeta is getting ready to fight the new 17. In Hell, Goku is knocked down to a level below Hell where he is put through a series of tortures by an old woman.

Episode 44
The Ultimate Android! The Two #17s Unite

Android 17 kills both Krillin and Android 18. In Hell, Goku uses an ice machine to turn Frieza and Cell into ice and then shatters them. On Earth, Vegeta and the new 17 are fighting when the old 17 arrives.

Super 17 is formed and Piccolo goes down to Hell to help release Goku.

Episode 45
Hurry, Goku!! The Plan to Escape From Hell!

Super 17 is easily defeating all of the Z warriors; while in Hell, Piccolo and Dende are trying to create a link from Hell to Earth. Finally their plan works and Goku escapes to Earth. At the same time, Super 17 destroys Dr. Gero and says that Dr. Myuu is now its sole master. Goku shows up and the fight begins.

Episode 46
Crash!! SSJ4 vs Super #17

Goku isn't able to beat Super 17 because Myuu has programmed the 17 to read all of Goku's attacks. Goku goes SSJ4, though, and Myuu has never seen this form. Super 17 proves to be better than Goku, so Goku doesn't mind dying and going to Heaven.

Episode 47
The Big Reversal! Goku's and Android 18's 2-Step Attack Explosion!!

Goku prepares to self-destruct while holding 17. However, 17 creates a

Dragon Ball GT - Episode Guide

barrier and Goku reverts back to his child form. Super 17 then kills Myuu, and Android 18 shows up. Goku realizes that when 17 absorbs energy, he is open to attack. When 18 attacks, Goku uses his Dragon Fist to kill Super 17. The Z gang uses the Dragon Balls to wish back Krillin, but when summoned, an old dragon appears.

Episode 48
This is a Surprise! Shenlon is the Enemy?!

The old dragon releases seven other dragons, each holding a Dragon Ball. We learn that because negative energy is created by each wish and so much energy has built up, that only evil has been released. Goku, Pan, and Gill run into the first dragon, the Dragon of the Water.

Episode 49
The Strongest Enemy!? The Fear of the Underhanded-Trick Using Dragon

Ryan Shenlon is being defeated by Pan, but he then shows his true power. He explains how the minus energy works. With their knowledge, Goku and Pan clean up the polluted water so Ryan Shenlon's power is taken away. Goku and Pan kill him with energy blasts, and then collects the two star Dragon Ball.

Episode 50
Saiyan Power Dies in Honorable Defeat!? Electrical Fighter Uu Shenlon!!

Pan and Goku run into a city that has slime everywhere, and the two meet Uu Shenlon. He electrocutes Goku and Pan and Goku goes SSJ4. After Goku and Pan pass out, a storm shorts out Uu. Goku uses a Kame Hame Ha to finish off Uu, and they collect the five star Dragon Ball.

Episode 51
Ryuu Shinlon! Looking for the Big Tornado Attack's Weak Point!!

In a fishing town Bisshu explains that since Odo-hime-sama has arrived, all the fishermen are supplied with food, so now they sit around and drink. Pan and Goku confront Odo-Hime-sama, who is actually Ryuu Shenlon, but they can't seem to get to the Dragon. Finally, Goku and Pan defeat Ryuu Shenlon and recover the six star Dragon Ball.

Episode 52
Pan, Look Out! To be Possessed by Chii-Shenlon

The three run into Chii Shenlon, but Chii does not want to fight, he only wants to make earthquakes. Chii explores the city, but realizes that Pan and Goku have fixed all of the destruction. Chii becomes angry and attacks. Chii sucks Pan into the Dragon Ball, so its true form can be released.

Episode 53
Pan Dies!? The Tears of 10x's Kamehame-ha!!

Goku goes SSJ4 and begins to beat up on Chii, but feels bad because he is also hurting Pan. Goku plans to use his 10x Kame Hame Ha, which causes Chii to panic. Goku doesn't hit Chii full power because he doesn't want to hurt Pan. Goku tricks Chii and is able to save Pan from Chii's body. Goku uses a 10x Kame Hame Ha to get the seven star Dragon Ball.

Episode 54
6000 Degree Celsius Power! The Fighter of the Sun!!

Next, the three encounter Suu Shenlon, who comes from the Sun. Goku and Suu fight, but Suu is able to make his body temperature rise to the temperature of the Sun. Goku is not able to attack Suu because of the heat, so he keeps running away. After running, Goku goes SSJ4 and Suu becomes its true form.

Episode 55
Bulma Begins Working on Vegeta's Makeover Plan!

Suu and Goku fight while Vegeta trains in the Gravity Room. Vegeta is thinking about his past fights and how Goku has always bested him, which makes him mad. Bulma has found a way to make Vegeta go SSJ4 with her brute ray.

Episode 56
After the Sun, Comes the Freeze! The Fire and Ice Dragon Brothers!!

During the fight, Goku has the chance to kill Suu, but lets him go because he spared Pan's life. As they prepare to fight again, an ice blast freezes Goku hand. It is Suu's brother, San, who has attacked Goku. Suu tells his brother to butt out because it's his fight. San Shenlon

Dragon Ball GT - Episode Guide

doesn't care and encases Goku into a statue of ice. Suu uses a blast to melt the ice.

Episode 57
The Overwhelmingly Strong Enemy!! The Ruling Evil Dragon!!

Goku attacks San and is ready to kill him. San begs for his life and Goku relents. San attacks again, and Goku uses his Dragon Fist to kill San. Suu and Goku begin to fight again when Il Shenlon appears and attacks. In an effort to protect Goku, Suu dies. Il Shenlon easily beats up Goku and not even the 10x Kame Hame Ha hurts Il Shenlon.

Episode 58
Counterattack Returned! SSJ4 is Surpassed!!

Goten, Trunks, Ubuu, Gohan, Chi Chi, and Videl all arrive to help Goku. Goten, Trunk, Ubuu, and Gohan know that they cannot defeat Il, so they give all of their power to Goku. Goku is now maxed out with energy and easily handles Il. Goku thinks he has finished him off with a Kame Hame Ha, but Il absorbs all seven Dragon Balls to become perfect.

Episode 59

Vegeta and Goku are attempting to fuse, but they don't have enough time. Everyone watches as Goku and Vegeta fight Il. The two use a ton of one patterns to trick the dragon, and they both end up far away from it. Finally, they have enough time to fuse.

Episode 60
Fusion!! The Ultimate Super Gojeta!!

SSJ4 Goku and Vegeta fuse to form Super Gojeta. Compared to Super Gojeta, Il is weak and is badly beaten. Gojeta uses a Big Bang Kame Hame Ha to knock six of the Dragon Balls out of Il Shenlon. When the fusion wears off, Vegeta and Goku prepare to fight again as Il attempts to suck the Dragon Balls back up.

Episode 61
I WILL Win!! Goku Swallows the Four Star Dragon Ball!!

To save the four star Dragon Ball, Goku swallows it, but Il easily pummels Vegeta and Goku. Goku and Vegeta attempt the Fusion Dance, and, after several tries, they finally have enough time to complete it. However, it does not work for some unknown reason.

Episode 62
To the Rescue!! Goku's Final Assistant Appears!!

The four star Dragon Ball emerges from Goku's forehead in the shape of Suu Shenlon. Suu and Goku both attack Il. Suu grabs Il from behind and forms a huge fire ball. Il enters Suu's body and kills him and this causes Il to get all the Dragon Balls and become perfect again. Vegeta falls out of SSJ4 mode and it looks as if Vegeta and Goku will die.

Episode 63
The Miracle Turnaround Victory!! Goku Pleads with the Galaxy for Help!!

Il forms an energy ball to blow up the Earth, but Goku protects the Earth by taking the blast. Goku appears to have died. Vegeta attempts to continue to fight Il Shenlon. Goten, Trunks, Gohan, and Ubuu also prepare to fight. While Il fights Vegeta, Goku forms a Genki Dama with the energy of everyone in the universe. Goku kills Il Shenlon and the real Shenlong appears.

Episode 64
Goodbye, Goku... Till the Day We Meet Again

Shenlong explains that no more wishes can be made, but Goku asks for one more. He wishes for everyone who was killed in the fighting to be brought back to life. Shenlong tells Goku to come with him. Goku gets on Shenlong's back and says his final good-byes to all of his friends. While on Shenlong's back, all of the Dragon Balls enter into Goku's body and he disappears. We are brought 100 years in the future when Vegeta Jr. and Goku Jr. are fighting in the Tenkaichi Budoukai. Pan sees Goku in the crowd, but she cannot catch up to him. All the highlights from the series are then shown. ★

Video Game Reviews

— By Douglas Vanderveer

Legacy of Goku

Rejoice "Dragon Ball Z" fans; there's finally a domestic release worthy of the DBZ name. That is, if you happen to enjoy the repetitive parts of the anime episodes. While the realm of this game is not totally negative, the combined force of the drawbacks most certainly negate any of the positive perks that the title offers. It's truly a shame that this game's potential has gone to the waste basket; however, before you write this game off as an ignorable cartridge, we recommend reading the entire review; you may want this game whatever the downsides.

At its heart, "Legacy of Goku" combines RPG and action elements to form a very Zelda-like feeling, but

with the addition of experience points. On paper, this is a suitable idea, but concepts are only one half of the battle. The other half, execution, was apparently too much for the developers, as the idea falls face first into the dirt a few minutes into the game. We are by no means implying that the gameplay is a total flop, it's just very tedious. Long sessions with the title are exercises in frustration, seemingly indicating that the target audience is one who only pulls out his Gameboy Advance for short stints.

The experience system, which should be considered an integral part of this game, is actually rather disappointing. In standard RPG-form, you can gain valuable experience points by fending off the game's many fiends. Unfortunately though, the bulk of your experience comes from completing monotonous tasks which can be placed into two different categories: finding things and talking to people. When you receive a few hundred experience points simply by conversing with a character, you're left to wonder what the developers were thinking.

To be honest, the fighting isn't too much fun either. Instead of engaging in captivating battles, you spend most of your time living by hit-and-run attacks. The game serves you with three special attacks to compliment the standard punch/kick affair: a normal ki blast, the Solar Flare (Taiyoken, for all of you Japanese-version fans), and Goku's trademark Kamehameha. While the melee attacks are somewhat effective, you'll most likely end up chucking Ki blasts at the mostly-generic enemies and then hiding from their line of sight. Cheap, yes; but it's the only efficient way of not getting yourself killed by

the rampant amount of enemies thrown your way. Is this game supposed to be difficult or just frustrating?

The graphics offering from "Legacy of Goku" is on par with what you would expect from a Gameboy Advance title. You view the action from an overhead angle which, while initially awkward, proves to be quite efficient at its job. The only

noticeable visual downfalls that are easily spotted include some enemies that blend into their environments; and due to the way you view the action, it can be hard to determine what areas you can and cannot fly over. Despite the minor nags, the graphics are impressive and nicely compliment what could've been an awesome game.

Sound-wise, the game is adequate, playing well-suited but forgettable tunes. The only real standout sound effect is Goku's yell of "Kamehameha" after firing off a partial-to-full charge of the attack.

Non-hardcore fans need not apply unless their seeking an only slightly-above-average action/adventure title. Dedicated DBZ fans probably have already scooped this one up; but if not, buy it and hope that the developers can fix the problems in round two.

Collectible Card Game

Suffer from a fear of society? Or perhaps you simply don't know anyone who plays the card game? Hey, if any of those conditions are true, cheer up! You now have a reasonable

facsimile of the card game available to play on your Gameboy Advance. The fiercely popular card game (most likely due to the DBZ label) takes some blows on its transition from a physical card game to an electric one, so we'll pick apart the flaws one-by-one.

For starters, we don't really like the concept of having all of the cards available to you for deck-building from the start. We understand that a player can't just buy cards for the game, but maybe making some of the cards unlockable by defeating the computer would've been nice. In fact, this potentially could've increased the replay value by adding incentive to play through again and again. Of course, this is just petty nit-picking, so don't mind our opinion on the situation.

There's one large problem with the game that stops us from giving it our full recommendation: the interface, while visually pleasing, is slow and horrible unintuitive. Unless you're a master of the card game (or have extremely good memorization abilities), you'll find yourself constantly scrolling through your cards and making use of the game's "View" function. Under normal circumstances this wouldn't be a bad thing, but everything moves so slowly that

you want to rip your hair out. Not only that, but transition effects are abused as if some special effects-happy person got a hold of the game and started adding things randomly. Honestly, what's the point? We don't know, and we doubt there's a very good reason behind it.

Visually, there's not much that a card game can do to wow a player, so we can't hold anything against this title. The video cards feature the same images that are displayed on their paper counterparts, which we believe to be both a blessing and a curse. We're not huge on the idea of card images not always matching their appropriate titles. For instance, when did "Red Knee Strike" become

associated with Bulma? That's kind of confusing, if you ask us.

The same adequacy rule applies to the sounds; you really only get to hear one loop of music repeating over and over, as well as some random punch effects to indicate a hit.

If you're not a fan of the DBZ CCG in the first place, you obviously won't appreciate the GBA incarnation of the game. Otherwise, this title makes for a decent purchase marred only by its counterproductive and slow interface. Hopefully, we'll see a game including the cards from the newer sagas as well as some speed enhancements and such. If we do, you can bet that it will be a worthwhile addition to any DBZ fan's game collection. ⭐

The World of Dragon Ball Z
Collectible Toys

— By Dan Hancock of Dragon Balltoys.com

Very few cartoons and toy lines have as much worldwide appeal as Dragon Ball and Dragon Ball Z. From its origins in Japan, it has grown into a worldwide phenomenon, being dubbed into many different languages in dozens of countries. Of course, wherever the anime goes, a toy line follows closely behind.

A vast majority of this incredibly diverse toy line originated in Japan, where the Dragon Ball series ran for just over 10 years (1986-1996.) Dragon Ball toys are still being produced there today, to meet the demands of both a domestic and foreign market.

A number of companies in Japan contributed to the Dragon Ball toy line, but the main force behind it was Bandai, known in the US mainly for other Japanese properties, such as Mighty Morphin' Power Rangers and the Gundam series. It would be nearly impossible to catalog every Dragon Ball product that Bandai created over the 10-year span—there are far too many items to even try, especially from our vantage point in the United States. However, there are a few lines and individual toys that are especially prominent, or especially desired by collectors.

The first is, of course, the Super Battle Collection (SBC). Until Irwin Toy started creating its own figures in the US, this was the most extensive Dragon Ball action figure line available. With 49 figures in total (many having been released in multi-packs), spanning from the Frieza saga of Dragon Ball Z to the end of Dragon Ball GT, these figures are highly sought-after by casual and serious Dragon Ball collectors alike.

Let's go into some background on the SBC. Each release is assigned a volume number, so it is easy to track the order in which they were released. Vol. 01-27

Burger King™ Dragon Ball "Metals" Goku

Pojo's Unofficial ABSOLUTE Dragon Ball Z

This book is not sponsored, endorsed by, or otherwise affiliated with any of the companies or products featured in this book. This is not an official publication.

Bandai Super Collection Vol. 02 Vegeta

are Dragon Ball figures, and Vol. 28-42 are Dragon Ball GT figures. There is a marked difference between the Z and GT figures, as the GT figures are slightly larger, made with a heavier plastic, have a glossier finish, and are much more reliable in terms of quality control than their predecessors.

Vol. 00, Son Gokou Perfect Version, was released at the same time as Vol. 41 and 42, in early 1998, and has much more in common with the GT figures than the Z figures. The first ten figures of the line have been released in two versions, a "standard" release (which are similar to the rest of the line), and a "1992" release.

The 1992 releases have much more distinctive packaging, all-Japanese text, and are of somewhat higher quality (though this is debatable, and may just be the common excuse among collectors to justify the much higher prices they have to pay for these versions). Every figure from the Dragon Ball Z collection has been re-released multiple times, and the Super Saiyan figures re-released after 1996 have gold hair, as opposed to the yellow hair of the originals.

While all of the Super Battle Collection figures are desired by collectors, some are more valued than others. Vol. 5 Trunks is the first of these – before Irwin released their Trunks figures, this figure in a mint box could easily fetch $30-50 dollars. The 1992 version going for much more than that, simply due to the popularity of the character. This was the best Future Trunks figure available, and although Irwin has since made their own version, the SBC figure still holds a valued place in many collections.

Vol. 10 Brolly is another sought-after figure. It is much bigger than any other SBC figure—at almost 8 inches, it towers above the rest of them. Add to this the fact that the figure is more rare than most, and you have a collector's item. Another especially collectible figure, due to its scarcity, is the yellow hair version of Vol. 12 Super Saiyan Trunks, as only the gold hair version is readily available. Other especially collectible figures from the line are Vol. 39 Great Monkey Baby, and Vol. 38, 41 and 42, the Super Saiyan 4 figures, due to the fact that they were both extremely popular, and produced in lesser quantities.

The most collectible SBC item, however, is the Movie 7 3-pack. This multi-pack, released at a Toei Animation Festival in 1992, comes with exclusive versions of SS Goku, SS Trunks, and SS Vegeta, all with shiny gold hair. The SS Trunks is the only new mold in the set, as it is a Super Saiyan head on the Vol. 5 Trunks body. This set fetches between $150-400 depending on condition.

Bandai has a great deal more to offer to collectors than just the Super Battle Collection, however. Their Super Collection is a set of soft-vinyl figures, which come in diorama-style display boxes. Each figure measures 4-6 inches tall, and each will cost a collector quite a bit on the secondary market. Another challenge collectors find with this line is a wide variance on the quality of paint application, so finding a "perfect" specimen, especially when shopping online, is quite a quest. Especially sought-after units from this collection are Vol. 4 Son Gohan and Kililyn (one of the only Krillin figures available from

Bandai Super Collection Vol. 04 Piccolo

Collectible Toys

Bandai), and Vol. 9 SS Gohan (which seems to be more rare than the others). Expect to pay somewhere in the hundreds (or just under) for each volume.

Another set that comes in multiple versions like the 1992 and standard SBC figures is the Full Action Kit Series (FAKS). These are a set of 6 (one kit is a two-pack) action figure models, the standard versions of which aren't all that difficult to find. The versions with the Toei sticker, however, are another story. These feature all-Japanese packaging, and are molded slightly differently than the more easily found standard versions. The first two volumes in this series have flip-front boxes, so you can see the kit inside.

In addition to the FAKS, Bandai released many other models of the Dragon Ball Z gang. The Battle Z Collection, released as two sets of five 3-3/4" action figure models, are desirable collectibles, as are the set of characters from the original Dragon Ball series.

Yet another Bandai line that is both rare and collectible is the Full Action Pose Series. These 7-9" figures are still the most articulated figures out there (imagine an artist's doll), and they come with cloth outfits.

On the other side of the scale, the 3.5" Hyper figures are another line dear to collectors. These figures in their original boxes are nearly impossible to find outside of Japan. Many feature exchangeable heads, and some come with halos that can be inserted into their hair. These figures were re-released by Bandai under the Mini 1 and Mini 2 lines which were packaged on blister cards; these versions are much more common, though still rare.

Bandai Hyper Figures (many were re-released as Mini figures)

Going further down the scale in size, Bandai produced an innumerable amount of tiny, unpainted figures, similar to M.U.S.C.L.E figures from the 80's (Kinnikuman in Japan). The rarer releases of these command high-yen amounts on Yahoo Japan, so there are plenty of people in Japan still trying to finish their collections. Bandai even released the Red Ribbon Muscle Tower for these figures. If you're looking for the ultimate challenge in Dragon Ball collecting, try to make a complete set of these little guys!

Bandai's B-Club and Kaiyodo (whom American collectors know for their excellent anime figures, such as the Neon Genesis Evangelion series and other imports) produced a number of resin models, always prized among collectors. These static-pose models are nearly impossible to find, especially unassembled in their original boxes. In fact, it's easier to find bootlegs of these models, but collectors always want the real thing.

Dragon Ball was first exported to other Asian nations such as Korea. The few licensed toys that were produced for Korean markets included a series of Dragon Ball models made by Academy. The Academy models were once considered ultra-rare, but a few months ago, sellers began popping up out of the woodwork, selling the set of five models for less than $50, sometimes for as little as $12! However, now that the wave has subsided, these models should go up in value again, as new fans discover and try to obtain them.

Irwin 5" Series 8 Figures

After its amazing success in Asia, Dragon Ball was exported to Europe, where AB Groupe produced a fairly extensive toy line around it. Every line that AB produced was titled "Super Guerriers" (Super Warriors), the main difference between them being either size or gimmick.

AB's main action figure line is the Super Guerriers Articulé. This line of 25 figures draws from the latter half

50 Pojo's Unofficial ABSOLUTE Dragon Ball Z

Collectible Toys

AB Super Guerriers Model Kits: Minoshia and Tapion

Irwin figures are now highly collectible, as well).

At the same time, the anime on Cartoon Network was creating a huge following, and the demand for new product was there, so Irwin launched into a huge reissue campaign. They released 13 different sets of figures, all Bandai and AB reissues, in a wide-release (which means that they could now be found at discount stores such as Wal-Mart, K-Mart and others), along with multiple side lines, including Bandai blasting figures, AB 16" Super Warriors, 2" and 1" AB Super Warriors, etc. The majority of these sold well, and allowed Irwin time and funding to start their own, original Dragon Ball Z line.

In the spring of 2000, fans got their first glimpse of original American Dragon Ball Z figures when the story broke on Dragon Balltoys.com. There were more than a few significant aspects of this new line. First was the fact that Series 1, 2 and 3 of this new line featured only characters, such as Nappa, Bulma, King Kai and Krillin, that had never been made as action figures before (with the exception of Future Trunks).

Second was the fact that compared to the Super Battle Collection or the Super Guerriers Articulé, these figures truly were "Super-Articulated" as the title of the line suggests; some had elbow joints, others had ball-jointed shoulders (a feature which has since become standard to the line). Series 4 introduced more common characters such as Goku and Vegeta, but each series always features one or two more obscure characters.

Some of the more collectible figures of this line are series 2 ChiaoTzu and Burter, both of which are extremely rare, especially now that Irwin has ceased production of them. Two other sought-after figures are series 1 Bulma and series 3 Krillin, also both extremely rare. Also, there have been multiple "exclusives" produced from this line.

The first of these was an orange-coated version of Master Roshi, which was released with a Musicland-exclusive four pack. The ironic thing about this pack was that the first version to hit stores had a big sticker on it proclaiming the "Exclusive Roshi" figure, but the figure included in the pack was the

Irwin 5" figure Collector's Pack (Canadian Exclusive)

Collectible Toys

Irwin reissues of Super Battle Collection Vol. 08 Gohan and Vol. 03 Piccolo

standard, black-coated version!

Though the corrected packs made it into stores a few weeks later, the error packs are the more collectible, as they are much more scarce. The orange-coated version of Master Roshi also made it onto the market on the single card, and this version is also a rare find.

Later dealer exclusives, produced for Electronics Boutique, Beckett Dragon Ball Z Monthly and the FUNimation Z-Store were metallic variants on series 5 SS Vegeta (EB Gold-Hair version) and Teen Trunks (EB Gold-Hair version, Beckett Metallic Version); series 6 Android 16 (Z-Store Metallic version), Perfect Cell (Beckett Metallic version) and SS Trunks (Z-Store Metallic version); and series 7 Majin Vegeta (Beckett Gold-Hair version). Electronics Boutique was supposed to get a Gold-Hair version of series 6 SS Goku, but the special versions, in some sort of still-unexplained mix-up, have never made it to stores.

Series 7 Majin Vegeta is also the first "error" figure in the line. The original release of this figure has black hair; and as every fan knows, there's never a time when Majin Vegeta isn't a Super Saiyan in the anime. So, to appease fans, Irwin produced a corrected, Super-Saiyan version of the figure, which was released about two months later, making for three different versions of this figure and all highly collectible.

Irwin has also made multiple side lines for the Dragon Ball Z franchise, including 12-inch figures with cloth outfits, die-cast vehicles with mini-figures, figure model kits (similar to Bandai FAKS), vehicles, Secret Saiyan Warriors (figures that come with a rubber shell to simulate a power-up), Striking Z Fighters, Blasting Figures, Energy Glow figures, and more. However, one line stands out from a collector's standpoint -- the 9" Collector's Edition. The three figures in this series, Gohan, Goku, and Vegeta, are battered and bloodied. These figures were made with older collec-

tors in mind, and were the direct precurser to IF Labs figures.

IF Labs is a joint venture between Irwin Toy and FUNimation, intended to produce high-grade collectibles for older fans. They currently have two lines, a 6" Dragon Ball line, and a 9" Dragon Ball Z line. Each figure falls into the $15-$20 price range, but is worth the investment. The attention to detail on these figures is amazing, as are the paint applications and general likenesses and sculpting.

The Dragon Ball Z series goes for a more realistic look for its figures, while the Dragon Ball series has a cartoonier look. The first series of Dragon Ball Z figures were released in two different sets, one for specialty markets, and one for mass markets. They have slightly different packaging, and different paint applications (for instance, the mass version of Cooler has bone-white armor,

AB 2" Super Guerriers Christmas Set

while the specialty version has silver armor). These lines are a great hit among collectors, as they're made with a collector's exacting tastes and specifications in mind.

While the giants such as Irwin, Bandai and AB are producing the majority of figures, sometimes collectible figures come from unexpect-

Collectible Toys

Bandai Super Battle Collection Vol. 01 Son Gokou (1992 Box)

ed sources. The prime example of this is the Burger King "metals" series. These seven figures, available with Burger King kids' meals, were superbly sculpted. While they have no articulation, they are beautiful display pieces, and are a favorite among collectors.

Also, since they are unpainted, they are favorites for customizers as well, as they become even nicer-looking with a good paint job. For figures so cheap, these are still excellent collectibles, and are fetching higher and higher prices on the secondary market (the great thing is that since they're fast food toys, and have no accessories, you can generally find a few at thrift stores for pennies).

Unfortunately, the second set of BK figures was nowhere near the quality of the first (you should leave these at the thrift stores, they're not worth pennies). Other collectible American Dragon Ball Z merchandise includes goofy kids items such as Bop Bags, banks, pinball games, LCD games, and more made by MGA Productions; mini-skateboards made by Toycom, mini-busts made by Palisades, and the upcoming I-Men block figures made by Toynami.

There you have it—an overview of collectible Dragon Ball Z figures. The great thing about collecting DBZ toys is that there's something for everyone, regardless of age or financial power. Younger collectors enjoy finding the Irwin figures at Wal-Mart as much as an adult collector enjoys finding the rare, never-offered-for-sale Super Saiyan Goku Super Collection variant. You can spend as much or as little money as you like, and still enjoy your hobby. ✪

IF Labs Dragon Ball Z Series 1 Lord Slug

Bandai Super Battle Collection Vol. 01 Son Gokou (Standard Box)

For more information and images of Dragon Ball Z toys

Visit Dragon Balltoys.com
at http://www.dragonballtoys.com!

Dan Hancock is the creator of the dragonballtoys.com website

He has been cataloguing and reporting news on Dragon Ball toys since 1999.

Dragon Ball Z Collectible Card Game Beginner's Guide

- Trunks Reforged Starter Deck - $9.99
- 30 Booster Packs - $90
- Buying the Singles you need to complete your deck - $100
- Plane ticket to the National Championships at GenCon - $300

Holding two Non-Combats and an energy attack like this guy in the tournament... completely worthless.

Over 300 people competed for the Championship Belt at the 2002 World Championships including this guy who obviously doesn't read Pojo.

BY – JESSE ZELLER

As you draw your three Dragon Ball Z cards to defend with, your mind is racing. You need to win this game to guarantee a spot in the Top 64 at the World Championships. It's all or nothing. You've worked all year to get to this moment. But as you turn up your cards, your heart sinks. You realize the three cards leave you with no defense, two worthless Non-Combats and an energy attack. You ask yourself "Why did I put this Non-Combat in here? It's useless for me!"

You've made a critical error. And you might as well start packing your bags and making plans for next year, because your shot as World Champion is over.

An error such as this reflects back to a basic weakness in a fundamental concept of the Dragon Ball Z Collectible Card Game–deck building.

Deck building is the single most important concept of the Dragon Ball Z card game. Where will you go in the game without a good deck by your side? When you make your deck, you should always be sure that it is a deck that you will be satisfied with, and a deck you will enjoy.

The first question you need to ask yourself is, "How exactly do I want to win a game of Dragon Ball Z?" Currently, there are five ways to achieve victory:

Survival

Survival victory, achieved through the use of "Beatdown Decks", is outlasting your opponent. You achieve this victory by draining your opponent's life deck to 0 cards.

Most Powerful Personality

Most powerful personality victory is also known as "winning by anger." You achieve this victory by reaching your highest personality through the process of gaining anger.

Dragon Ball

This victory is achieved by collect-

ing all seven Dragon Balls of the same type.

Cosmic Backlash

One of two "instant" victories. You achieve this victory by meeting the requirements on the card, Cosmic Backlash. Not recommended for rookie players.

Dragon's Victory

One of two "instant" victories. You achieve this victory by meeting the requirements on the card,

Dragon's Victory. Not recommended for rookie players.

Which one suits you best? New players should stick to Survival, Most Powerful Personality, or Dragon Ball victory strategies. Cosmic Backlash and Dragon's Victory should not be your first choice of victory if you are a new player. Certain cards can directly remove Dragon's Victory and Cosmic Backlash from the game leaving you with no other chance to win if they were your main way of winning. Even some veteran players will not try and win by Cosmic Backlash or Dragon's Victory because they don't consider them "true" victories.

Let's say you've decided to try to win by Survival or Most Powerful or Dragon Ball. You now have developed your main strategy. It's not a smart idea, however, to dedicate every single card in your deck to your main strategy. You need to develop further sub-strategies so decks that counter your type of deck do not defeat you. Some sub-strategies you may want to consider using are:

Physical Beatdown

The act of defeating your opponent through the usage of physical attacks.

Energy Beatdown

The act of defeating your opponent through the usage of energy attacks.

Dragon Ball Retrieval

Retrieving Dragon Balls from your Life Deck, whether it be for increased power, or as a second way of victory.

Anti-Dragon Ball

Countering Dragon Balls through the use of stealing them, or removing them from the playing area.

Anger Increasing

Gaining anger, whether it be to use higher personality powers, or as a second way of victory.

Anti-Anger

Fighting anger with multiple anti-anger cards.

Allies

Playing with allies, whether they are for beatdown support or defense support.

Regeneration

Regenerating cards from your discard pile back into your Life Deck.

Hand/Deck Manipulation

Removing certain cards from your opponent's hand or Life Deck and totally destroying any strategy they have to win.

You should try to use at least one sub-strategy along with your main strategy. This will give you more support to defend against many diverse deck types in Dragon Ball Z. For local tournaments, you should build your sub-strategies around countering the most popular local deck types. This is called metagaming. If Dragon Ball decks are popular at your tournaments, you may want to consider running anti-Dragon Ball cards such as The Power of the Dragon or Huh???. For premier tournaments such as Regionals, or Nationals you should try and use a

DBZ CCG - Beginner's Guide

little bit of each sub-strategy so you will be prepared to battle all decks.

Now that you have decided how you want to win, and factored in any sub-strategies you wish to include, it is time to decide if you want to declare a Tokui-Waza.

Declaring a Tokui-Waza means you can only have freestyle, named (which are freestyle cards), and cards that match the Tokui-Waza you declared in your Life Deck. But with this limitation comes great power. The great power is in the form of a Mastery card. Simply put, a Mastery will supercharge

your strategy to win the game.

Declaring a Tokui-Waza also gives you an additional one PUR for your Main Personality. Currently there are seven Tokui-Wazas that a player can declare: Red, Blue, Black, Orange, Saiyan, Namekian, and Freestyle. Obviously, there are some styles that will assist in certain victories over others. For example, the Red and Blue styles are more likely to assist you in a Most Powerful Personality victory than the Saiyan or Namekian styles which are more likely to win by Survival. Make the choice wisely if you plan to declare a Tokui-Waza.

A new mechanic to the Dragon Ball Z card game is Sensei Decks. If you are familiar with "Magic: The Gathering," a Sensei Deck is simply another name for a sideboard, with a few differences. You may use one of five Sensei cards, each of which comes with a unique power, during the game.

However, each Sensei card has a Sensei Deck limit. The lowest Sensei Deck limit is one. The most is thirteen. There is one limitation with the Sensei Decks: you can only have "Sensei Deck" or "Sensei Deck only" cards in your Sensei Deck.

If a card just reads "Sensei Deck" on it, then you may play it in your Sensei Deck or in your regular Life Deck.

One of the most common questions I am asked is, "How much defense should I run?" My response is always, "It depends." It depends on many factors. The most common factor is what is the most popular deck type in your gaming area. If energy beatdown is popular, you should run more energy defense. If you will be participating in a premier level tournament, the amount of defense your deck contains should be determined on how confident you are against other Survival Decks.

In my last deck, I ran a meager 12 defensive cards. To make up for the small amount of defense, I had allies in play to soak up most of the physical damage. If you were to run a deck with no allies, then you'd certainly want to run more physical defense. One card you certainly do not want to leave out of your deck is Time Is A Warrior's Tool!

After you have a sufficient amount of defense, it is time to start working on what cards you should include in your deck. Look at different cards and ask yourself, "Will this card help me achieve victory?" Just because a card is an Ultra-Rare does not necessarily mean it will improve your deck.

Perhaps the most important three cards you need to have in your deck are three copies of Trunks Energy Sphere. This card is one of the few cards I will give a perfect rating, and it's the one card I will tell people to always include in their deck. Trunks Energy Sphere is a great card to include because it stops combat cards, which are very popular in play.

You now have a big pile of cards from which to make your deck. One aspect about Dragon Ball Z is that there is no finite size to your deck. You have the choice of 50 to 85 cards. If you declare a

DBZ CCG - Beginner's Guide

Namekian Tokui-Waza, you may have up to 90 cards! The majority of Beatdown Decks being used today run exactly at or near 85 cards.

More commonly, you will see Backlash and Dragon Ball decks aim to run approximately 50 cards. This is because the Backlash and Dragon Ball decks are going for a quick win. These decks require a far greater reliance on certain cards and thus need the better odds of drawing a certain card.

A Namekian Regeneration Deck does not rely on so many certain cards, allowing you to pack your deck to the full 90-card limit. If you wish to go balanced, or have really no clue how many cards you should put in your deck, try sticking to 65-75 cards.

It's time for the moment of truth. You have your new and improved Dragon Ball Z deck ready to win a tournament. However, before you can ever enter a tournament with it, you must do one thing—playtest!

Playtesting is the single most efficient way of improving and toning your skills with your Dragon Ball Z deck. Playtesting will reveal the decks you are weak to and the decks you can defeat with ease. Playtesting also shows if you are running too much defense or offense, non-combats, and other cards.

If someone ever has a suggestion to improve your deck, you should always listen. It can never hurt to listen to someone's thoughts on how to improve your deck.

Once you have playtested different decks and recorded your thoughts about your deck's performance, it's time to tweak it. Tweaking a deck is simply making changes to find the perfect synergy between the cards in your deck, and your playing style. One of the first things you should tweak is the balance between defensive and offensive cards.

Did you draw defense cards at the right time? Did you draw attack cards at the right time? Once you can answer "yes" to both questions, it's time to playtest again. If you are using an Anger Deck, was anti-anger giving you a problem? Were you gaining enough anger?

Once you can balance these problems you will need to wash, rinse, and repeat the steps of tweaking, then you are on your way to being the next

World Champion! This is where the journey ends! I hope I have helped you in your endeavors on the path to the World Championships! Good luck and remember to playtest, playtest, playtest! ★

Chipmonk, from Score, hustles players to their tournament games using a bullhorn at the 2002 World Championships.

Dragon Ball Z Collectable Card Game Top 10 Lists

— By Israel Quiroz

There have been 7 sets of Dragon Ball Z cards released for Score's Collectible Card Game. Also, a ton of Promos have been released. Let's have fun, and talk about the Top 10 cards from each set and Top 10 promos. These are the cards that had the biggest impact on the game, and are the top cards for your deck.

Saiyan Saga

1. Vegeta's Quickness Drill

After looking over the Saiyan Saga time after time, it's not hard to see why this is the best card in the set. This drill is a powerful card that allows you to draw one extra card every time you enter Combat, whether you're the attacker or the defender. Most cards that allow you to draw cards every turn usually hurt you in the long run, because you end up running out of cards. With this card you draw cards from your discard pile, so you'll never have to worry about running out of cards.

2. Earth Dragon Ball 7

This card is the best Dragon Ball out of the Saiyan Saga. It doesn't only end Combat to buy you more time, but it also allows you to set up your next turn. When you play this card you can choose any three cards from your discard pile and place them at the top of your Life Deck in any order. This is the best combo set up ever. You not only get to end Combat, but you get to set up your hand for your next turn.

3. Battle Pausing

This Combat card has been a powerhouse ever since it was released. Score slowly started to weaken this card by changing its power and restricting it to one per deck. After that, it's power was changed to draw the top two cards from your discard pile, remove from the game after use, limit one per deck and your opponent's Main Personality gained five power

stages. Still, despite these modifications, the card is still playable and it screams to be used in combo decks.

4. Teaching the Unteachable Force Observation

Being able to end Combat is usually good when you're trying to set up and finish off you opponent. However, being able to keep your opponent from attacking you is much better. There are times when you can't afford to have your opponent attack you, because you may run out of cards or your combo is almost ready. In that instance, this card comes into play as it gives you the ability to keep your opponent from attacking you. You'll have all the time you need to make a comeback or to set up a killer combo to finish him off.

5. Saiyan Truce Card

There may be a lot of cards that can end Combat and protect you from your opponent, but this card stills stands out among the rest. The ability to end Combat alone would make it worthwhile. By getting to keep all the cards in your hand while your opponent still has to discard his cards, it simply screams to be abused. This card was and is still being used in many decks. Before this card was restricted to one per deck, Beatdown Decks were able to crush their opponents. With this card they were able to keep up to twenty cards in their hand.

6. Vegeta's Physical Stance

It's not often that one can find a card that will shut down your opponent in a heartbeat. If your opponent is trying to take you out with big, fat physical attacks, this card is all you need to stop him. No matter how strong your opponent is, Vegeta's Physical Stance stops all of his Physical attacks for one turn. When you're facing a Physical Beatdown Deck, you'll be glad you have this card because it'll help you if you're in a tight spot. It can turn the tide of the game, since your opponent won't be able to harm you while you can still hit him with your Physical attacks.

7. Orange Focusing Drill

One of the hardest things to deal with in this game is a good Non-Combat set up. This drill might not do much alone, but once you start getting your other drills in play, it's all you need to keep them safe. This drill protects your other drills from being discarded, and it forces your opponent to destroy it first before he can do anything to your other drills. This is the card set up players have been dreaming about because it will frustrate your opponent in more ways than you can imagine.

8. Goku's Capturing Drill

This drill is the reason Dragon Ball Decks have been around so long. With this drill in play, your opponent will never be able to steal your Dragon Balls and there won't be anything he can do to stop you. It really is that simple. Get this drill in play and you can start to play your Dragon Balls without worrying about them being captured by your opponent. This drill works even if he deals you five or more Life cards of Damage. When it comes to Dragon Ball

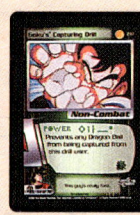

Deck cards, it just doesn't get any better than Goku's Capturing Drill.

9. Ally Wins

If you like to hit your opponent with cards he won't be able to stop, you'll love this card. This Combat card forces your opponent to discard one life card for each ally you have in play. It might not do a lot of damage in  the early game, but later on it can be a game finisher. The one thing that makes this card great is the fact that only one card in the entire game can stop it. If your opponent doesn't have it when you play this card, it will be fifteen life cards he won't be able to stop.

10. Red Back Kick

This card is greatly underestimated and, for some odd reason, not many players use it. It is a Physical attack dealing +3 power stages of damage that stop  all energy attacks for the remainder of Combat and lower your opponent's anger one anger level. The card is decent and is a must in every Red Deck, because that style doesn't have a lot of cards that can stop Energy attacks. Red Back Kick is one of those cards that can protect you while beating down your opponent. It would be silly not to use it.

Frieza Saga

1. This Too Shall Pass

Ladies and gentlemen, set your eyes on the best card in the game. It is not best because of what it can do, but because of what it can keep your opponent from doing. This card simply cancels any card that your opponent uses against you, and he will lose all the effects from that card. It's no surprise that it is not legal in tournaments (but it's still the best card in the game.)

2. Time is a Warrior's Tool

 Talk about cards that just say no to your opponent's attacks, Time is a Warrior's Tool is a master. This card stops all of your opponent's Energy and Physical attacks without even removing itself from the game. Its only downside is that it's limited to one per deck. However, when you keep in mind how strong it is, that is hardly a drawback.

3. Orange Destruction Drill

The Saiyan Saga was all about playing Dragon Ball Decks and using decks with a lot of Non-combat cards. This card changed the environment because of its ability to destroy any Non-Combat card in play at the beginning of every turn. What may take your opponent several turns to set up is destroyed by this card in a matter of seconds. As long as there are playable Non-Combat cards in the game, there will always be room in a deck for this card.

4. Frieza Smiles

The Frieza Saga doesn't have a lot of strong attacks, but it does have what you need to stop them. This card is one of many that can completely shut down your opponent and keep him from harming you during Combat. It is also the kill card in a lot of Dragon Ball Decks. With this card, you can stop all of your opponent's attacks while you use Non-Combat cards to get your Dragon Balls into play.

5. Guldo Lv. 1

 This card is the best personality the Frieza Saga brought to the table. The green guy's Physical attack might not deal a lot of damage, but it allows you to draw two more cards from the bottom of your discard pile every time you use it. Guldo has made what would be long games last less than ten minutes. His power allows you to overwhelm your opponent by drawing an insane amount of cards per turn.

6. Mommy's Coming Dear

This card's image is a reminder of how scary women can be. Just kidding. Although this card may not seem like much because it stops all the damage from your attacks, it can save you if you're trying to stay alive or have no attacks in your hand. Combo it off with Earth Dragon Ball Seven and you won't take any damage from your opponent's attacks.

7. Jeice's Style Drill

This drill is one of those cards that seem ok when they are released, but get better as time goes on. It used to be just another drill that can stop attacks from your opponent, but now it's better than all the new defense shields. Since it's not a defense shield, it can stop focused attacks. However, you have to make sure it's the first Energy attack played or it won't work.

8. Vegeta's Jolting Slash

If you're using a villain, this card is a definite must. It's a nice Energy attack that stops all Physical attacks against villains, and it also lowers your opponent's anger two anger levels. Once you 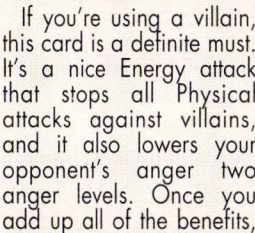  add up all of the benefits, you have a card that can do three really nice things and it only costs two power stages. Use Vegeta as your Main Personality, plus you can have up to four of these babies in your deck.

9. Straining Focusing Move

We've seen a lot of cards that can stop Physical attacks, but there aren't a lot of cards that can do the same for Energy attacks. This Straining Move is one of the few cards that can stop Energy attacks. If you think about how Energy attacks usually deal life cards while Physical attacks deal power stages, you realize how much better a card is that stops Energy attacks compared to a card that stops Physical attacks.

10. Yamcha's Skillful Defense

Last but not least, we have a card that's been seen in a lot of decks since it was released. We can think of cards that can stop either a Physical attack or an Energy attack, but they're all Combat cards. It  might not seem like much, but Combat cards can be canceled by Trunks Energy Sphere, even when they're blocks. Cards like this one can't be canceled by anything.

Dragon Ball Z Collectible Card Games: Top 10 Lists — By Isreal Quiroz

Trunks Saga

1. Chiaotzu's Psychic Halt

This card is wrong in many ways. When you play it, your opponent can't do a single thing at all. They can't use Non-Combat cards, allies, play attacks or anything. This card alone used to determine games because of it's amazing power. You won't be seeing it in tournaments anymore, but it's still the best card in the Trunks Saga.

2. Trunks Energy Sphere

Say hello to one of the few "counter spells" that Score hasn't banned, and it doesn't look like it will be banned in the near future. This card is what gamers call "counter spells"  because it can stop your opponent from doing anything he may be trying to achieve. This card can cancel the effects of any Combat card, and the only card that can stop it is itself. Given that fact, the odds of it being stopped are really low.

3. Breakthrough Drill

Up until the release of the Trunks Saga, Stasis Decks were everywhere and dominated the environment. This card was one of the few weapons the players could use against Dragon Ball Decks. If you could keep your opponent from ending Combat, the game was yours. This card changed the environment and now a lot of games are determined by it. The Breakthrough Drill shows you that there's always a way to fight a dominant deck.

4. Where There's Life There's Hope

This card falls in every deck. There's no reason a player wouldn't play it. Who can say no to keeping your opponent from winning when he thought he had already defeated  you? This Non-Combat card sits in play until your opponent wins the game then it says "no, you have to wait one more turn." This card keeps your opponent from winning until the beginning of his next turn. It should be treated as your last chance to make a comeback and defeat your opponent.

5. Black Water Confusion Drill

This card was Score's answer to the players who were tired of losing to Dragon Ball Decks. The Trunks Saga has a lot of cards to fight Stasis Dragon Ball Decks and many ways to slow them  down. This drill brought Beatdown Decks back, because while it's in play, no one can play Dragon Balls. If you're opponent is using a Dragon Ball Deck, he needs to find a way to deal with this drill before his Life Deck was gone. Some players argue that Score made a statement in the Trunks Saga that it doesn't like Dragon Ball Decks.

6. Black Style Mastery

The Black Mastery was the return of Beatdown Decks. This Mastery is nothing more than a drill that stays in play the entire game and improves all of your attacks to deal more damage. If you play a Black styled attack, it deals +2 power stages and +4 Life Card of Damage. With this card, all of your attacks can do an extra +4. When combined with big Physical and Energy attacks, it deals a ton of Life Cards of Damage.

7. Namek Dragon Ball 4

In the Trunks Saga, we get a new set of Dragon Balls and once again one of them stands out among the rest. Namek Dragon Ball 4's power allows you to discard all of your opponent's Non-Combat cards in play. With so many  set-up decks in the environment, the Namek Dragon Ball 4 usually means game over and thanks for playing. The only major drawback of this Dragon Ball is if your opponent captures it, they make you discard all of your Non-Combat cards. Despite this concern, it's a risk worth taking.

8. Red Style Mastery

This is the 2nd best Mastery in the set. It introduced a deck archetype that dominated the environment until the release of the Androids Saga. This Mastery provides the ability to gain two  anger every turn by removing a card from your discard pile from the game. A small price to pay to be able to win in less than seven turns.

9. Android 20 Absorbing Drill

This drill is one of the cards that keeps players complaining. With this drill in play, you can stop any Energy attack by simply discarding two Life Cards. It's a really powerful card that can destroy your opponent if he's trying to beat you down with Energy attacks. This card is so powerful that I wouldn't be surprised if it were restricted in the near future.

10. Hero's Way

Here's the sleeper of the set. This card has so much potential and so much power it's not even funny. It can crush just about any Namekian Deck and it stops all of those decks  that try to combo off their discard pile. The cool thing about it is if you're trying to set up your discard pile, this card is the best way to get rid of all the stuff you don't need. The ability to remove both discard piles from the game is a lot better than you can imagine.

Dragon Ball Z Collectible Card Games: Top 10 Lists — By Isreal Quiroz

Androids Saga

1. Android 18's Stare Down

It was cards like this one that allowed the villains to take over the tournament scene when the Androids Saga was released. No one can resist a card that allows you to look at your opponent's hand and make him discard any card. If you're using Android 18 as your main personality, you get to draw an extra card every turn and you can use up to four copies of this card. It gives you the hand advantage you need to take out your opponent.

2. Cell's Threatening position C6

Tired of Anger Decks? Do you wish there was a way you could stop them once and for all? You'll find what you are looking for in this card. You'll be able to make your opponent go back to square one. This villain's only card allows you to set your opponent's Main Personality to level one. Wait for your opponent to get to his level four and use this card to set him back to level one. It'll take him too long to recover and give you enough time to take him out.

3. City in Turmoil

Say hello to the Battleground you'll find in most Survival Decks. This card turns off all Non-Combat cards in play and makes sure nobody can use them for the remainder of the game. The big drawback is that it will also turn off your Non-Combat cards. However, if you're using a pure Beatdown Deck, you shouldn't have many Non-Combat cards in play.

4. Piccolo the Trained Lv. 1

This card is the best personality the Android Saga has to offer. He has decent power stages and a power that will crush your opponent's strategy in seconds. Piccolo's personality power turns off your opponent's Main Personality power and doesn't let them use it for the remainder of the turn. Your opponent won't know what to do without it because his deck is built on being able to use personality power.

5. Blue Terror

This Energy attack is like having two cards in one. When you play it, you can search your Life Deck for any card and place it in your hand. It's ability to let you get any card you need at any given time makes this card almost broken. Cards that allow you to tutor for any other cards in your Life Deck are a welcome addition. The fact that this tutor can deal three Life cards to your opponent is just an added bonus.

6. Black Searching Technique

This card is so good I don't even know where to begin. The card deals two unblockable Life cards of Damage to your opponent, it allows you to look through your opponent's Life Deck, and you can remove any two cards you want from the game. It's not even limited to one per deck so you can pack three of them and pick your opponent's Life Deck. If you want, this card lets you get rid of all the blocks he has left and throw every attack you have at him.

7. Orange Stare Down

Once again we see how much Non-Combats hate what the Android Saga brought to the game. This card doesn't only remove Non-Combats in play from the game, but it's also an Energy attack. When combined with the Trunks Saga or Cell Saga Masteries it can capture a Dragon Ball. What more could you ask for when facing a Dragon Ball Deck? With this card you could remove their Goku's Capturing Drill and steal their Dragon Ball while you're at it.

8. Saiyan Inspection

Here's the sleeper of the set. Every set has a sleeper card that only gets better as time goes on. This card is like having an off switch to your opponent's personality card power. The only drawback is that after the release of World Games, there's a Sensei card that can nuke any Non-Combat cards in play. We all know how easy it is to deal with Non-Combat cards, but cards like this one are still worth using. You'll know what I mean when your opponent loses control of the game because he can't use his personality card power.

9. Namekian teamwork

Here's the new card Ally Decks received in the Android Saga. This card is the most recent button to nuke all of your opponent's Non-Combat cards in play. The catch is that you need to have in ally in play in order to use this card. If you're already using an Ally Deck, that shouldn't be a problem. The good thing is you don't have to discard any of your Non-Combat cards when you play it because you could lose board control.

10. Severe Bruises 112

I know most of you are wondering what this card is doing in the top 10 right? Well, if you're using a hero as your main personality, you can't use Cell's Threatening Position. But you still need to find a way to fight anger. This Non-Combat card is the best Terrible Wounds variant in the Android Saga. Not many Anger Decks use a lot of drills, so this card should be able to keep your opponents from gaining any more anger. In the meantime, you can focus on taking them out.

Dragon Ball Z Collectible Card Games: Top 10 Lists – By Isreal Quiroz

Cell Saga

1. Android 18 Lv. 1

This card has been dominating the environment ever since it was released. Her power allows you to set up your hand before you even draw it, plus you get to draw a card. Being able to look at the top six cards of your Life Deck and place them back in any order before you enter Combat is extremely powerful. When you add the ability to draw a card to it, it makes this card so much more appealing. The second reason why this personality is used by every gamer is the fact that she's Android 18. It's just amazing how silly kids can be nowadays.

2. Blue Style Mastery

Before the Cell Saga was released, the player base was asking for a good, playable Blue Style Mastery. This Mastery has a lot of potential because it turns any card in your hand into a Physical or Energy block that can lower your opponent's anger two anger levels. Having this Mastery in play is like having a block in your hand every time you enter Combat. Many say a good defense is a good offense. This card will prove them wrong.

3. Z Warriors Gather

Here's the mother of all ally tutors. This card doesn't let you use one or two allies and bring them into play. With this card, you can get up to seven allies in play at three power stages above zero. It easily translates into having seven extra cards you can attack and use to defend while your opponent only has his one Main Personality. If you can get this card into play at turn one, the game will be over before you know it.

4. Cell's Presence

Cell's Presence is one of the best ways to deal with Ally Decks, and it gives heroes a decent card instead of having to use The Plan. What makes this card playable is the current environment. If it wasn't for the card Z Warriors Gather, this card wouldn't be that great. It is just a card that has a lot of power and can be really strong when it needs it to counter an even stronger card.

5. Vegeta the Last Prince Lv. 3 HT

This has to be the best card ever made when entering Combat power. Nothing can top it. It allows you to look at your opponent's hand and make him discard any card when entering Combat. With this guy on your side, you'll always know what your opponent is planning and you'll be able to force him to discard the best card in his hand. You can't ask for anything more from a card.

6. Namekian Energy Focus

This Namekian card both turns itself into any Energy Combat card and lets you draw the bottom card of your discard pile at the same time. It is one of the few cards that will allow you to get two more cards in your hand. When used in the right deck, it can turn itself into an attack and become any Energy Combat card you might need at that time. Try it out with Pikkon in a Beatdown Deck. You'll see how strong this card can be.

7. Orange Energy Discharge

As far as Energy attacks go, this is the closest thing you can get to a Krillin's Heat Seeking Blast. This Energy attack might not be unblockable, but it hits for at least six Life cards of Damage. You can capture a Dragon Ball even if you don't have other modifiers in play. It also gets around two of the best cards that can stop Physical and Energy attacks: Yamcha's Skilful Defense and Goku's Super Saiyan Blast.

8. Orange Haulting Drill

I know what you're thinking and the answer is no, the editor didn't make a mistake and misspell the title of the card. This card was actually misspelled by Score and it's one of the mistakes that has never been fixed. However, spelling aside, this card is fairly decent. It can help you deal with Physical Beatdown Decks by minimizing the amount of damage you take from Physical attacks. While you have this drill in play you'll never take more than three power stages from a single Physical attack your opponent performs.

9. Krillin's Solar Flair

Krillin's Solar Flair is one of those cards that works well in theory. You might want to call this card a small Tapkar. The perfect set-up for it is a Saiyan Physical Beatdown Deck. When it's successful, your opponent can't play any Physical Combat cards for the remainder of Combat. Once you actually play the card, you realize that since your deck is packed with Physical attacks, your opponent will always have an Energy block in his hand. The only reason this card made the list is because it works well in a Backlash Deck.

10. Stunned

Every time a new set comes out, all the players must get together to pick the one card about which they are going to complain. The card for the Cell Saga has to be Stunned. This card causes a lot of players to never want to use Trunks, Piccolo and Krillin. Stunned is a strong card because it can win you the game when you face certain personalities. The rest of the time, it's a dead card that sits in your deck. Before you decide to use it, make sure there are players using those characters in your local area.

Dragon Ball Z Collectible Card Games: Top 10 Lists — By Isreal Quiroz

Cell Games

1. Straining Rebirth Move

It's not always how powerful a card is or how much damage a card can deal that makes it one of the best cards in the set. This is one of those cards. It's worded a little different than most cards for a very special reason. IQ's (me) daughter was born on 5/9/01 and that handsome devil just had to work those numbers into a card power. This card is the result of many hours of re-wording and playing around with card effects. Hope you like it. =)

2. Gohan's kick

This card changed the tournament environment for good. Dragon Ball Decks fear this card. Even some of the Survival Decks have to watch for it because once this card has been played,  Combat will not end until both players can't do anything else. This card keeps your opponent from playing a card that can end Combat or cards that can mass block all the attacks you perform. It will also stop you from doing the same things, but if all you have in mind is beatdown, it turns out to be a pretty good trade off.

3. Caught Off Guard Drill

If this card wasn't heroes only, it would probably be the strongest card in the set. This drill allows you to name any card that cannot be played or used as long as the drill stays in play. It is the best way to deal with cards that can hurt you or cost you the game. With this drill in play, your opponent won't even be able to play those cards. You have to know what cards your opponent is using, and make sure you don't hurt yourself when you name a specific card.

4. Power of the Dragon

Expect to see Power of the Dragon repeatedly played until Score bans  all Dragon Balls ever made. This card is the equivalent of Cell's Threatening when facing Dragon Ball Decks. It can be the game breaker because if you're opponent can't recover quickly, it'll be too late. There are a lot of cards that hurt Dragon Ball Decks but nothing like this card. Just don't waste it early or it may cost you the game.

5. Aura Clash

Ever since the game was released, there was a small flaw in it. The problem was that the main personality would always stay on  his level one if he wasn't trying to win by anger. When this card hit the scene, it quickly changed the game because you were finally able to force your opponent to go to his level two. This meant that players could no longer make decks based on their level one alone. Aura Clash may have brought disruption to the environment, but it also allowed you to use your level two or level three powers, even if you weren't trying to win by anger.

6. Cosmic Backlash

As I've stated before, every time a new set is released, the players complain about a new card. When this card was released, it was considered the new broken card that would kill the game. Similar to the way that Android 18 was supposed to kill the game in Cell Saga. Cosmic Backlash was designed to help players fight Dragon Ball Decks because they were taking over the environment. It worked like a charm. A deck was finally built around this card and it completely crushed Dragon Ball Decks. It was also able to take down other decks that didn't rely on the Dragon Ball victory.

7. Goku's Dragon Ball Quest

How about a Dragon Ball Deck fast enough to race Anger Decks without having to end Combat? This card gave the Dende Dragon Ball Decks a  huge boost in speed and allowed them to combo a lot easier. When this card is used correctly, it can win the game in a matter of turns without your opponent being able to stop you.

8. Dragon's Victory

This is one of the two new victory conditions Cell Games brought to the table. It may not have seemed like a great thing at first, but  it was later used in different decks. Anger Decks started using it and it eventually became a deck of its own. Those decks are still being used today. This card has a lot of potential because it can be splashed into other decks to surprise your opponent. It also changed the Tuff Enuff environment because anger didn't matter before, but now you need to keep it in mind while building your deck.

9. Namekian Quick Blast

This card has to be the best focused attack ever made. It deals enough damage to allow you to steal a Dragon Ball, and you can recover any two cards while setting up your discard pile. It is a must for every Namekian Deck. Not only can it recover itself, but it's one of the best Energy attacks the Namekian Style has to offer.

10. Goku's Farewell

This is just one of those cards that are fun to use. With this card, you can surprise your opponent and he won't know what to expect. It allows you to go to your highest personality level, so you can beatdown your opponent with your super high power stages. However, be careful, because once you use this card you only have five turns to win the game. As the old saying goes, with great power always comes a great drawback.

Dragon Ball Z Collectible Card Games: Top 10 Lists – By Isreal Quiroz

World Games

1. Goku's Blinding Strike

This huge Energy attack is a must in almost every deck. It can hit your opponent's Life Deck for a lot of damage and get rid of his best cards. It's a Sensei only card that can hit your opponent for a total of seven Life Cards. If it's successful, you get to name any three cards and force your opponent to search his Life Deck and remove them from the game. You just can't go wrong with this card. It is one of the few playable Sensei Deck cards so always make room for it.

2. West Kai Sensei

West Kai Sensei is another card that can easily fall into any deck. This card can remove any two Non-Combat cards in play from the game during your attacker attacks phase. If your opponent has a Vegeta's Quickness Drill in play that's been hurting you or any other Non-Combat card, you can deal with them by using this card. The beauty of it is that it's a Sensei, which means you get to start the game with it in play. Non-Combat cards will not be able to harm you while you have this Sensei on the table.

3. Hero's Drill

This card is what many players are calling Dragon Ball hate 101. This drill gives Physical Beatdown Decks a chance when facing those annoying Dragon Ball Decks. While you have this drill in play, all of your successful Physical attacks can remove the bottom card of your opponent's discard pile. If any of your opponent's Dragon Balls are at the bottom of his Life Deck, you'll be able to remove them from the game. You may keep him from winning with this card alone.

4. Orange Style Mastery

Here's a brand new deck archtype waiting to happen. Orange has always focused on Energy beatdown in the past, but things have changed thanks to this Mastery. When it is combined with Cell HT level one, you get two Physical attacks doing +5 power stages of damage every turn. It can only get bigger when you perform more Physical attacks. Expect to see this Mastery in your local tournament scene. Be wary of the power of this Mastery, with it your opponent can take you out in one turn.

5. Krillin, the Great

Krillin's Heat Seeking Blast anyone? Krillin has gone from a level three to the best personality level in the World Games Saga. His level three Constant Combat Power makes all of your Energy attacks do tons of damage. When you combine it with Energy attacks, it can't be stopped. What you have created for yourself is a killing machine. Expect this guy to take over the Florida environment, because you never know what'll come out of the Bag of Beans.

6. Namekian Style Mastery

This Mastery looks a lot like the Saiyan Saga Mastery from the Cell Saga, but there's a hidden deck archtype it brings to the table. Dragon Ball Decks have taken a huge hit in the World Games Saga which is why this Mastery was created. With it you get to draw the bottom card of your discard pile when entering Combat. When in play, you'll be able to recover the Dragon Balls placed at the bottom of your Life Deck in no time.

7. Energy Drain

This card is a small preview of how strong the Majins will be once the new set is released. We have already seen how strong Majin Vegeta's level one is, and how much potential there is when you combine him with this card. This card might bring back the Saiyan Lockdown Deck, because if you can keep your opponent at zero power stages, they won't be able to do anything.

8. Free Style Mastery

This Mastery is one of the craziest cards ever released. It allows you to tear apart your opponent's Life Deck without him being able to do anything, but you have to build your deck around this card alone. Goku the Puppet can be a lot of help when building the deck and there is so much you can do with this card. Try it out and you'll see what I mean.

9. Red Heat Seeking Blast

Every Style has a way to hurt Dragon Ball Decks and, for once, Red didn't get stuck with the worst card. This Energy attack will tear apart all the Blue Dragon Ball Android 18 Decks because they can't deal with this card. If you get one off against a Blue Dragon Ball Deck, it should be enough to finish it off. We're talking about a Focused Energy attack that can deal eight to ten Life Cards of Damage.

10. Goku's Quickness Drill

This card is the best metagame card in the set. It will take out the annoying Tapkar Backlash Decks that cause so many complaints. Whenever your opponent forces you to discard a card, Goku's Quickness Drill allows you to draw a card for every card you were forced to discard. You just can't go wrong with it. Even if it's discarded from your hand, you get to place it into play instead of discarding it.

Dragon Ball Z Collectible Card Games: Top 10 Lists – By Isreal Quiroz

Promos

1. Trunks HT 1

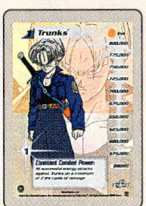

This card took over the tournament environment when it was released back in the Trunks Saga and it's still going strong. Trunk's level one Constant Combat Power turns all of your opponent's Energy attacks into Energy attacks for two Life Cards of Damage. Once you have this guy in play, you take a maximum of two Life Cards from any Energy attack your opponent performs. It is great for a Dragon Ball Deck, because your opponent will never be able to capture your Dragon Balls.

2. HUH???

This Non-Combat card was just released in the World Games Saga and it's already a staple. A staple is a card that you have to play in your deck irregardless of what type of deck you use. What makes this card a staple is that it can remove a Dragon Ball in play from the game, and it's the best way to deal with Dragon Ball Decks. What makes the card even better is that it's a Sensei Deck Only card. If you know your opponent is not using a Dragon Ball Deck, you don't even have to put it in your deck.

3. Fatherly Advice

This card is the best tutor in the game. With it you can get almost any card from your discard pile or from your Life Deck. What makes it even better is that it's a Non-combat card, so you can let it sit there until you really need a card to stay alive or finish off your opponent. Having this card in play is like having any card at will. How can you go wrong with a card like this one?

4. Confrontation

This is one of the few playable heroes only cards ever made. It is a weaker version of the Android 18 Stare Down, but in the end it still gets rid of a card from your opponent's hand. Once played, you get to look at your opponent's hand and force him to shuffle a card back into his Life Deck. He may still draw the same card later in the game, but if you're trying to get rid of your opponent's blocks in order to hit him with your big attacks, this card is all you need.

5. Cell HT Lv. 1

This guy has been used and abused ever since he was introduced. He works well with the Black Trunks Saga Mastery and with the World Games Orange Style Mastery because his power allows you to perform two Physical attacks doing +3 power stages of damage. When you combine it with either one of the Masteries, his power can do insane amounts of damage. You can also try him in a Saiyan Lockdown Deck, because his power will help you keep your opponent's Main Personality at zero power stages.

6. King Kai's New Home

This Location only made the list because of the current environment. With this card in play, you can completely shut down any Tapkar Deck or any other deck that relies on heavy card drawing. This Location doesn't let a player draw more cards once that player has four cards in his hand. It can save you from those decks that try to build up a huge hand to overwhelm you.

7. Foreboding Evidence

Foreboding Evidence is another really good and strong card for villains. With this card, any villain can shuffle all the Combat cards in his discard pile back into his Life Deck. It's like starting the game all over again, because if you do it at the right time, you can get about twenty cards back into your Life Deck. If you like to use combo decks, use this card with a hero as your Main Personality. You'll be able to take any three cards from your discard pile and place them in any order on top of your Life Deck. This card is similar to an Earth Dragon Ball Seven only smaller.

8. Emotional Baggage

This card didn't make the list because of how strong it is or for how it can be abused in a certain combo. This card made the list just because I've been wondering if it really is the worst promo card ever made. After thinking for hours and hours, I can't come up a worse one. What makes this card awful is that only Vegeta can use it, if he has Trunks in play as an ally and your opponent discards him or removes him from the game. I'd rather use a Physical attack doing +1 power stage than this card. It's useless.

9. Team Work Kamehameha

Who wouldn't want to be using an Energy attack that does ten Life Cards of Damage? This attack deals a lot of Life cards of Damage to your opponent and your Main personality doesn't even have to pay any power stages. You do need to have an ally in play with at least four power stages, but that's not as hard as it sounds.

10. Gohan's Nimbus Cloud

There's no good reason why you wouldn't want to play this card. When you play it, you get to draw a card and there's nothing your opponent can do to stop it. You also get to search your Life Deck for a Location and place it in play. You're actually getting two cards from your deck with one card. If you ask me, that's a pretty good deal. ★

Cheap @$$ Deck
Guldo's Low Budget

— BY ISRAEL QUIROZ

We all know what it feels like to be broke and how hard it is to build a deck when you don't have a lot of cards. Our green friend Guldo found himself in the same situation after spending all of his allowance on snacks, so he decided to build a deck with nothing but common and uncommon cards. I can't wait to see Goku's face after he gets crushed with this piece of art.

Top Cards

Don't think that because there are no rare or promo cards in this deck, there aren't any good cards. One of the best cards that will frustrate your opponent is Saiyan Inspection. This Non-Combat card will keep your opponent from using his Main Personality's card power until he plays a Dragon Ball. You'll be shutting down his main weapon and he'll cry if he doesn't have any Dragon Ball cards in his deck.

Orange Joint Restraint Drill is another powerful card. This Drill makes all of your Physical attacks do four extra power stages of damage. Get it in play in the early game and you'll be hitting your opponent for more Life Cards than you can imagine.

As you can see, there a lot of great cards in this deck but nothing can compare to the power Guldo brings to the table. His level one power is a Physical attack that can allow you to draw the bottom two cards of your discard pile. With a power like this one, you should have no trouble overwhelming your opponent.

How It Beats You

When using this deck, you have to make sure you let your opponent know that you aren't using anything but common and uncommon cards. Make him think you don't have any

good cards in your deck and then hit him when his guard's down.

After looking over the deck a few times, you'll realize that most of the attacks you play can stop your opponent's attacks or keep him from performing any attacks. The deck was made so you'll have more options during Combat, and to make sure you will always have enough attacks in your hand to call your opponent into Combat.

When using this deck, your worst nightmare can be pure Anger Decks because you don't have a lot of cards that keep your opponent from gaining anger. When facing an Anger Deck, go on the defensive until you have enough cards in your hand to lower his anger. Use all of the cards that allow you to recover cards from your discard pile and hope you recover some cards that lower your opponent's anger.

The deck is not hard to work because it is Combat-oriented. Try to attack your opponent at every turn and play attack after attack. Don't give your opponent any time to recover and you'll have him begging for mercy before you know it. If you can apply enough pressure in the early game by attacking at every turn and using Guldo's power, no amount of rare cards will be able to save your opponent. Who needs those silly rare cards anyways?

After you use this deck a few times you'll see how much fun it is because it's basic and effective. Guldo's power can win you the game if you use it correctly. Make sure that you always have good cards at the bottom of your discard pile and you'll be ready for anything your opponent can throw at you. The best thing about this deck is that with all the money you're saving, you can spend hours upon hours at the arcade. =)

Guldo's Low Budget

Main Personality: (3)
Guldo Lv. 1
Guldo Lv. 2
Guldo Lv. 3

Physical Combat Cards: (26)
1x Vegeta's Physical Stance
1x Nappa's Physical Resistance
3x Red Power Lift
3x Blue Round Throw
3x Red Back Kick
3x Black Defensive Stance
3x Black Defensive Burst
3x Gohan's Kick
3x Red Shattering Leap
3x Namekian Side Kick

Energy Combat Cards: (20)
1x Nappa's Energy Aura
3x Yamcha's Skillful Defense
1x Good Advice
3x Black Turning Kick
3x Blue Arm Blast
3x Black Energy Web
3x Krillin's Kamehameha Outburst
3x Namekian Quick Blast

Combat Cards: (16)
1x Time is a Warrior's Tool
3x Blue Awakening
3x Blue Leaving
3x Mother's Touch
3x Prepared Dodge
3x Trunks Energy Sphere

Non-Combat Cards: (20)
1x Earth Dragon Ball 3
1x Earth Dragon Ball 5
1x Black Water Confusion Drill
1x Jeice Style Drill
1x Orange Burning Aura Drill
1x Orange Destruction Drill
1x Orange Off Balancing Drill
1x Orange Steady Drill
3x Orange Joint Restraint Drill
3x Break Through Drill
3x Saiyan Inspection
3x Power Up The Most

Killer Deck
Perfect (Valdez) Backlash

— By Brian Valdez

Anybody who has played with or against a high quality Backlash Deck knows that the deck is all about speed. Android 18 is the best Main Personality when it comes to Backlash Decks. We have used the controversial Tapkar, but he's not that great anymore. Tapkar's biggest strength was speed, which made him great for Backlash Decks, but after the recent change in the Current Rulings Document, Android 18 is the best personality for this deck archetype.

Although I may be retired, I still know how to make a deck or two. When trying to think of a deck to make for this particular book, I wanted to create a World Class tournament deck that is fun to play, and causes my opponent to get incredibly nervous before the first card is drawn. Once I apply my "Valdez Deck Theory," I feel like no other deck can do the job like Cosmic Backlash.

The advantages of having a deck that is extremely small and fast are numerous. First of all, whenever you have a small deck with the power to draw many cards, you are able to consistently set up your main strategy at a much faster pace. With this consistency, you are less likely to have an unwanted draw, and with enough playtesting, it may seem that no bad draws even exist in the deck. This eliminates a great deal of luck, which in turn, allows a player to utilize much more of his skill. By default, the smaller, quicker deck is going to have two of the most sought after advantages during the game – card advantage and consistency. Don't forget, with enough speed advantage, you are able to nullify many defenses against you.

Having a fast, small deck is not without its weaknesses. With a lower amount of cards, you are not able to fit in as many answers to potential problems you may face during certain game situations. This means the overall potential of the deck is limited; however, although the overall potential isn't as high as bigger decks, it will play closer to its full potential more often than the "heavyweight" and "middleweight" decks.

Another weakness is that the faster decks are often extremely strong early game, but lose their strength during the late game. These factors and considerations amount to what I call the "Valdez Deck Theory," and determine the contents of the deck and the reason certain card attributes are called upon in play.

A Cosmic Backlash Deck's primary base of cards are fairly well known, since my days of playing a Cosmic Backlash Deck at three of my four world tournaments. Staples make up 50% of the deck, with cards such as the obvious Cosmic Backlash, as well as the other cards that help make up the "Perfect Backlash" combo: Piccolo's Fist Block, Red Shielded Strike, and Krillin's Solar Flare. Gohan's Kick, Black Scout Maneuver, and Confrontation help soften the opponent for the eventual backlash. This allows for very aggressive playing of the deck.

The defense system of the deck appears to be totally demolished after the opponent plays a Gohan's Kick, since the only pure defensive cards are all omni blockers or combat enders. This isn't entirely true,

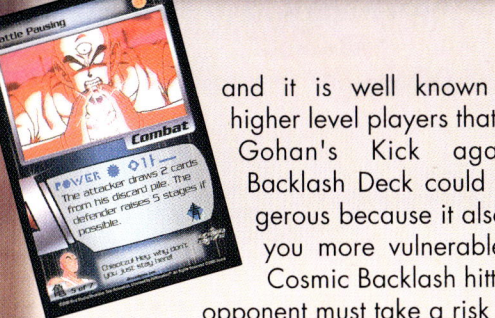

and it is well known among higher level players that using a Gohan's Kick against a Backlash Deck could be dangerous because it also makes you more vulnerable to the Cosmic Backlash hitting. The opponent must take a risk in order to play a Gohan's Kick.

While we are on the subject, if you are ever in a mirror match against a Cosmic Backlash Deck, and the Cosmic Backlash Deck enters with a Gohan's Kick, it isn't a bad idea to follow up with a Cosmic Backlash of your own. Cards such as Krillin's Solar Flare and Red Shielded Strike are also defensive cards, and will work even if Gohan's Kick is in effect.

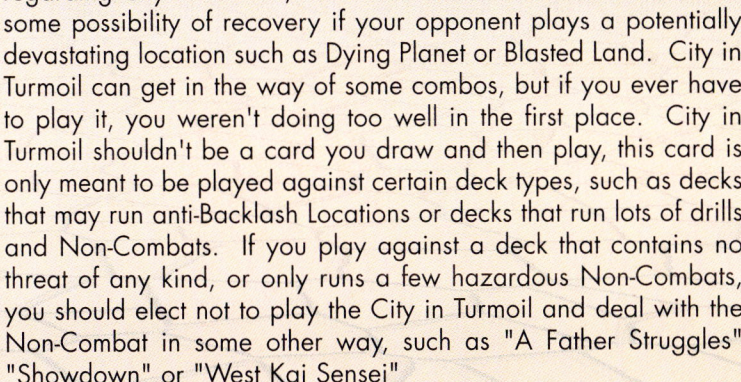

There are some controversial aspects to this deck. Some players may wonder about my reasoning for choosing the West Kai over the North Kai as my Sensei, and why I choose to run City in Turmoil as my bg/loc while leaving Caught Off Guard Drill out of the deck list entirely.

Well, I believe the West Kai is a better Sensei for the deck. The only time the North Kai may be better than the West Kai in this deck is against a CS Blue Mastery deck. On the other hand, this deck can still chain a double backlash together early in the game against a blue deck, while the West Kai Sensei can help defend against any Caught Off Guard Drills which may enter play early in the game.

Overall, I believe the West Kai Sensei is a much wiser choice for tournament play than the North Kai Sensei. As for the decision regarding City in Turmoil, I feel there must be some possibility of recovery if your opponent plays a potentially devastating location such as Dying Planet or Blasted Land. City in Turmoil can get in the way of some combos, but if you ever have to play it, you weren't doing too well in the first place. City in Turmoil shouldn't be a card you draw and then play, this card is only meant to be played against certain deck types, such as decks that may run anti-Backlash Locations or decks that run lots of drills and Non-Combats. If you play against a deck that contains no threat of any kind, or only runs a few hazardous Non-Combats, you should elect not to play the City in Turmoil and deal with the Non-Combat in some other way, such as "A Father Struggles" "Showdown" or "West Kai Sensei".

I have filled my allotted space, so I'll leave some of the cool tricks in the deck for you to find. Special thanks to IQ (Israel Quiroz) for helping me tweak this deck. ;-)

Perfect Valdez Backlash

Sensei (1)
x1 West Kai Sensei

Main Personality (4)
x1 Android 18 (CS)
x1 Android 18, the Model
x1 Android 18, the Machine
x1 Android 18, the Survivor

Combat (21)
x3 Confrontation
x3 Trunks Energy Sphere
x3 Blue Leaving
x3 Black Scout Manuever
x3 Piccolo's Fist Block
x2 A Father Struggles
x1 Saiyan Truce Card
x1 Super Saiyan Effect
x1 Time is a Warrior's Tool
x1 Battle Pausing

Physical Combat (11)
x3 Cosmic Backlash
x3 Red Shielded Strike
x3 Gohan's Kick
x1 Nappa's Physical Resistance
x1 Vegeta's Physical Stance

Energy Combat (4)
x3 Krillin's Solar Flare
X1 Nappa's Energy Aura

Noncombat (8)
x3 Tien's Mental Conditioning
x2 Showdown
x1 Victorious Drill
x1 Expectant Trunks
x1 Fatherly Advice

Dragon Ball (4)
x1 Earth Dragon Ball 3
x1 Earth Dragon Ball 4
x1 Earth Dragon Ball 5
x1 Earth Dragon Ball 7

Battleground (2)
x2 City in Turmoil

This 3D is Comin' At Ya!

Duck!

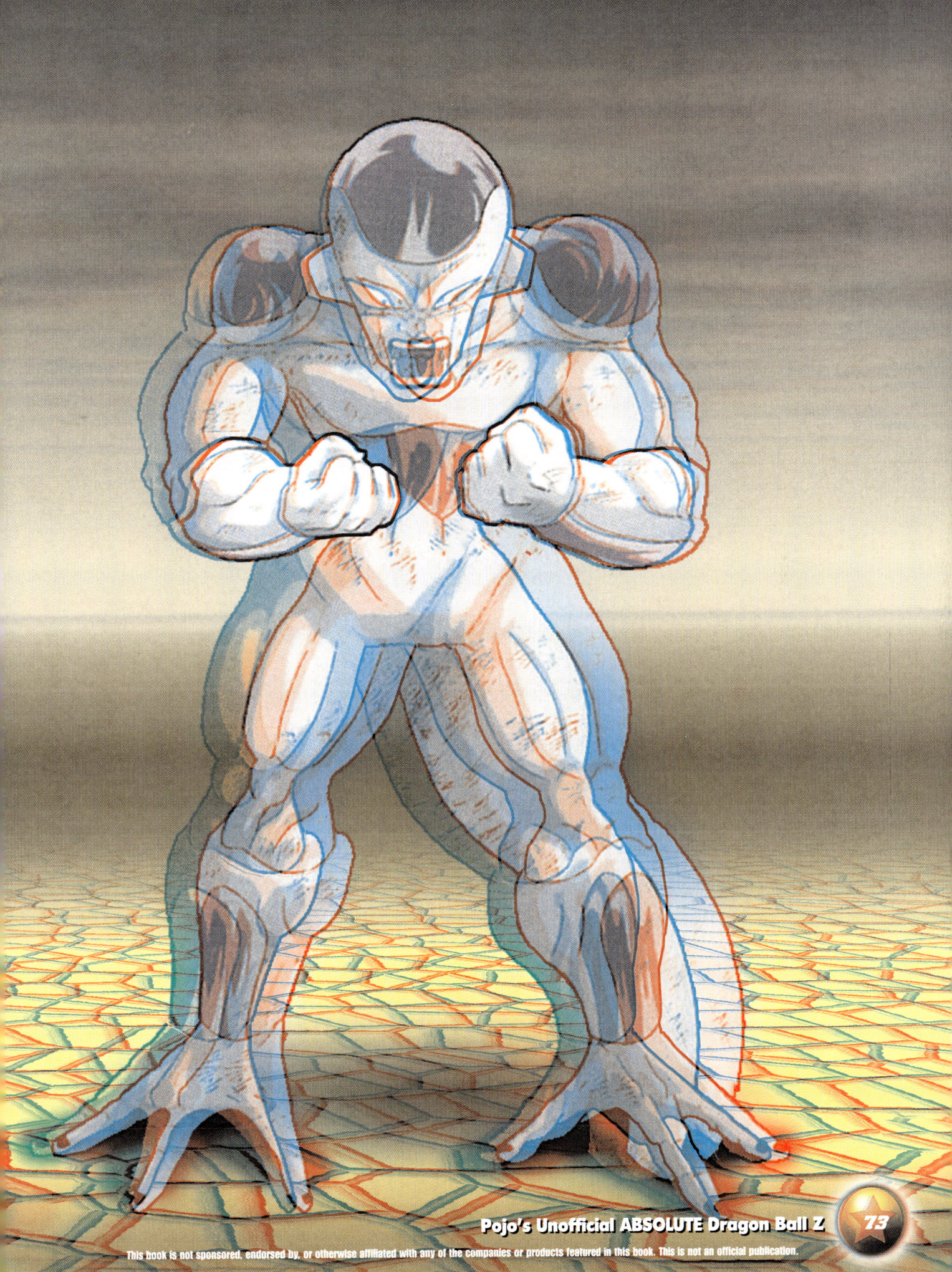

Dragon Ball Character BIOs

— By Eric R. Gerson

Advisor Black
Second in command of the Red Ribbon Army, Advisor Black helped Commander Red collect the Dragon Balls thinking Red's wish was world domination. When learning that Red's plan was to wish to become taller, Black shot him and took over the Red Ribbon Army. Though it was only momentary, as Gokou killed Black and destroyed the terrorist organization.

Aerobics Woman
Watched by Muten Roshi, the aerobics woman has a daily exercise program on television. Roshi, Oolong, and sometimes Yamcha all like to watch her show.

After-Life Martial Arts Tournament Announcer
Announcer for the afterlife tournament that Gokou competes in following the Cell Games, he has a mushroom-like head.

Agent Purple
He is a Master of Martial Arts and a pervert. Gokou defeated Agent Purple in Muscle Tower in the original Dragon Ball series.

Agent Purple's Brothers
The brothers of Purple are called upon to assist in killing Goku. Each has a weapon more lethal than the brother preceding him.

Akane Kimidori
Appearing in the Dr. Slump/Dragon Ball crossover, Akane Kimidori is a tomboyish main character of Dr. Slump.

Akkuman
The fourth, and previously final, fighter of Uranai Baba. Akkuman looks like a devil. Because Akkuman was Baba's final fighter, Roshi was surprised to see that Akkuman was Gokou's next opponent. Roshi was worried about who was stronger. Akkuman would have been able to kill Gokou, but Gokou possessed no evil within him. Akkuman's technique of blowing people up by awakening their inner evil didn't work on Gokou.

Akira Toriyama
Making random appearances in the manga and series, Akira Toriyama expresses himself as a robot-like character.

Alien Dinosaur
A giant dinosaur that Goku and the others encounter in their search for the black star Dragon Balls. The dinosaur eats a Dragon Ball by mistake. Not wanting to wait for the dinosaur to digest the ball, Goku flies into dinosaur's mouth and down to its stomach. Finding the Dragon Ball, Goku forces his way out of the dinosaur's stomach, creating a hole that causes the dinosaur to deflate and shrink. After bandaging the dinosaur up, Goku apologizes.

Amondo
Amondo is Tauras' henchman, whom Goku kills in the third Dragon Ball Z movie.

Android 8
A Frankenstein-looking android, Android 8 was ordered to kill Child Gokou when he went to defeat the Red Ribbon Army. Given that he didn't like to fight, Android 8 refused and instead teamed up with Gokou. After the defeat of the Red Ribbon Army, Android 8 went to live a peaceful life with Suno.

Android 13

Created by Dr. Gero's secret computer, Android 13 was designed to kill Gokou. After Dr. Gero died, the computer drew upon its hatred for Gokou, creating the three androids sent to kill him in movie seven. Gokou was a match for Android 13 only when he was Super Saiyajin. After Androids 14 and 15 were destroyed, Android 13 assembled various parts from them to transform itself. As Super 13, none of the Z Senshi could even hurt him. Once creating a giant Genki Dama, and turning Super Saiyajin once more, Gokou was able to win the fight.

Android 14

Formed from Dr. Gero's hatred for Gokou, Android 14 was big and gray. Immensely powerful, Android 14 fought against Trunks and beat him, until Trunks transformed into Super Saiyajin. He then kills Android 14 with his sword.

Android 15

Dr. Gero's computer also created this short, blue Android to kill Gokou. While helping Android 14 in its fight against Trunks, Android 15 was told to take care of Vegeta once he arrived. Although it gave Vegeta a great fight, it was no match for the Saiyajin Prince once he changed into a Super Saiyajin.

Android 16

Mirai No Trunks was unaware of Android 16 because it was not awakened in the future timeline. Android 16 doesn't fight any of the Z Senshi as it is programmed that Gokou is its only enemy. It is shattered by Cell, but rebuilt by Buruma and her father. However, when attempting to blow up Cell with an internal self-destruct bomb, Android 16 is shattered again leaving only its head. The bomb failed to ignite because Dr. Briefs removed it. He thought it too dangerous for the Android to possess. The Android's final words were encouragement to Gohan to let his anger explode so Gohan's hidden power would be released. After it finished this speech to Gohan, its head was crushed by Cell.

Android 17

The most evil of all the Androids, Android 17 turned on his creator, Dr. Gero, and kicked off his head. It then proceeded to smash Gero's head with his foot. The Android was unwillingly absorbed by Cell to help Cell reach perfection, and died when Cell did. Android 17 was then wished back to life without its self-destruct bomb, which all of the Androids possessed, including Cell. After being absorbed into Cell, it isn't heard from again until Dragon Ball GT, when it fused with Artificial Android 17 to become Super 17. At that time, it kills its creator once again.

Android 18

Android 18 was also absorbed by Cell, unwillingly, in order for Cell to reach perfection. However, she is spit out when Super Saiyajin 2 Gohan punches Cell hard in the stomach. Kuririn was in love with Android 18, and

DBZ Character BIOs

wished for the self-destruct bomb within her to be removed. They eventually marry and have a daughter named Marron. Android 18 was originally human, but given enhancements that made her into an android. In the future timeline of Trunks, she and Android 17 are responsible for the death of the Z Senshi and most of humanity.

Android 19

The weakest android, next to Android 20 of course, its best technique is to absorb energy through its palms. Both Android 19 and 20 were the first to search for Son Gokou, and were mistaken for the Androids described by Mirai No Trunks. Android 19 almost succeeded in killing Gokou due to Gokou's heart disease. Just when the Android is about to finish him, Vegeta interferes because he feels it is his right alone to kill Gokou. Vegeta easily fights 19, and eventually kills it with his lethal technique, the Big Bang Attack.

Angel

Angel develops a crush on Gohan after seeing him in his underwear. Gohan agrees to go on a date with her only because he thinks she knows he's the Great Saiyaman. However, she quickly loses interest in Gohan and moves on to a new guy.

Angira/Angel

A henchman of Lord Slug, Angira was killed when Gokou fired Angira's mouth blast back at him.

Annin

Annin is the guardian of the Furnace of Eight Divinations found at the border between Earth and the afterlife.

Aoi Kimidori

Appearing in the Dr. Slump/Dragon Ball crossover, Aoi Kimidori is the sister of Akane.

Apple/Apura

Apple is a henchmen of Frieza, and was responsible for bringing Vegeta back to full health after his defeat at the hands of Zarbon. Unfortunately for Apple, he was unaware of Vegeta's ability to mask his ki. Apple assumed Vegeta wasn't getting better and insulted the Saiyan prince. Vegeta let out a ki blast, destroying the rejuvenation chamber he was in and killing Apple.

Arale Norimaki

The main character of Dr. Slump, Arale is a robot built by Senbe. During the Dr. Slump/Dragon Ball crossover, she saves Goku by defeating Commander Blue.

Aruhuan/Aruhuajin

A planet destroyed by Majin Buu five million years ago.

Arqua

A fighter of the East galaxy, Arqua faced Gokou in the semi-finals. He was doing poorly until he used a special technique causing the ring to turn into a large lake. Once this occurred, he began to beat Gokou. However, once Gokou used the taiyoken to blind Arqua, he escaped the water to fire a kamehameha; Gokou returned the ring to normal and knocked Arqua out of the ring. Being the good sport that he is, Gokou congratulated Arqua on nearly defeating him and said he hoped to fight him again in the future.

Atla/Atora

Atla is an Arlian who Vegeta and Nappa meet after willingly surrendering to the Arlian army. He was betrothed to Lemlia, but lost his future wife to the dictator of the planet. After Vegeta and Nappa kill the entire Imperial Army and the dictator, Atla thinks

DBZ Character BIOs

that his planet will finally be at peace and he and his wife can once again be together. This was short-lived, however, since Vegeta destroyed the planet before returning on his journey to Earth.

Baba/Uranai Baba
The sister to Muten Roshi, Uranai Baba is a gifted fortuneteller. She has often helped out by seeing battles when the TV could no longer pick up the camera signals.

Burter/Baata

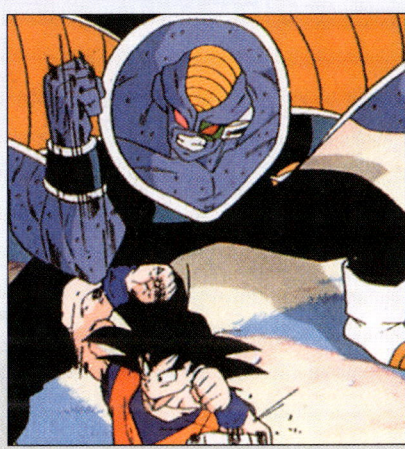

A member of the Ginyu Tokusentai, Baata believed himself to be the fastest warrior in the universe. His opinion changed after Son Gokou, using the 100 times gravity training, easily defeated him. When in an actual battle, he usually fights alongside his teammate Jeice.

Babi-Di
The son of Bibi-Di, Babi-Di is a small, old-looking sorcerer. He resurrects Majin Buu with the help of Dabura, in hopes of ruling the universe with Buu's power. However, Buu quickly gets tired of his constant insults, and kills Babi-Di.

Babidi's Subordinate Staff
They are a group of low-level fights who were easily defeated by Gohan on Babidi's ship.

Bacterian
The only participant in the Tenkaichi Budoukai that never bathed. Bacterian was a disgusting and weak fighter. His only attacks were his smell and breath. When competing against Kuririn, he was defeated.

Bank Robbers
When robbing a bank in Dragon Ball GT, the Bank Robbers caused an area to be secured by the police. Since this was the only way to the movie theatre where Pan planned to go to with her boyfriend, she beat them all up.

Bardock
The lone Saiyajin who fought against Furiza, Bardock is the father to both Son Gokou (Kakarotto) and Radditz.
While on Planet Kanassa, Bardock acquired the ability to foresee the future. He was able to see the destruction of Planet Vegeta and the future of his son, Kakarotto. Bardock attempted to battle Furiza to save his son and his home. Unfortunately, he was no match for Furiza, and was destroyed along with his planet. His last words to his son were to kill Furiza so that he would die by a Saiyajin's hand.

Barry Kahn
He is a teen superstar. Barry is seen by Buu on a poster when Buu is trying to kiss a girl. When she refuses, he thinks it is because of his looks. Buu shifts his face to resemble Barry Kahn. When the girl still won't kiss him, Buu kills her.

Bartender A
A man in a bar who serves Lunch a drink when she makes her first appearance.

Bartender B
A happy bartender who serves Lunch after the death of Tenshinhan. He almost passes out when Lunch pays for her drinks with thousands of dollars.

Battle Robot
These were Cooler's Drones from DBZ Movie 6. They had exceptional strength, and were only able to be defeated when the Z Senshi fought at full power.

Bear Thief
Bear Thief is the first enemy Goku encounters outside his home. He is a giant bear with the uniform of a samurai. Since he is hungry and has a taste for sea turtles, Bear Thief threatens to eat Umigame. Not wanting to lose his new friend, Goku beats Bear Thief without much difficulty.

Bebi

The last of the Tsufurujins, Bebi is the DNA of the Tsufurujin king. Genetically created by Dr. Myuu, Bebi's only goal is to kill all Saiyajin to avenge the extinction of his race. Given that he is a parasite, he infests people by entering through a wound or other

DBZ Character BIOs

body opening when their bodies have reached full power. After taking over Trunks, and not being strong enough to keep control, Bebi traveled to Earth while Gokou and the others were still searching for the Dragon Balls. He first targets Goten and is easily defeated. However, he eventually succeeds in taking him over. He then moves on to Gohan and to his final target, Vegeta. When Gokou returns to Earth, all of humanity, except Mr. Buu and Mr. Satan, had been brought under Bebi's control. After taking over a body, Bebi lays an egg inside it, so he still has control over the body when exiting.

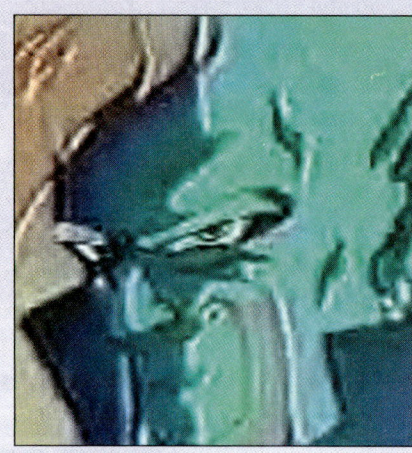

revealed. When trying to fight Super Saiyajin 2 Gohan, he is punched in half.

Bee/Biru

Biru is Mr. Satan's dog. He was brought to Mr. Satan by Buu. Buu couldn't understand why he wouldn't run away from Buu in fear as most humans do. When he found out that Biru's leg was broken, Buu healed him and Biru became fond of his savior. Some humans, attempting to kill Buu, shot Biru. Buu almost completely lost his temper, but was salvaged when he learned that Biru was still barely alive. He quickly healed him. Biru never seems afraid of enemies, particularly the evil Buu. He always runs and bark at them.

Bibi-Di

Bibi-Di is both the creator of Majin Buu and the father of Babi-Di. He is killed by Kaioshin because of his evil actions. Before being killed, he is forced to seal Majin Buu because he couldn't control him. Once Majin Buu was out of the picture, Kaioshin was able to kill Bibi-Di.

Bido

Bido is one of the strong arms of Bojack's henchmen. Like all of his companions, his past is never

Big Ghetti Star

A giant ship created by Cooler, the Ghetti Star needs other planet's cores to power it. At the center of the ship is Cooler's brain, which controls the ship. After capturing Goku and Vegeta, Cooler attempts to drain their Saiya power. After turning Super Saiyan, the two warriors give Cooler all the energy he wants, which in turn, destroys the ship.

Bio Brolly/Bio Burori

In DBZ Movie 11, Jaga Badda and his scientists create a clone of Brolly from the blood cells Priest brings them. After fighting Trunks, Goten, and Android 18, Bio Brolly is engulfed in acid. Instead of killing him, the acid merely deforms him, making him a green monster. Gohan, Krillin, and Trunks think they have defeated Bio Brolly and are about to go home, when he rises from the ocean as a giant. However, he is susceptible to salt water, so the three warriors fire kamehameha into the ocean, covering Brolly and defeating him.

Bio Men

Appearing in DBZ Movie 2, the Bio Men were Dr. Wheelo's henchmen who attacked Roshi and Piccolo. They looked almost similar to Saibamen, but they didn't have a mouth and were blue.

Bio Warriors

Created by Jaga Bada in the 11th DBZ movie, the Bio Warriors probably would have easily defeated Mr. Satan, if it weren't for Goten, Trunks, and Number 18.

Black Star Shenron

Black Star Shenron is a dragon summoned when the black star Dragon Balls are gathered. It is much larger in size and power than the Shenron of DB and DBZ. The other major difference between this Shenron and the other Shenron is that if the Dragon Balls are not gathered within a year of the wish being granted and the wish being reversed, the planet from where he is summoned will explode.

Blind Boy

A blind kid looking for milk, he runs into Buu while walking on a cliff. Buu can't understand why the boy doesn't fear him, and the boy explains that he is blind and can't see. Buu wants the boy to run in fear, so he heals his eyes so he can be frightened by Buu. However, being able to see for the first time in his life, the boy thanks Buu and they sit down and talk for a while. After hearing that the boy was looking for milk, Buu flies into a nearby city and turns a person into milk and brings it back to the boy. The boy thanks him and leaves. After their talk, Buu destroys the city behind him. This scene foreshadows the struggle of the good and evil within Buu.

Blue's Group Leader

One of Blue's top men, the Group Leader enjoys picking his

DBZ Character BIOs

nose. When he finds this out, Blue kills him.

Blueberry

A henchman of Furiza, Blueberry is dog-like in appearance. When searching for Vegeta and the Dragon Balls, he and his teammate, Raspberry, encounter Bulma, who has a Dragon Ball. After learning what the balls can do, Blueberry decides to find them himself and take over the galaxy. A giant crab eventually kills him after he mistakes its eggs for Dragon Balls.

Bojack

Bojack is an incredibly strong warrior who was sealed within a star by the Kaio. After Gokou destroys Kaiosama's planet, Bojack is freed and takes over the Tenkaichi Budoukai. After he easily defeats Trunks, Vegeta, and Piccolo, Bojack fights Gohan. When Bojack is about to kill Gohan, Gokou saves him and helps Gohan release his inner power. As Super Saiyajin 2, Gohan is able to easily kill Bojack.

Bongo

King Gurumesu's Terminator-like henchman in the first DB movie, Bongo follows orders without question. When battling Goku, he is defeated but not killed.

Bon Para, Son Para, Ron Para

Bon Para, Son Para, and Ron Para are the three brothers hired by Mutchy-Motchy to gather the Dragon Balls. They use a strange dancing technique to cause their enemies to unwillingly dance until they run out of energy. When Goku asks for the universe's energy, they help out.

Bora

Bora is the father of Upa and protects Karin tower. When attacked by Tao Pai Pai, he is killed, but is later restored when Gokou gathers the Dragon Balls. Bora doesn't make that many more appearances in DBZGT, but he helps when Gokou asks everyone on Earth to give him energy to kill Majin Buu.

Boss Rabbit

Boss Rabbit is a gang leader who has the ability to turn people into carrots. When confronted by Goku, he is defeated.

Bra/Bura

Vegeta and Bulma's second child, Bra doesn't have much of a role in either DBZ or the GT series. She has the ability to control ki, as seen when she flies to help Bebi, but she never transforms into a Super Saiyajin.

Brolly/Burori

DBZ Character BIOs

The legendary Super Saiyajin, Burori was born with a power level of 10,000. He hates Gokou, because Gokou is the only one who ever made him cry. It happened while they were infants. Burori and Gokou were born around the same time. He makes three movie appearances in movies eight, ten, and eleven.

Bubbles

A small monkey friend of Kaiosama, Bubbles is used in the first step of Kaio's training. To overcome the uncomfortable gravity of Kaio's planet, students must chase Bubbles until he was caught. It took Gokou two weeks to catch Bubbles.

Budoukai Announcer

The announcer for all Tenkaichi Budoukai, expect for the Budoukai held one-hundred years after the end of Dragon Ball GT. The announcer has great appreciation for martial arts, He is always excited to see Gokou and his friends compete, since he believes they are the only true martial arts masters on Earth.

Bujin

The most psychically powerful of Bojack's men, Gohan kills after transforming into Super Saiyajin 2.

Bulma/Buruma

The second most important character in Dragon Ball Z GT, Buruma is responsible for many essential inventions, such as the dragon radar. In the original Dragon Ball series, she told Gokou what Dragon Balls were. Without her, much of the story line would never have occurred, such as Gohan and Kuririn traveling to Nameksei in search of Nameksei's Dragon Balls. Moreover, Trunks wouldn't have been able to return to his past or even existed without Buruma.

Bun

Bun is the leader of the stealth ship that Kuririn, Gohan, and Bulma accidentally board. Bun's hatred for Furiza and his men dates back to when his parents were killed right in front of him.

Bus hijackers

Three men hijack a bus of senior citizens, and Videl gets called to help. When the bus is about to fall off a cliff, the Great Saiyaman rescues everyone and defeats the hijackers.

Butter

Butter is a participant in the 25th Budoukai. He is one of Kuririn's opponents. Butter underestimates Kuririn because of his size, but Kuririn easily whips him.

Buyon

Buyon is a fat monster Goku meets in muscle tower. He is defeated when Goku punches a hole in the wall, causing the cold air to freeze him.

Captain Chicken

Captain Chicken is a superhero who participated in the twenty-eighth Tenkaichi Budoukai. He forfeited after seeing the Gokou and Uub fight. He pretended to hear the cries of a damsel in distress and ran away.

Captain Ginyu/ Ginyu Taicho

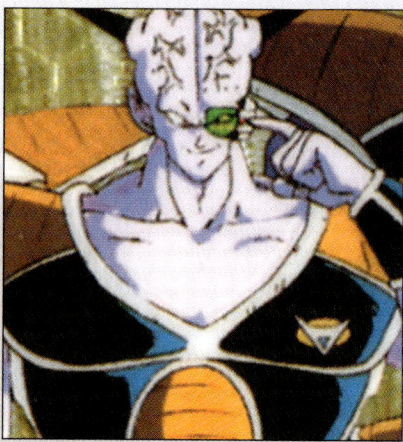

Before Goku underwent his 100 X Gravity training, Captain Ginyu was second most powerful next to Furiza. His special ability is the body switch, which, as the name implies, allows him to switch bodies with his opponent. He is never killed, but must live his entire life as a frog after Goku tricks him into switching bodies with one.

Cardinal Mutchy-Motchy

As the high priest of Lude, Mutchy-Motchy terrorizes anyone who fails him and his God, Lude.

DBZ Character BIOs

He uses a whip and a device that turns people into dolls. He hires the Para brothers to obtain the Dragon Balls for him, so he could resurrect their god. He is killed when his pet Leon is defeated and blown up.

Cashew

He is one of the minions of Garlic Jr. When Garlic Jr. returns, Cashew, despite his strength, is killed like all the others.

Catapy

Catapy fought against Gokou in the first round of the afterlife Budoukai. He got Gokou in a hold and tried to tickle him until Gokou gave up. After Gokou freed himself, he called Catapy a weakling. Catapy got mad and created a cocoon around himself. Given that he wouldn't hatch from the cocoon for twelve hundred years, Gokou won the match.

Cell

Cell is Dr. Gero's master creation. He is supposed to be the perfect fighter, created from the DNA cells of the universe's greatest fighters. Because the project is too long for Dr. Gero, he leaves his computer to complete the project. He is Dr. Gero's twenty-first Jinzonigen. Cell is actually Android 21. In the future, he kills Mirai No Trunks and uses his time machine to return to when Trunks first arrived. He does this so he can absorb Jinzonigen 17 and Jinzonigen 18 and reach perfection. Cell has to go back in time because Trunks killed them in his time. His first form is reptilian, his second is more human with some lizard qualities retained. Once reaching perfection, Cell looked much more human. Gohan eventually kills him in his Super Saiyajin 2 form.

Cell Juniors

Cell created the Cell Juniors to attack the Z Senshi and get Gohan angry. Cell wants to see the hidden power within Gohan that is boasted about by Gokou. Even Vegeta couldn't even hurt them at full power. After transforming into Super Saiyajin 2, all the Cell Juniors are killed.

Chachai

He is one of the contestants in the first match of the afterlife Budoukai. He is matched against Olive. He is incredibly fast and fights very well, but he is defeated after using the split form technique and slamming his head against the heads of his other forms.

Chaozu

The weakest ki-controlling Z fighter, Chaozu is left behind from the Cell fight. However, his telepathic powers are fantastic, but that usually doesn't help him win a fight. In the original Dragon Ball, Chaozu was an emperor. Throughout all of Z and GT, he follows Tenshinhan around, and treats him like a brother.

Chibi

He is short, drunk, and harasses Lunch when she first appears in the anime.

Chibi

A child Pteradon, Chibi is kidnapped by a greedy Circus owner for the show in Satan City. Great Saiyaman eventually saves Chibi.

Chi Chi

Chi Chi is the wife of Gokou. She first meets Gokou as a child, and asks Gokou to marry her. Thinking that marriage was a type of food, Gokou agrees. Together they have two sons, Gohan and Goten. She seems to possess a large amount of stress, and shops to make up for it. Her highest hope is for Gohan to grow up and become a scholar. She never wants Gohan to go into battle, fearing that it will

DBZ Character BIOs

interrupt his studies. When Gohan does fight, however, she is proud of him, but never admits it.

Chii Shenron
Created from the wish to restore those killed during the twenty-fifth Tenkaichi Budoukai, Chii Shenron used other life-forms to hide his true body. He is a small and weak-looking pig-like dragon. After pretending that he died from an attack intended to hit Goku and Pan, Chii Shenron took over Pan's body and grows into a large and powerful dragon. To retrieve Pan, Goku acts as though he is defeated and Chii let Goku see Pan one last time before killing him. Counting on this, Goku pulls Pan away from Chii, returning Pan to his true form. After seeking revenge of all those he hurt, Goku kills him, restoring the 7-star Dragon Ball.

Chindai Ken
Owner of a martial arts school, Chindai Ken is a master of the Seikyokuryuken. Unfortunately, he suffers from a disease that quickly drains his energy.

Chinshyou Ken
The son of Chindai Sensei, Chinshyou Ken (like Vegeta) is very proud of his strength and thinks Goku is weak. To prevent Goku from participating in the Budoukai, he puts a laxative in his soup.

Chunshi
Another person Goku meets on his trip around the world during Mr. Popo's training.

Chyao
Goku saves this little girl during his second trip around the world. After he saves her, she asks him to save her entire village from Ginkaki and Kinkaku.

Chyuri
She meets Goku in the Goro Goro Mountains and asks for his help in finding her bird Pi Pi.

Chyuri's Mama
The mother of the girl who Goku helps find Pi Pi.

Circus Trainer
A circus trainer who treats the Pteradon Chibi harshly, using whips on him.

Clothing Store Man
After the androids steal clothes from his store, he calls the police to report them. The police chase them, but are blasted away by Android 18's ki blast. They are not killed.

Cocoa
A small child, she is to be sacrificed to the mountain God to save the village from the monster in movie 10. When Videl, Trunks, and Goten arrive, she is spared as they promise to take care of the monster.

Commander Blue

Incredibly powerful, Commander Blue's weaknesses are his fear of mice and hatred of women. He and Goku fight in mid-air after he tries to kill everyone with a time bomb. They both crash into the mountains near Penguin Village. When Blue returns to Red Ribbon Headquarters, Tao Pai Pai kills him.

Commander Red

He is the leader of the Red Ribbon Army. Commander Red secretly wants to use the Dragon Balls to become taller, not to take over the world as his minions think. When Advisor Black learns this, he shoots Commander Red and takes over the Red Ribbon Army.

Commander Red's Cat
Odd-looking pet of Red's, he enjoys attacking people for no reason.

Cooler

The brother of Furiza, Cooler goes to Earth to exact revenge for his brother's death. Cooler's power is much greater than

88 Pojo's Unofficial ABSOLUTE Dragon Ball Z

DBZ Character BIOs

Furiza's, and he has one additional transformation. He makes two movie appearances, in movies five and six. In movie six, he returns as a metal cyborg and attacks the new Planet Namek.

Copper Shogun

Commander Shogun never makes an actual appearance. He is a commander of the Red Ribbon Army.

Crane master/Tsurusennin

The teacher of Tenshinhan and Chaozu, Tsurusennin is a rival of Kamesennin. At the twenty-second Tenkaichi Budoukai, his students face off against Gokou and the others. When they learn of Tsurusennin's evil side, Tenshinhan and Chaozu leave the school. Tsurusennin is not happy with their actions and is about to attack his former pupils, when he is blown away by Kamesennin's kamehameha.

CQV Reporter

A television reporter for CQV, he reports on the strange disappearances in Ginger Town.

Cymbol

Cymbol is the second child of Piccolo Daimoa. He is sent to discover who killed Tamborine and to exact revenge. However, Yajirobe is still hungry and kills Cymbol and cooks and eats him.

Dabura

The overlord of the demon world, Dabura travels to Earth with Babi-Dee hoping to gather enough energy to resurrect Majin Buu. With his special ability, Dabura turned Kuririn and Piccolo into stone before being eaten by Majin Buu. After this occurred, Kuririn and Piccolo returned to normal. His past is never revealed and he is said to be as strong as Perfect Cell.

Dai Kaio/Grand Kai

Recognized at the strongest in the afterlife, Dai Kaio is the head of the Kaio. He also has his own planet of the same name. He presides over the afterlife tournament, and promises to personally train the winner (who would have been the first person he ever taught.) When Gokou defeats Paikuhan and wins the tournament, Dai Kaio disqualifies both of them for touching the ceiling during the fight. He would have overlooked this infraction if he hadn't been neglecting his own training. Dai Kaio would not have been able to keep up with Gokou.

Dai Kaioshin

The god of gods, Dai Kaioshin is a kindly and fat god. When East Kaioshin was fighting against Majin Buu, he saved him from a blast and blew Buu to pieces. When Buu reformed himself, he absorbed Dai Kaioshin, which resulted in Fat Buu (Mr. Buu). Some of Dai Kaioshin's kindness still exists in Buu, changing him from a demon into a laid-back demon who always wants tasty foods.

Daigorou Kurigashisa

He appeared in the Dr. Slump/Dragon Ball crossover.

Daisuko

Daisuko is a sumo wrestler-like fighter who has competed in nine movie tournaments. After reach-

DBZ Character BIOs

ing the finals, he is sent with the others to island two to compete. Matched against Bido, he is instantly killed.

Daizu
Goku kills Taurus' minion Daizu in the 3rd DBZ movie.

Debu
Debu is a fat drunk. He harasses Lunch in the bar where she makes her first appearance in the anime.

Dende
Dende is a small Namekseijin who is rescued by Son Gohan and Kuririn after being attacked by Dodoria. Dende is taken away from his village when his family is killed. When Cell is discovered, and Kamisama fuses with Piccolo, Dende is sent to become the new God of the Earth and create new Dragon Balls.

Dinosaur
Dinosaur is a large T-Rex who continuously tries to eat Gohan during his training with Piccolo. It eventually becomes a playmate for Gohan, and even a source of food, when Gohan cuts off pieces of his tail to eat.

Dirty Boy
A foul-smelling thief, Dirty Boy steals the dragon radar as Goku bathes. The smell leads Goku to Dirty Boy's location, and he gives up his booty when caught.

Dobermen
The Dobermen are a group of fierce dogs that are commanded by Shuu to attack Goku, Yamcha, Oolong, Bulma, and Puar.

Doctor A
Doctor A is the chief doctor of Planet Frieza No. 79. He takes care of Vegeta after his fight on Earth.

Doctor B
Doctor B is the chief doctor on the hospital planet that Goku, Pan, and Trunks land on during their search for the black star Dragon Balls in Dragon Ball GT.

Dodoria

Dodoria is a pink-purplish, fat henchman of Furiza. He is a weak fighter. Vegeta kills him after Dordoria reveals to Vegeta the truth about Planet Vegeta's destruction.

Doll-Tucky
This reclusive prophet of Lude is fascinated with dolls, especially the Pan doll. During his infrequent public appearances, Doll-Tucky performs phony miracles to dupe his followers. He eventually turns all of Lude's followers into dolls, so Lude can steal their energy and revive himself.

Dolphin/Isuka
Appearing in the Dragon Ball series, Dolphin helped Goku and Chichi by showing them the direction to Muten Roshi's house.

Domma
Domma is Lenne's bethrothed, and he joins Goku and the others when they face Zunama. He joins them, despite his fear that he wouldn't survive the battle.

Doore

A member of the Cooler Tokusentai, he is killed by Piccolo.

Dorodabo
A gargoyle-like henchman of Lord Slug, Dorodabo is killed by Piccolo.

Dr. Briefs
The father of the annoying Buruma, Dr. Briefs built three ships that the Z Senshi used during DBZ. The third one was used by Vegeta to train and become Super Saiyajin. He also helped repair Android 16.

Dr. Frappe
Android 8's creator, Dr. Frappe

DBZ Character BIOs

is a brilliant scientist whose genius is exploited by the Red Ribbon Army. When Android 8 refuses to kill Goku, the Saiyan saves both Frappe and Android 8. Afterwards, the doctor removes Android 8's bomb.

Dr. Gero/Android 20

Gero is one of the better scientists of the Red Ribbon Army. Unfortunately, Gokou destroys the Red Ribbon Army in Dragon Ball. Dr. Gero continues plotting against Gokou, eventually building a couple of androids designed to kill him. He turns himself into an android as well, Android Number 20, and goes hunting for Gokou with Android 19. However, he is killed by Android 17. He returns in Dragon Ball GT, but is once again killed by Super 17 upon orders from Dr. Myuu.

Dr. Kochin

Assistant of Dr. Wheelo, Dr. Koshin's job is to find someone strong enough for Dr. Wheelo to take over. He becomes too old after Dr. Wheelo is imprisoned, and is built into a robot.

Dr. Kori

Dr. Kori is a scientist from the 11th DBZ movie who helps create Bio Brolly.

Dr. Myuu

A genius scientist, Dr. Myuu is responsible for the genetic creation of Bebi. After being killed by Bebi, Dr. Myuu goes to hell and meets Dr. Gero. Conspiring together to complete the unfinished Android 17, they create the Hell fighter Number 17 who merges with the original Android 17, to create Super 17.

Dr. Raichii

This scientist is the main villain of the DBZ OVA Special. In an attempt to rid the universe of the Saiyajin, Dr. Raichii sends Destron gas-emitting machines to Earth to destroy all life. The Z Senshi destroy all but one of the machines, which is protected by an unbreakable energy shield. Traveling to the dark planet to face Raichii, the Z Senshi fight and kill the doctor; however, his cyborg proves more difficult. Combining all of their ki attacks, the heroes destroy the cyborg, causing the final gas machine to explode.

Dr. Wheelo

One of the smartest men on Earth, Dr. Wheelo uses his genius for evil and is imprisoned in ice. After dying, his brain is preserved. The plan is to transfer it into the body of the world's strongest man. After his assistant Dr. Koshin uses the Dragon Balls to melt the ice surrounding his laboratory, Dr. Wheelo searches for Muten Roshi, believing that he is still the strongest man. After learning that Gokou is now the strongest, he tries to obtain Gokou's body.

Dracula Man

The first fighter of Uranai Baba, Dracula Man is fast and has the ability to change from man to bat. His first battle is with Kuririn, and he wins by sucking blood from Kuririn's head. Upa and Puar defeat Dracula Man by using crosses and garlic to trick him into flying out of the ring, and then they smack him into the water.

Drum

Created to finish off Tenshinhan, Drum was Piccolo's third child after being released from the Denshi jar. When Gokou arrives to help, Gokou kills Drum.

East Kaio/East Kai

The Kaio of the eastern galaxy, East Kaio is the only female Kaio. She loves racing and uses her jet bike to race. Gokou has to race and beat her, in order to compete in the afterlife tournament.

DBZ Character BIOs

East Kaioshin/Supreme Kai
Kaioshin is one of the higher Gods of the universe, and even has his own planet, Kaioshin Kai. He kills Bibi-Dee after Majin Buu is sealed away. He is the only surviving Kaioshin of his generation, because the other four were either killed or absorbed by Majin Buu.

Ebichiyu
A contender in the GT Tenkaichi Budoukai, Ebichiyu makes it to the semifinals.

Ebifurya
One of the Bio Warriors who works for Dr. Wheelo in the 2nd DBZ movie, Ebyfuria looks very similar to Recoome from the Ginyu Force. His special attack is a freeze blast that can immobilize opponents. Goku eventually kills him.

EC3
This robot from planet M-2 faces off with Goku after he and Trunks escape from the scanner. Like most of the robots of M-2, he has special abilities, such as sinking into walls and floors. When Goku blasts all of the M-2 robots with ki attacks, they combine and form the Mega Cannon. After Goku learns the Mega Cannon's techniques, he becomes bored and destroys it with a kamehameha.

EC4
Another robot from planet M-2, EC4 learns her fighting techniques from Giru's data and is sent to destroy Pan. Unfortunately, even Giru doesn't know Pan's true power; upon learning what Giru has done, Pan cries and releases her anger on EC4, destroying him.

Elderly Couple
Appearing in Dragon Ball GT, Pan and Goku meet the Elderly Couple while searching for Uu Shenron. When Pan can't buy a can of juice, they give her one and explain the strange red liquid found throughout the city and the reason why the city is abandoned.

Eliza
A classmate of Gohan's at Orange Star High School, Eliza is attracted to Gohan and asks him to sit next to her and for a ride home.

Emi
Emi is one of the orphaned children aboard the stealth ship where Kuririn, Gohan, and Bulma become trapped on their way to planet Namek. When Kuririn and Gohan try to convince the orphans that they are not enemies, Emi kicks Kuririn in the shin.

Emperor Pilaf
The first major villain in Dragon Ball, Emperor Pilaf believed he was destined to rule the Earth. He uses his fortune to search for the Dragon Balls to have his wish granted. He also believes in sophistication, and often blames his minions whenever he would fart or burp. Though he comes very close to ruling the world, his plans never succeed.

English Teacher
He taught Gohan at Orange Star High School.

Eyeglass Pig
Eyeglass pig is near-sighted and sits atop a tree announcing news for Penguin Village.

Fake Z Senshi
These illusions of Gohan, Piccolo, and Gotenks appeared only in the anime, when Goku and Vegeta encounter them while in Buu's stomach. Since they aren't real, Goku and Vegeta are able to beat them. However, they don't feel pain and can't be defeated. They eventually just disappear.

Fire Fighter
He is a fire fighter in Satan City. He tries to put out a fire in a large building.

First normal man to give his power to the Genki Dama
Because he wanted to see what would happen if he raised his arms to the sky as Vegeta pleaded, this man is the first normal

DBZ Character BIOs

human to give his power to Goku's genki dama. It happens when Goku is creating the genki dama to kill Buu.

Followers of Lude
These are a group of people who pray to their God Lude. They are all eventually turned into dolls by Doll-Tucky to revive the Lude Monster. When Goku and Pan destroy the Lude Monster, they are freed.

Freshwater Turtle Monster
The freshwater turtle monster lives near Karin Tower.

Frieza Planet Number 79 Communications Leader
The Communication Leader is the first to recognize that Vegeta's space pod is approaching the planet, and he reports that Vegeta coming and in need of medical attention.

Frieza's Scouts
These are two followers of Frieza who Gohan and Krillin encounter after landing on Namek. They think Gohan and Krillin are weak, as they are unaware of Gohan and Krillin's ability to hide their ki. Gohan and Krillin kill them both.

Frog
A fighter of the South galaxy, Frog fights against Mariko in the semi-finals of the afterlife Budoukai. To win, Frog tries to expand his body to a point that will push Mariko out of the ring. However, Mariko lifts Frog off the ring and throws him into one of the hovering planets, causing Frog to deflate and land outside the ring.

Furiza/Frieza

Furiza is one of the most important, if not the most important, villains in DBZ. He destroys almost all of the Saiyajin race, their home planet, and many other people. He goes to Planet Nameksei to search for the Dragon Balls when he hears Radditz's message in the beginning of the series. He wants to use the Dragon Balls to gain immortality, but never succeeds because he doesn't know the Namekseijin language. He has multiple forms, which he uses to keep his true power hidden. His power increases with each transformation. His first form is short, and kind of mega man looking. The second is much taller and looks like his father. His third form is similar to the queen in the movie "Aliens." His fourth and final form is short and much better for fighting. After being defeated by Son Gokou, he is rebuilt by his father and travels to Earth, only to be killed by Mirai no Trunks. He is again killed in movie twelve when the dead return, this time by the Great Saiyaman Gohan.

Future Bulma/Mirai No Buruma
Mirai No Buruma builds a time machine for her son Trunks to travel back in time to give Goku curing medicine for his viral heart disease. Though scared for her son's safety when battling the androids, she is very proud of Trunks.

Future Gohan/Mirai No Gohan
Mirai No Gohan is the only surviving warrior from the battles with the androids. He spent his entire life training to defeat the androids that killed his friends and become as powerful as his father. Trunks asks him to train to help with the battle, and Gohan accepts. When the androids attack the Western Capital, Gohan goes to battle, but is knocked out by Trunks. Trunks is afraid that if Mirai No Gohan also goes to battle and they both die, there will be no one left to protect the Earth. After a valiant effort, Gohan is killed. When Trunks finds Gohan's corpse, his rage explodes, causing him to transform for the first time.

Future Trunks/Mirai no Trunks

One of the most important characters in the DBZ story, Mirai no Trunks is the son of Vegeta and Buruma. He comes from the future where Androids 17 and 18 have

DBZ Character BIOs

killed all of the Z Senshi and are causing havoc and destruction all over the Earth. Son Gohan, the only warrior who survived, trains Trunks but is killed four years before Trunks travels back in the time. Gohan's death is what causes Trunks to become Super Saiyajin. When he arrives from the future, he kills Furiza and King Cold. He tries to keep his identity secret, except from Gokou, to preserve his existence. Trunks also carries a sword given to him by Tapion.

Gajira Norimaki

A pair of angels who speak a language understood only by Arale, Gajira Norimaki appear in the Dr. Slump/Dragon Ball crossover.

Garlic Jr.

Garlic Jr. attempts to gain the position of God of the Earth but he is unsuccessful. He first appears in movie one, where he is sent into his own dead zone by Gohan's incredible power. He returns in between the Freezer and Android sagas, where he tries to turn everyone into demons to exact revenge on Gokou and Gohan. However, Gohan once again knocks him into his own dead zone.

Gasuteru

This giant demon from the 2nd DB movie travels by way of clouds and fights using ribbons.

General Silver

The first member of the Red Ribbon Army who faces off against Goku, General Silver is beaten but not killed.

Ginger

A henchman of Garlic Jr., Ginger is short and green. He is killed by Gokou's kamehameha.

Ginger Town's Prominent Rich Man

A rich man who is being attacked by Cell when Piccolo first meets the android, he offers Piccolo as much money as he wants to save his life. Before Piccolo can act, Cell absorbs him.

Ginkaku

Ginkaku is the younger brother of Kinkaku. Both are defeated by Goku, who forces them to work for the people of a village.

Giran

He participates in the twenty-first Tenkaichi Budoukai. Giran is Gokou's opponent. He uses the Guruguru Gum to paralyze Gokou. When Gokou shows his incredible strength to break the gum, Giran forfeits the fight.

Giran's Townspeople

Pteradon-like creatures, these townspeople help Goku try to find Giran.

Ghost Usher

A small ghost, he directed people where to go in Uranai Baba's house.

Giru

Goku, Pan, and Trunks meet this robot, also known as T-2006, on planet Imegga. After Giru eats the dragon radar, the heroes have no choice but to take him with them. The gang eventually discovers that Giru is Dr. Myuu's servant. The robot betrays his master to help his new friends. After finding all seven dark star Dragon Balls, they return to Earth. Accompanying Trunks back to Capsule Corp., Giru meets Vegeta. When he learns that Bebi has taken control of Vegeta, Giru attempts to confront Bebi but is destroyed in a ki blast. Giru doesn't return until the evil Shenron are defeated and the original Shenron restore all life.

Gogeta

Gogeta is the fusion of Gokou and Vegeta via the fusion dance. He makes two appearances, one in movie twelve, and one in Dragon Ball GT in the fight against Ii Shenron. He is extremely powerful, though not as power-

DBZ Character BIOs

ful as Vegetto in DBZ. He resembles Son Gokou, and has a dual voice, just as all Saiyajins do when fused. His special technique is a ball resembling a rainbow that causes his opponent to explode five seconds after impact. Like all fused warriors, he wears a black and orange vest.

Gohan

Gohan is the son of Goku and excels in both fighting and studying. After the battle with Radditz, he is taken by Piccolo to train for the arrival of other Saiyajin. Gohan's innocence changes Piccolo from a demon into a good person. His power comes from anger, and the angrier he is, the stronger he is. Gohan is the first warrior to transform into Super Saiyajin 2, and by doing so, he is able to defeat Cell. After defeating Cell, he stops training to study and attend high school. When Buu appears, he is once again forced to battle.

DBZ Character BIOs

Goku/Son Gokou

The main character of DBZGT, Son Gokou is originally sent to Earth to clear it off for purchase. The reason for his mission is lost when he falls off a cliff. After the fall, he becomes a loving child and a courageous person. Compared to all of the other characters, Son Gokou has the most abilities and is the strongest. He marries Chi Chi and has two sons, Gohan and Goten. In the original Dragon Ball, Gokou is introduced as a kid. For most of the series, he doesn't change until the twenty-fourth Budoukai when he trains with God and Popo. After the Budoukai, Gokou marries Chichi. In the following series, Dragon Ball Z, Gokou becomes more of a fighter than an innocent kid, but he still keeps some of his innocence. Through the duration of the DBZ series, Gokou undergoes three Super Saiyajin (Saiyan in English) transformations. The first transformation occurs during the Furiza fight after Kuririn is killed. The transformation causes Gokou to skyrocket in power, and causes his hair to stand on end, and his hair color to change from black to gold, his eyebrows to gold, and his eyes to blue. He doesn't reach Super Saiyajin 2 until after the Cell fight. The transformation of Gokou isn't shown until the Majin Vegeta fight. He doesn't look that much different than when he transformed to Super Saiyajin 1,

DBZ Character BIOs

but his hair is more defined and hard, and instead of five strands of hair over the face, there are only three. Gokou transforms to Super Saiyajin 3 in the afterlife. He could have used this form against Majin Vegeta, but it drains too much energy and would have lessened his time back on Earth. With no choice, Gokou transforms to delay Majin Buu from destroying the western capital and the dragon radar. The Super Saiyajin 3 form is entirely different from the previous two in that Gokou's eyebrows disappear, his hair becomes much thicker and longer, and his eyes are more defined. In Dragon Ball GT, Gokou is transformed back into a kid by the black star Dragon Balls. In that series, Gokou also reaches the final, and true form of Super Saiyajin, Super Saiyajin 4. This level is only reachable through Oozaru (the Giant Were-monkey). In DBZGT, Rou Dai Kaioshin pulls Gokou's tail out so he can return and have a fighting chance against Bebi. He is on the Tsufurujin planet that Bebi used the Dragon Balls to recreate. After being beaten, Gokou looks up at the Earth, and since the Earth is full, it has the same effect as looking at a full moon. This causes Gokou to transform into an Oozaru, and since he can become Super Saiyajin, the Oozaru becomes Super Saiyajin as well. He is not able to control the form because his tail is pulled out, and he is in the process of destroying everything. However, his granddaughter Pan helps him regain control of his mind. Once that happens, Gokou transforms into Super Saiyajin 4. The Super Saiyajin 4 transformation makes him look more like an ape. He grows a bit taller (and he returned to his adult body in that form), and has long black hair, red hair covering his torso, his tail is red, and his eyes become hazel. Whether Gokou ever dies is unknown, since it appears in the final episode of Dragon Ball GT that he merges with Shenron.

Goku Jr.

A third-generation descendant of Goku, Goku Jr. is the grandson of Pan. The identity of his parents is never revealed. He only makes one appearance in the Dragon Ball GT series – during the Tenkaichi Budoukai that occurs 100 years after the end of the GT series. Goku Jr. is the main character of the Dragon Ball GT TV Special, and at first, he is cowardly. When Pan is hospitalized, Goku Jr. goes on a mission to Mount Paozu to recover the four-star Dragon Ball to wish for Pan to get better. The bully, Pahku, who picks on Goku Jr. at school, goes with him. They become friends after saving each other's lives. When Goku Jr. finds the Dragon Ball, Goku confronts him and explains that he needs all seven balls to make a wish. Goku also tells him that to save a loved one, you need courage and not mystical balls.

Gokua

The swordsmen of Bojack's team, Gokua is very strong and is able to fight Trunks to a draw. However, once he transforms into a Super Saiyajin, Gokua is defeated.

Gora

A tall ogre, Gora guards the entrance to the underworld with Mera.

Goremu

The Goremu are a group of people who appeared only in the anime.

Goten

The second son of Gokou, Goten is conceived just before the Cell Game. He has amazing power for a six-year-old and can already transform into a Super Saiyajin. This feat surprised and made Gohan angry, since it took him a long time to master it. Goten and Trunks are best friends, probably because they can play together and not hurt each other. When Buu is resurrected, and Vegeta and Gohan fail to defeat him, Goten is the world's last hope. He trains to master the fusion technique, so he can merge with Trunks. In Dragon Ball GT, he is more of a lady's man, and he is always worrying

DBZ Character BIOs

about dates and never focusing on his training.

Gotenks

Gotenks is the result when Goten and Trunks fuse together. He has an attitude that he can take on anyone. This is due to his age and immaturity. Gotenks has two very powerful and unique attacks, Super Ghost Kamikaze Attack and the Shine Shine Missile. He has many other attacks that aren't very affective. He is also the second and last person to reach the Super Saiyajin 3 form. He has an incredible amount of strength, and almost defeats Buu, but the fusion wears off because he waits to become Super Saiyajin 3. He procrastinates so the fight will be cool and exciting.

Gozu

Gozu is the blue demon of hell, and he hits Gokou over the head when Gokou attempts to take one of Lord Enma's special fruit. Once he learns who Gokou is, he decides to have fun with him, pretending to help Gokou escape and return to the path of the snake. After playing for a while, his partner Mezu wants to play also, and Gozu watches Gokou compete against Mezu.

Grandpa Gohan

A kindly old man, Grandpa Gohan finds Gokou in the Saiyajin pod and adopts him as his own grandson. At first, Gohan has trouble keeping Gokou under control, but after accidentally dropping him off a cliff, Gokou becomes a loving grandson. When he teaches Gokou the art of kempo, Gohan awakens the power within Gokou. Unaware of Gokou's transformation when he sees a full moon, Gohan is crushed when Gokou transforms. He later returns in the Dragon Ball series when Gokou goes to see Uranai Baba, Gohan uses his only day back on Earth to see his grandson.

Grandma Hakkake

Grandma Hakkake lives by herself in the northern forest, and taught Chi Chi how to be a good wife. She also provides the Basho Sen that is used to extinguish the flames that imprisons Gyuu Mao's castle.

Grandma Paozu

Grandma Paozu lives near Mt. Paozu, and she rewards Goku and Bulma with the five star Dragon Ball after they rescue her daughter.

Great Elder

He is a village elder who holds celebrations for a Mountain God. Krillin, Chaozu, Yamcha, and Tenshinhan save his village from a volcanic lava flow.

Great Octopus

While trying to locate his friends, Goku discovers an octopus that he kills with a kamehameha. He eats his find.

Great Saiyaman

The defender of Satan City, the Great Saiyaman is the identity Gohan assumes to maintain justice. He uses strange poses to express his power, like the Ginyu Tokusentai, and he isn't taken seriously at first. When participating in the Tenkaichi Budoukai, Gohan dresses as the Great Saiyaman to avoid being recognized. However, when Videl is nearly killed, he transforms into Super Saiyajin, which removes the bandana on his head. While competing against Kibito, Gohan is recognized.

Great Saiyaman 2

Great Saiyaman 2 is the identity Videl uses when she joins Gohan to fight crime in Satan City. She only appears as the Great Saiyaman 2 once in the series, and in DBZ movie 13.

Gregory

A small cricket-like alien, Gregory is the second step in Kaiosama's training. The student is given a large mallet is supposed to chase Gregory around trying to hit him with it. Bubbles' training is used to conquer the gravity, whereas Gregory's training is to develop speed.

GT Tenkaichi Budoukai Announcer

The announcer for the Tenkaichi Budoukai that is held one hundred years after the end of DB GT. He introduces Goku Jr. and Vegeta Jr. for their battle.

Guard Man

The Guard for the Satan City circus, he fights Great Saiyaman to prevent him from saving Chibi.

DBZ Character BIOs

Guidance Robot
A robot onboard the Ghetti Star, his job is to calmly guide prisoners to their cells and to explain politely that they are going to die. He is destroyed along with the Ghetti Star.

Guldo/Gurudo

Gurudo is the weakest member of the Ginyu Tokusentai. The only reason he is on the team is because of his unique ability to freeze time for as long as he can hold his breath. His other special ability is to freeze the mind of his opponent so he can't move. With these skills, he can kill any warrior, but he is decapitated by Vegeta before his head is destroyed in a ki blast.

Guru/Senior Elder
Gura is the only surviving Namekseijin after the weather catastrophe on Planet Nameksei. He gives birth to every Namekseijin to repopulate the planet. Guru is also the creator of the Nameksei Dragon Balls. A kindly old man, he powers up Gohan and Kuririn hoping they will help them in his battle against Furiza.

Gyoshu
A devil-looking henchman of Lord Slug, Gyoshu is killed by Slug when he insults Slug's age.

Hacchi
A Chinese orphan, Gohan met him when he escaped from Piccolo.

Hand Axe Wielding Man
Goku meets him in the beginning of Dragon Ball, and he hits Goku over his head when Goku attempts to enter his house.

Hasukii
A thief employed by the Red Ribbon Army, Hasukii is hired for 1 million Zeni (DB currency) to steal Goku's Dragon Ball. However, she fails.

Head Guard
The personal bodyguard of Kokuou, Piccolo Daimoa kills him by dropping him out of Kokuou's escape plane.

Heishi
They are soldiers of the underworld who fight with swords.

Hejji, Hogu and Rii
Oolong kidnaps Hejji, Hogu and Rii in the beginning of Dragon Ball, the three girls are intended to be Oolong's servants. However, they disobey and live in Oolong's house like queens.

Hercule's/Mr. Satan's Fan Club
A group of young girls who love Mr. Satan, they almost run down a bunch of people in order to meet him.

Hikui Bird
An endangered bird, Hikuis live in volcanoes and their feathers are used to make Basho Shen.

Hiredugarn

A monster created by the Black magicians, Hiredugarn was amazingly powerful, but had a flaw in that a special ocarina can immobilize him. Once immobilized, a warrior can slice him in half with a special sword forged by Gods. When this is done on the Planet Konack, one half is sealed within Tapion and the other within Minosha. Unfortunately, when Tapion is released from his seal on Earth, the two halves joined again. After cocooning and re-emerging as a more powerful monster, all seems lost until Gokou goes Super Saiyajin 3.

Hoi

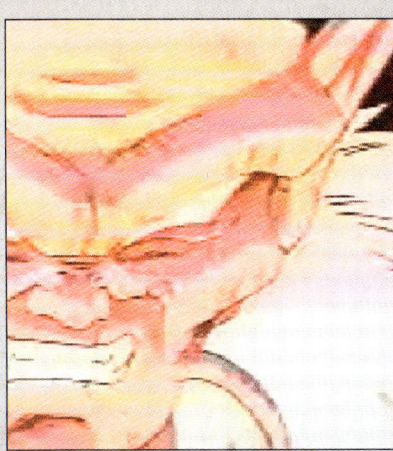

One of the Black magicians responsible for the creation of

DBZ Character BIOs

Hiredugarn. Hoi comes to Earth to seek the other half of his creation so he can wreak havoc and destruction throughout the universe. Hiredugarn kills him after becoming whole.

Hospital boy

Hospital Boy appears in Dragon Ball GT as a patient on the hospital planet. Goku, Pan, and Trunks land there in search of the black star Dragon Balls. Gaining their trust, the boy attacks Trunks and Bebi leaves the boy's body to try to take over Trunks. Later in the series, he gives his energy to Goku to create the mega Genki Dama to finish off Il Shenron.

HTV's Woman Interviewer

A reporter for HTV, she covers the twenty-fifth Tenkaichi Budoukai. When she tries to interview Vegeta, she is ignored. When she tries to interview Piccolo, he destroys her camera.

Huge Fish

The first enemy that Goku battles in the manga, anime, and movies. The fish is caught and eaten by Goku.

Human Gunman

A trigger-happy human, the Gunman and his associate kill two old people for fun. When they come to Buu's home, they shoot his dog Bee and attempt to kill Buu with a bazooka. When the smoke clears, an unharmed Buu heals his dog and the men run. Later, they return and shoot Mr. Satan in the chest. Before losing control, Buu heals Mr. Satan, but before they can escape, Buu's anger creates another Buu, Evil Buu. Evil Buu brutally kills the Gunman and his associate.

Human Gunman's Associate

The associate of the Human Gunman, he kills an old man and tries to kill Buu. When Evil Buu is created, Buu enters the Associate's body and explodes it from the inside.

Icarus/Hire Dragon

Hire Dragon is Gohan's best friend. He appears in movies 3, 4, and the Garlic Jr. Saga. Chi Chi forbids Gohan from being friends with a dragon, since it will disturb his studies. In movie 3, Hire Dragon helps get control of Gohan's mind while he is Oozaru.

Idarsa

Idarsa is a rude kid who participates in the youth division of the twenty-fifth Tenkaichi Budoukai. He is angry that his first opponent is Trunks, so he constantly insults him. Trunks defeats Idarsa with even trying.

Idarse and Ikose's mother

Incredibly annoying and loud, Idarse and Ikose's mother is responsible for Babi-Di discovering the names of the warriors Buu faced during his fight with Vegeta and the fact that Trunks lives in the western capital. Humiliated by how easily Goten and Trunks defeated her sons, she reveals this information to Babi-Di. However, her annoying voice and chronic complaining causes Babi-Di to threaten to kill her. This is the last time she is heard from again in the series.

Iedei

A giant mutant bug, Iedei is the last resort of the Arlian king to defeat Nappa and Vegeta. However, he is no match for the Saiyans and is killed.

Ii Shenron

The strongest and most evil of the Shenrons, Ii Shenron is the last Shenron Gokou faces. Even as Super Saiyajin 4, Gokou can't beat him, especially when he absorbs the other Dragon Balls. When Vegeta arrives and becomes Super Saiyajin 4, they fuse together and become the strongest warrior ever, Super Saiyajin 4 Gogeta. Gogeta could have easily killed Ii Shenron had the fusion not ended as quickly as it did. Because of the immense power of Gogeta, the fusion lasts only a couple of minutes. Thinking that he has finally killed Gokou, Ii Shenron proceeds to destroy Earth. After beating Gohan, Vegeta, Goten, and Trunks, there appears to be little hope. All seems lost, until Gokou arises with the genki dama. Gathering energy from all over the universe, Gokou defeats Ii Shenron and restores the original Shenron.

Illusion Saiyan/Maboroshi Saiyajin

Two Saiyans that Krillin and the others encounter in God's Pendulum room during the Saiyan Saga, they have incredible power compared to Krillin and the others and defeat the Z Senshi

DBZ Character BIOs

without much difficulty. After being defeated, Krillin and the others awake to learn that the Saiyan on their way to Earth are much stronger than the ones they fought.

Ikose

The brother of Idarsa, Ikose also participated in the youth division of the twenty-fifth Tenkaichi Budoukai. Like his brother, he is rude and angry that his opponent is a little kid. Unfortunately, the little kid turns out to be Goten. Ikose is defeated without much effort by Goten.

Imeggan/Imeggajin

A planet of merchants, the Imeggans were originally an ordinary people. However, when King Don Kea took control, the taxes he imposes make everyone have to act as businessmen. They must constantly sell their wares to survive. They also provide energy to Goku during his fight with Ii Shenron.

Imeggan elderly couple

An older couple that Goku and the others meet while hiding from the Imeggan police, they tell Goku the story of what happened on their planet and why everyone seems so greedy. They also provide food for Goku and the others.

Imeggan Receptionist

A friendly receptionist at the Imeggan hotel in Dragon Ball GT, he promises Goku and the others that he won't try to rip them off like the other merchants. After they check into their room, Goku, Pan, and Trunks learn that everything costs additional money.

Inferior Machine

Pan meets the Inferion Machine on Dr. Myuu's planet, and he explains why the planet is nothing but machines. He also tells Pan why he is constantly being teleported from inside Myuu's main building to the outside of the building. Later, he helps Pan find Goku and Trunks.

Inoshikachyou

Inoshikachyou is a large boar that Tenshinhan and Chaozu use as part of their con act. Inoshikachyou destroys a town, then Tenshinhan and Chaozu come forward and pretend to kill him for money. They travel from town to town performing this con, until Goku interferes and ruins it.

Interviewer

Working for ZTV, the interviewer is sent to be a commentator for the Cell games and Mr. Satan's fight with Cell. Like most everyone on Earth, he thinks of Goku and his friends as a nuisance, getting in the way of Mr. Satan saving the world.

Invisible man

The second fighter of Uranai-Baba, the invisible man battles Yamucha. Because he is not able to see him, Yamucha is losing. Kuririn gets a good idea and positions Buruma and Roshi in a certain manner. He pulls off Buruma's top, causing Roshi to shoot blood from his nose. Roshi gets nosebleeds whenever he sees nudity. The blood covers the Invisible man, and allows Yamucha to see him.

Jackie Chun

A play on Jackie Chan, Jackie Chun is the identity Muten Roshi assumes when competing in the Tenkaichi Budoukai to avoid being recognized. He wins the twenty-first Budoukai after beating Gokou, but in the twenty-second, Tenshinhan defeats him.

Jaga Badda

The cousin of Mr. Satan, Jaga is jealous of Mr. Satan's popularity and stature. He blackmails Mr. Satan by threatening to tell that world that he used to wet his pants, and forces him to go to his island to face his bio warriors. Jaga, being short and weak, can't fight Satan on his own so he's responsible for the creation of the Burori clone.

Janemba

The result of all evil that has passed through Hades, Janemba is formed because a kid demon neglects to watch the evil cleansing machine. At first, Janemba is a playful, extremely large and

Pojo's Unofficial ABSOLUTE Dragon Ball Z

DBZ Character BIOs

yellow spirit-like demon. After being defeated by Gokou as Super Saiyajin 3, he transforms into a smaller, red demon, which neither Gokou nor Vegeta is able to beat. Once Gokou and Vegeta succeed in the fusion dance, Gogeta kills Janemba.

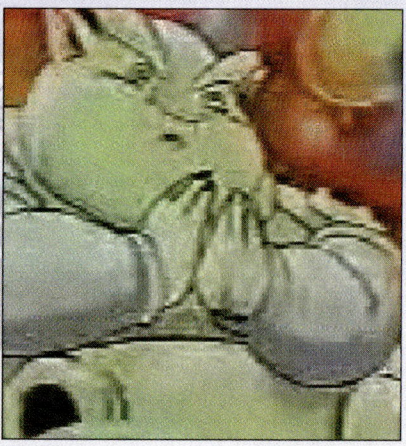

Jeice

Jeice is a member of the Ginyu Tokusentai. He is afraid of Gokou because of how easily he defeated Recoome and Baata. Jeice seeks the assistance of Ginyu Taicho to help with his fight with Gokou. He later fights Vegeta, thinking Vegeta is weaker than him. However, this proves to be a mistake, as Vegeta easily defends against all his attacks, and finishes him off with a ki blast.

Jewel
The runner up in the 24th Tenkaichi Budoukai, Jewel thinks of himself as a ladies man. In the 25th Budoukai, Android 18 knocks Jewel out of the ring during the Battle Royal for trying to hit on her.

Jinku
Jinku is an orphan Gohan meets after escaping from the wilderness. He has the physical features of a fox. He, like the others, is taken to the orphanage.

Kaichyuu Oyaku
A family of giant wormlike creatures that Vegeta and Goku encounter while searching for Gohan and others in Buu's body. The Kaichyuu Oyaku have incredibly powerful exoskeletons – the head of the family took ki blasts from both Goku and Vegeta without even being stunned. Once they discover that the Kaichyuu Oyakyu aren't enemies, Goku and Vegeta leave them alone.

Kaizoku Robo
Kaizoku Robo is a giant robot constructed by pirates to guard their treasure. His main weapons are a machine gun for an arm that never runs out of ammo, and a flame-thrower. Goku defeats him.

Kaka
The painter for the Red Ribbon Army, Kaka paints Red very tall which pleases the Commander.

Kakao
The android member of Tauras' team in DBZ movie 3, Kakao battles Yamucha and beats him. Goku eventually kills Kakao.

Kakujya
Kakujya is a scientist who works for Slug in DBZ movie 4.

Kami/Kamisama (God)

Kamisama is the God of the Earth. He tried to become God of the Earth long ago, but was denied because of the evil within him. To resolve this problem, Kamisama split himself into two beings, one good and one evil. The evil side of him is Piccolo Daimoa, and they both share a spiritual link. If one dies, the other is supposed to die as well. However, when Gokou kills Piccolo Daimoa, Kamisama survives because of Daimoa's offspring, Piccolo of DBZ. He is also the creator of the Dragon Balls and like Piccolo, Kamisama will die if any of the Dragon Balls die.

Kanassajin
Bardock and his group attack the Kanassajin in the beginning of the Bardock story. The Kanassajin have powerful psychic abilities and know that the Saiyajin are going to kill them.

Kanemochi Fuufu
Kanemochi Fuufu and his wife come out of Uranai Baba's place after having their fortune told, while Goku and the others are waiting in line to see Uranai Baba.

Kargo
Kargo is a Namekseijin child who is killed when Dodoria

DBZ Character BIOs

attacks Dende and Muuri's village.

Karin/Corin
The grower of the Senzu Beans and protector of the sacred water, Karin lives in a tower near God's palace. He is very wise and intelligent, and helps Gokou when fighting Tao Pai Pai. He is seen very little in Dragonball Z, but always ensures that the senzu beans are grown.

Karinto
Goku meets Karinto during his training with Mr. Popo. He is the one Goku is looking teach him "Quiet Like the Sky".

Karoni
One of Mr. Satan's best students, Karoni attempts to fight Cell. Since this is an annoyance to Cell before the fight with Goku, Cell shoots Karoni into the sky with his ki. When he finally lands, Karoni's teeth are knocked out and he is badly beaten.

Kenpau Ka
A street fighter who offers people 100,000 zeni if they can beat him, Kenpau Ka fights Goku and loses. Goku uses the money he wins to find Bulma's house.

Kibitto

Kibitto is Kaioshin's assistant. He is killed by Dabura. He is later resurrected when Buruma summons Shenron after Vegeta kills many of the spectators of the Tenkaichi Boudukai. His special ability is souki idou – instantaneous movement to any lower planet or Kaioshin's world. He later fuses with Kaioshin to demonstrate the power of the potera.

Kid Gamera/Ko Gamera
After giving his kinto to Goku, Muten Roshi needs a new ride. He wants to use Kid Gamera as a ride. However, Roshi can't stomach it since Kid Gamera's method of travel is spinning quickly.

Kid Katsu
A contender in the GT Tenkaichi Budoukai, Kid Katsu makes it to the semifinals.

Kidnappers
After kidnapping Goku, these two men threaten to kill him unless Capsule Corporation pays them five billion zeni. While trying to declare their ransom to Bulma, their time runs out on the pay phone. Later, they call again and reach Vegeta who doesn't care what they do to Goku. After Goku flies out of the car and brings the men a pay phone, they are too scared to continue and let Goku go.

Kigurumi Z Senshi
During the twenty-fifth Tenkaichi Budoukai, a movie is shown to commemorate Hercule's defeat of Cell. The movie features actors wearing gigantic masks of Hercule, Cell, and the Z Senshi. Using pathetic special effects of wires, buttons, and switches, the actors are able to fly, make explosions, and shoot ki blasts. The movie ends with the Z Senshi beaten and Cell getting killed by a kick from Hercule.

Killer
Killer is a tall black man who competes in the 25th Budoukai. He makes it to the Battle Royal, but is knocked out of the ring by Mighty Mask.

King Chapa/Chapa Ou
A fighter in both the twenty-first and twenty-third Tenkaichi Budoukai, King Chapa attempts to defeat Goku, but loses both times.

King Cold

The father of Furiza and Cooler, King Cold looks like Furiza's second form, except he wears battle armor. He is killed by Mirai No Trunks in our timeline by first getting blasted near the heart, and then completely blasted. He makes about two more appearances in the Z timeline, one after Gokou dies in the Cell saga, and during the Buu/Gokou fight.

King Don Kea
King of the planet Imegga, Don Kea is a ruthless and greedy leader. He is dethroned after his bodyguard Ledgic is beaten and he leaves Don Kea to take care of Goku himself. Not being very strong, he can do nothing to Goku and the others, so he gives up.

DBZ Character BIOs

King Gurumesu
Appearing in DB movie 1, King Gurumesu is a normal person who becomes corrupt when he finds rubies that give him an insatiable hunger.

King Yama/Lord Enma
The overseer of Hades, Lord Enma decides whether a soul goes to heaven or hell. He is short-tempered, and loses it often in the series.

King Kai/North Kaiosama
The God of the northern galaxy, Kaiosama lives on a small planet with his friends Bubbles and Gregory. When the Saiyajin are on their way to Earth, Gokou ventures the path of the snake to seek training from him, since he is considered the greatest martial artist of the northern galaxy. He isn't very serious and constantly makes bad jokes. When Kaiosama's planet is destroyed by Cell, Kaio and Gokou leave for Dai Kaiosama's world to visit old friends and meet strong fighters.

King Kuresu
The father of Princess Miisa, King Kuresu's kingdom is constantly being attacked by demons. When Goku arrives, he saves the kingdom by sealing all the demons in hell and saving Princess Miisa.

King Moai
The dictator of the Planet Arlia, King Moai is killed by Vegeta after pleading for his life.

King Vegeta
King Vegeta is the father of the proud Prince Vegeta. Unlike most Saiyajin fathers, he decides to keep his son with him rather than send him to a planet to conquer. He hates the tyrant Furiza, and he gathers all the elites to kill him when Furiza attempts to destroy Planet Vegeta. Though very strong, he is killed by Furiza with only two hits. After he dies, Furiza kills the other elites with little difficulty.

King Wonton/Ounton Ou
To decide who has the greatest martial arts dojo, King Wonton hosts a Budoukai in the village where he is king.

Kinkaku
Kinkaku is a thug who Goku meets when he's traveling around the world. Kinkaku and his brother Ginkaku force the people of a mountain village to give them food once a month. His weapon of intimidation is a man-eating gourd that sucks people in and turns them into sake.

Kinoni Sarada
Appearing in the Dr. Slump/Dragon Ball crossover, Kinoni rides around on a tricycle. He has a light-hearted but strange personality.

Kirano
A participant in the Tenkaichi Budoukai at the end of DBZ, Kirano is must face Captain Chicken.

Kishime

A Bio Warrior in DBZ movie 2, Kishime's main attack is the use of electric tentacles that he attaches to his arms. Goku kills him.

Kokuou
The King of the Earth, Kokuou doesn't have much of a role in any of the three series. Although he does care about his people, and he is a popular ruler. When attacked by Piccolo Daimoa, he is forced to renounce his throne. After Gokou kills Piccolo, he becomes King once more.

Kokuou's Castle Guard
He is a large guard who protects the door to the king's quarters. When he tries to stop Piccolo Daimoa from entering, he is killed when Piccolo Daimoa puts his hand through the guard's chest.

Konkichi
A little fox-like kid that Goku encounters on his trip around the world, Konkichi is a thief, but only steals to survive. Because Goku saves his life, he treats Goku like a king.

DBZ Character BIOs

Kouryu
Kouryu is a 10-year-old competitor in the 25th Tenkaichi Budoukai's children's' division.

Krillin/Kuririn
Kuririn is a monk who trains with Kamesennin and Chibi Son Gokou. He has no nose, and no hair until later in the series. Kuririn is the strongest human, but he is never as strong as a Saiyajin, let alone a Super Saiyajin. He marries Android 18 later in the series and has a daughter named Marron. He plays a semi-important role in the series, as his death by Furiza causes Gokou to become a Super Saiyajin for the first time.

KTV's Female Interviewer
The anchorwoman for KTV television network.

Kui
Kui goes to Planet Nameksei to face Vegeta who is in search of the Dragon Balls. Vegeta kills Kui after he begs for his life.

Kung Fu Man
A competitor in the twenty-fifth Tenkaichi Budoukai, Kung Fu Man has a striking resemblance to Bruce Lee in both appearance and fighting technique.

Kurikinton Soramame
Appearing in the Dr. Slump/Dragon Ball crossover, Kurikinton Soramame is a barber.

Kyo Jin
A large man who fights Krillin in the twenty-second Tenkaichi Budoukai, Kyo Jin is defeated when Krillin grabs his finger and throws him into a wall.

Lanfan
Lanfan participates in the twenty-first Tenkaichi Budoukai and fights against Namu. Lanfan uses her sexuality to distract her opponent, leaving him open to attacks. When Namu remembers his mission to get water for his village, he closes his eyes and knocks her out.

Large Complaining Girl
A large and impatient woman, Goku brings her to Roshi as a maid. However, Roshi wanted a bouncy girl, not a fat one.

Ledgic
The first enemy encountered in Dragon Ball GT, Ledgic is the bodyguard of King Don Kea and the only reason he is still in power. When he fights Goku, he beats him pretty badly until Goku goes Super Saiyan. Once he realizes Goku's superior strength, he stops fighting and leaves the warrior in peace.

Lemlia
The betrothed of Atla, she is forced to marry King Moai. After the king's forces are killed, she hopes that Atla and she will be together until Vegeta destroys the planet.

Lenne
Forced to marry Zunama, Lenne wears a Dragon Ball in her hair. In exchange for taking care of Zunama, she promises Goku and the others that they can have the Dragon Ball. Trying to trick Zunama, Trunks dresses up like Lenne to infiltrate Zunama's lair, so he can cut off his antennas.

Leon
A gigantic lion-like monster, Leon is Mutchy-Motchy's pet. He destroys any problems Mutchy can't take care of himself. Leon is easily beaten when Goku fires a ki blast into the wall, causing a huge boulder to crush him.

Lime
Lime is a small girl that Gohan meets prior to the Cell Games. Her entire family, except for her grandfather, was killed by Cell. After the announcement of the Cell Game, her village gives all of their money to a greedy businessman who creates a dome to protect himself from Cell. Once he realizes the businessman's true intentions for the dome, Lime's grandfather bravely stands up to him, and must fight General Tao. After the grandfather is beaten, General Tao is about to kill him when Gohan intervenes. When he learns Gohan's identity, General Tao flees. Lime is grateful to Gohan for saving her grandfather and village, and says goodbye and wishes Gohan luck in the Cell Game.

Lucifer
A vampire-like demon in DB movie 2, Lucifer attempts to destroy the sun to create a world of absolute darkness. When he is about to fire a laser cannon at the sun, Goku's kamehameha pushes the cannon so it fires directly at Lucifer, killing him.

Lucifer's Servant
A servant to Lucifer in DB Movie 2, he not only has a taste for blood, but also a vast knowledge of it.

Lude Monster
The creation of Dr. Myuu, the monster is an idol said to be God. In order for it to receive full power, it must absorb energy from people. It has three stages of power, and is revived at stage two when Goku and Trunks defeat Mutchy. In order to reach level three to beat Goku and Trunks, Lude changes Doll-Tucky into a doll and throws he and Pan into the monster for it to gain needed energy. He is defeated

DBZ Character BIOs

when Goku and Pan hit its cell at the same time, freeing all who were absorbed.

Lunch

Possessing no ki power, Lunch has the ability to transform from a good-hearted young girl into a machine-gun-wielding gangster. During Gokou and Kuririn's training by Muten Roshi, she is a cook. She is rarely seen in Dragon Ball Z but she has a thing for Tenshinhan. After Tenshinhan dies in the battle with Nappa, she gets drunk in a bar. (This scene was cut from the American version)

Magical Errand Witch

A witch who works for the Kaioshin, she puts on Rou Dai Kaioshin's potara earring and is permanently fused with him. Though he becomes ugly, he learns the ability to raise an individual's ki. He uses this technique on Gohan during the Buu Saga.

Mai

A servant of Pilaf, Mai, along with her teammate Shu, attempts to aid Pilaf in his mission to conquer the Earth.

Maid Robot

Maid Robot works for the Capsule Corporation.

Majin Buu

Majin Buu is the final and most powerful villain in DBZ. He is a demon created from magic by Bibi-Dee. Buu is sealed away by Bibi-Dee because he's uncontrollable. In the final chapter of DBZ, Babi-Dee and Dabura gather enough energy to resurrect him. Buu is responsible for the death of almost every Earthling, and he destroys the Earth itself.

During the course of the Buu Saga, he undergoes six transformations. His first form is that of a fat and jolly demon, obsessed with tasty foods.

After the near death of Mr. Satan, the only human to have ever been Buu's friend, the evil within Buu is expelled, creating an extremely bony, but stronger Buu. Fat Buu loses to Skinny Buu and turns into chocolate, and Skinny Buu eats him. Skinny Buu transforms again and his body is lean and much better for fighting. He also experiences a drastic climb in power and develops the ability to sense ki. He finds God's palace, and upon discovering everyone there, requests to fight the one Gokou promises is stronger than him. Given that Goten and Trunks are sleeping, and even with fusion wouldn't have been a match for this newer Buu, Piccolo convinces him to wait one hour for the fighters to get ready. Buu agrees, but states that he will kill everyone after the hour. Trunks and Goten leave to train in the room of spirit and time as Buu waits. Not being able to wait any longer, Buu screams to fight the warriors. Piccolo convinces Buu that he can't fight them because so many people are still alive on Earth. To compensate, Buu fires thousands of ki attacks from the palace killing everyone except the three who dodged the attacks – Mr. Satan, Tenshinhan and Chaozu. Having given the kids as long as he could to train, Piccolo leads Buu to the room by taking the long way. They eventually reach the room, and Goten and Trunks fuse together to fight Buu as Gotenks. After a long and interesting battle, Gotenks pretends to have lost, causing Piccolo to destroy the entrance to the room. Buu becomes so angry at the loss of tasty treats that he creates a temporary portal from the room to Earth. Upon returning to Earth, he turns Buruma and the others into chocolate and eats them. After Gotenks goes Super Saiyajin 3 and creates a portal of his own, he and Piccolo also escape.

Fighting again, Gotenks nearly defeats Buu, but the Super Saiyajin 3 wears off, as well as the fusion. Just as they are about to be defeated, the newly powered up Gohan arrives. After being severely beaten by Gohan, Buu self-detonates. He returns to the battlefield and taunts Trunks and Goten to fuse again and finish the fight with him. They do so, though Gohan tells them not to do it. Buu secretly sends parts of himself behind Gotenks and Piccolo, and uses them to absorb the two. Gohan doesn't stand a chance against the super-powered Buu. Gokou is given his life back by

DBZ Character BIOs

Rou Dai Kaioshin, and returns to Earth. Buu absorbs Gohan before he can put on the potara earring and fuse with Gokou. With no one left to fuse with except Dende and Mr. Satan, all hope seems lost until Lord Enma lets Vegeta back on Earth. Once Gokou fuses with Vegeta to become Vegetto, Buu doesn't have a chance. Vegetto tricks Buu into absorbing him, and Vegetto enters Buu's body to free the others. Unaware of the magic within Buu, the permanent fusion of Gokou and Vegeta wears off. Everyone is freed, and Vegeta pulls Fat Buu away.

Transforming again, Gokou and Vegeta rush out of Buu with Gohan and the others. Buu returns to his original, and most evil and powerful, form. He proceeds to destroy the Earth. Gokou, Vegeta, Dende, and Mr. Satan barely escape with the help of Kaioshin and are brought to his planet. Without enough time, Gohan and the others are left on Earth and killed when it explodes. Sensing Gokou and Vegeta's ki on Kaioshin's planet, Buu teleports there to finish them. Rou Dai Kaioshin, Kaioshin, and Dende leave the planet using souki idou, but forget Mr. Satan. After a long and amazing battle, Vegeta devises a plan to use planet Nameksei's Dragon Balls to wish for Earth and its inhabitants to come back to life. Once done, Vegeta asks for the Earth's energy so Gokou can create a giant Genki Dama (translates to energy ball, but dubbed spirit bomb in English.) The Earth people don't trust Vegeta and won't help until Mr. Satan screams for their assistance. Thinking it is Mr. Satan fighting Buu, the whole Earth donates their energy, creating a huge Genki Dama. With it, Gokou finally kills Buu.

DBZ Character BIOs

Man-Wolf
A participant in the twenty-second Budoukai, his first match is against Jackie Chun. Man-wolf wants to exact revenge against Jackie for destroying the moon and keeping him in his wolf form. By using a special technique – Kuririn's head – Jackie Chun changes Man-wolf back into a man. Once this happens, Man-wolf no longer has any ill feelings towards Jackie, and forfeits the match.

Mariko

A fighter of the west galaxy, Mariko faces Gokou in the finals of the afterlife Budoukai. He gives Gokou a good match, but is eventually defeated when Gokou kicks him in the ribs and throws him out of the ring by the tail.

Maron
As Kuirin's first girlfriend, Maron is unintelligent and uncommitted. She is also very frank about her feelings. She calls Chi Chi and Bulma old ladies, and they nearly kill her. She thinks that Kuririn will never marry her, so she leaves him. Later in the series, she goes to Kame House looking for Kuririn and tells him he is the only man she has ever loved. After being groped by Muten Roshi and learning that Kuririn isn't at the Kame House, she leaves and is never heard from again.

Married couple that find Ma Junior's egg
The couple finds Piccolo Daimoa's egg that he shot out of his mouth before dying. When the egg hatches, Piccolo of DBZ is inside. After climbing out of the egg, Piccolo burns the couple's house down.

Marron
The daughter of Kuririn and Android 18, Marron doesn't play a major role in either DBZ or DBGT. She is named after Kuirin's first girlfriend, Maron. In DBZ, she looks exactly like a combination of 18 and Kuririn, with blond hair, no nose and a large forehead. In DBGT, however, she looks more like her mother.

Master/Muten Roshi

Also known as Kamesennin because he is a well-known martial arts teacher, Muten Roshi trains Child Gokou and Kuririn. He spends fifty years mastering the kamehameha, and Gokou learns to do right after seeing it. He is also the biggest pervert in the Dragon Ball world. He is killed when trying to defeat Piccolo Daimoa using mafuba, but is resurrected after Gokou defeats Piccolo. He lives with his sea turtle, Umigame, on his small island.

Mayor of Jingle Village
The Mayor of Jingle Village is kidnapped and held captive, until the townspeople find the Dragon Ball the captors want as ransom.

Medametcha

An extremely strange frog, Medametcha is a henchman of Lord Slug and has the ability to create energy-sucking clones of himself. However, he isn't strong enough to battle Gokou and is killed.

Meetian/Meetjin
The Meetians are race of people eradicated by Bardock's group. Bardock learns of Frieza's intentions to kill off the Saiyans from his dying comrade Toma. Toma is killed by Dodoria on Planet Meet.

Megane Buta
Appearing in the Dr. Slump/Dragon Ball crossover, Megane is a pig who announces the town news from a tree.

Men from the Orphanage
The Men from the Orphanage try to take the orphans Gohan meets while training with Piccolo

DBZ Character BIOs

back to the orphanage. They fail at every attempt until Pigero leaves.

Menmen
A nephew of Jaga Badda, Menmen was sent to Hercule to deliver Jaga's challenge. He is extremely clumsy and constantly falls down.

Mera
A beautiful demon of the underworld, Mera helps Goku and Princess Miisa escape.

Mermaid/Ningyo
Goku attempts to give Ningyo to Roshi to be a housemaid, but she can't live on land.

Metallic

A large Terminator-like android, Metallic battles Gokou in Muscle Tower but loses when his batteries ran dry.

Mezu
A red demon of hell, Mezu wants to play with Gokou, but instead must work when he loses to Gozu in rock, paper, scissors. After doing some work, he whines that Gozu is having all the fun, so Gozu lets him play with Gokou. He promises to show Gokou a secret way out of hell if he wins a race against him, but doesn't think Gokou has a chance since he is the fastest demon in hell. But, after tricking him, Gokou wins the race and is shown the way out of hell.

Midori Norimaki
The teacher of Arale, Midori eventually marries Arale's creator Senbe. Together they have a son named Tanbu.

Mighty Mask
He competes in the 24th and 25th Tenkaichi Budoukai, but Mighty Mask isn't very strong. In the 25th, Trunks and Goten want to fight as adults, so they knock Mighty Mask out and assume his identity.

Migoren
A dog-like alien from the northern galaxy, Mirogen is 7000 years old and fights evil aliens. Migoren trains on Dai Kaio's planet and hope to one day be trained by Dai Kaio himself.

Mikokatsun

A bio warrior in DBZ movie 2, Mikokatsun's main technique is to use his obesity. He is defeated when Gokou uses Kaioken and flies through him, causing him to deflate like a balloon.

Minosha
The younger brother of Tapion, he and his brother seal the two halves of Hiredugarn within themselves, and then seal themselves into separate oracles. When Minosha is freed, the half of Hiredugarn is eventually freed as well. Being a noble warrior, he attempts to battle the half of Hiredugarn that escapes, but he is killed.

Minto
While living in a small mountain village, the young boy Kuririn meets a little girl named Minto and has a thing for her.

Miss Piza/Pizza
Pizza is the ditsy announcer for Mr. Satan at the Cell Game. She obviously sees how much stronger everyone is than Mr. Satan, but she still thinks of him as the strongest and admires his power. Her only appearance is during the Cell Game.

Mohikan
A participant in the twenty-second Tenkaichi Budoukai, he is defeated by Yamcha after getting elbowed in the chin.

Monban
The soldiers of the underworld who hurl spears.

Monkey Family
Goku saves the Monkey Family from the Red Ribbon Army. They thank him for his valiant effort.

Monster
Monster is a Dragon carrying a Dragon Ball. Roshi, Yamcha, and some of the others try to defeat him to get the Dragon Ball. He is finally beaten when Roshi farts on him.

Moose Family
The Moose has 12 family members, and Goku meets them when he is training with Mr. Popo. The family consists of Moose, Éclair,

DBZ Character BIOs

and their nine children: Pudding, Cookie, Donuts, Biscuit, Jelly, Crepe, Sugar, Chocolate and Babaro. The grandfather's name is Karintou (Fried Dough Cake.)

Mou Kekko
Defeated by Mr. Satan in the second match of the twenty-seventh Tenkaichi Budoukai, Mou Kekko tries his luck again in the twenty-eighth Budoukai. Unfortunately, his opponent is Pan and he thinks she is just a weak little brat. He completely underestimates her. With two hits, he is defeated.

Mr. Buu

Originally part of the Majin Buu, Mr. Buu is the good part of the Majin. He becomes friends with Mr. Satan. When Buu is restored to his original form, and about to kill Mr. Satan, Mr. Buu expels himself from within Majin to protect his friend. Although he isn't strong enough to hurt Majin Buu, he is able to distract him long enough for Gokou and Vegeta to gather energy for the Super Genki Dama. In Dragon Ball GT, he remerges with Uub, who is the reincarnation of Majin Buu, to fight Bebi-Vegeta.

Mr. Doctor
After his fight with Vegeta, Mr. Doctor takes care of Goku.

Mr. Money
In movie nine, Mr. Money sponsors the tournament as a gift for his son who is a huge Mr. Satan fan. He originally plans for the finalists to compete against students of Mr. Satan dressed as aliens. His plans are ruined when Bojack and his men take over the competition.

Mr. Popo
God's best friend and apprentice, Mr. Popo is the caretaker of God's palace. Though he looks weak, he is actually very strong.

Mr. Robot
Although he has never appeared in the American Dubs to date, Mr. Robot is a character Gohan meets during his six-month training with Piccolo. Gohan is trapped in a cave that is empty, except for a robot who is turned off. Gohan turns it on to ask for help, but Mr. Robot feels that he has to stay off forever. Like Piccolo, Mr. Robot is charmed by Gohan's innocence and he starts to care for him. When a boulder almost smashes Gohan, Mr. Robot catches it and lets Gohan escape. After he gets away, Gohan realizes his new friend is crushed by the rock and walks away crying. (You may remember the scene after the dinosaur dies and Gohan walks away crying, and is stronger for the experience. The scene used in the dinosaur episode was from cut and pasted from this one with Mr. Robot.)

Mr. Satan/Hercule Satan
Though very annoying, Mr. Satan is one of the most crucial characters in DBZ. Without his presence, the entire universe would have been destroyed. His influence over the people of the Earth gives Gokou the energy he needs to complete the genki dama and kill Majin Buu. He is also the father of Videl who is the future wife of Son Gohan.

Mr. Shu/Su Saiaku Sensei
Gohan's evil tutor, Mr. Shu considers himself the greatest tutor on Earth. He uses a whip to control his students. When insulting Goku, Gohan rebels against him and destroys his whip. Gohan is about to punish Shu when Chi Chi walks in. After Shu requests more money, insults Goku, and criticizes Gohan's intelligence, Chi Chi throws him out of the house.

Mrs. Briefs
The mother of Buruma, Mrs. Briefs has a small role in each of the three Dragon Ball series. She mainly buys cakes and brings everyone drinks. She isn't as intelligent as her husband or her daughter, but she is very beautiful.

Musuka
The Circus owner in Satan City, Musuka steal a Pteradon baby named Chibi whom Gohan has played with since he was a kid. When Chibi's parents come to

DBZ Character BIOs

save him, Gohan is forced to knock them out to stop them from hurting anyone in the city. Unfortunately, before doing so, he screams that he is Gohan and they need to calm down. This confirms Videl's notion that Gohan is the Great Saiyaman. After knocking out the Pteradon parents, Gohan brings them back home along with Chibi. Musuka promises never to kidnap animals again.

Mutchy

The high priest of Lude, Mutchy disguises himself as a whip that Cardinal Mutchy-Motchy uses. He is extremely powerful and controls anything that his whips touch. He is killed by a ki blast from Trunks.

Mutaito

Mutaito is the martial arts elder of a small village. He faces off against Tao Pai Pai, who is hired by village's richest man to be his bodyguard. Though strong, he is no match for Tao Pai Pai and would have been killed had it not been for Gohan's interference. Once he learns who Gohan is, Tao Pai Pai runs away. Mutaito is grateful to Gohan for saving him and his village, and tells him he knows the world is going to be made peaceful again with warriors like Gohan going to battle Cell.

Muuri

The village elder, Muuri is very wise and brave. When Furiza and his men attacked his village, Muuri destroys the scouters to prevent Furiza from locating the other villages. However, he angers Dodoria, who after killing the other Namekseijin, kills him.

Myra

The third fighter of Uranai Baba, Myra is able to defeat Yamucha by beating him up. He forces Yamucha to either to forfeit the match or be dropped off a platform to his death. However, when fighting Gokou, he is defeated.

Nail

The only warrior Namekseijin, Nail is the protector of the Senoir Elder. To delay Furiza from returning to his ship, Nail fights bravely, but unsuccessfully against the tyrant. His power level is 45,000, above most of the Ginyu Tokusentai. When found half dead by Piccolo, Nail gives Piccolo the gift of himself, allowing Piccolo to merge with him. He greatly increases Piccolo's power level.

Namekian/ Namekseijin

A race of reptilian-like creatures, the Namekians are nearly wiped out from a catastrophic weather event. Luckily, one Namekian survives and gives birth to one hundred Namekians. He also recreates the Dragon Balls of his world, which unlike the Earth's Dragon Balls, are larger in size and greater in power. After again being wiped out by Frieza, the race seems nearly extinct until Kaiosama and God devise a plan to use the Earth's Dragon Balls and Namekian Dragon Balls to bring back all souls killed by Frieza and transport them to Earth. After a year living on Earth, the Namekians use their Dragon Balls to transport themselves to a new planet that is almost identical to their original home. Throughout DBZ and DBGT, the Namekians help Goku and the Earth in any way they can, but usually by donating energy to help create super genki dama.

Namu

A participant in the twenty-first Tenkaichi Budoukai, Namu wants to win the prize money so he can buy water for his village. His first match is against the seductive Lanfan, and he wins by closing his eyes and knocking her out. When fighting Gokou, he puts up a good fight, but when attempting a second Diving X, he is knocked out of the ring.

DBZ Character BIOs

Nappa

A partner of Vegeta and one of the Saiyajin elite, Nappa is very large in size, but very small in intelligence. He defeated all of the Z Senshi, including Piccolo, and was about to finish them all when Gokou arrives to save his son. Nappa is defeated when Gokou unleashes the great power of the Kaioken and paralyzes the large Saiyajin. Unable to fight any longer, and for losing to a low soldier, Vegeta kills Nappa since he isn't needed any longer.

NBS's Announcer

The anchor for NBS, this announcer alerts everyone to the existence of Piccolo Daimoa.

Neizu

A member of the Cooler Tokusentai, Neizu is a turtle-like alien. He is killed by Piccolo.

Nikki

A henchman of Garlic Jr., Nikki is tall and blue. He is killed along with Ginger by a kamehameha fired by Gokou.

Niko Chan Daiou

Appearing in the Dr. Slump/Dragon Ball crossover, Niko is an alien who becomes stranded on Earth.

Nok

A participant in the twenty-eighth Tenkaichi Budoukai, his opponent is Vegeta. When he greets Vegeta by shouting insults, Vegeta knocks him across the arena with one hit. After feeling how strong his opponent was, Nok forfeits.

Noppo

Noppo harasses Lunch when she makes her first appearance. He is a tall drunk and appears only in the anime.

North Kaioshin

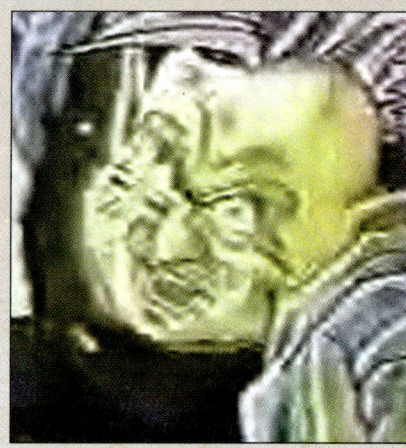

The God of the northern universe, North Kaioshin fights with a sword against Majin Buu. Unfortunately, he is unaware that cutting Buu in half doesn't hurt him and he is quickly killed by Buu.

Nurse

After his fight with Vegeta, the nurse takes care of Goku. Roshi grabs her butt, as he does with many girls he meets.

Obo Chyaman

Obo Chyaman is an inhabitant of Penguin Village who shows up during the Dr. Slump/Dragon Ball crossover.

Ogre Intern /Anai Oni

The Ogre of Hades, Anai Oni escorts Goku to the path of the snake after Goku's death fighting Radditz.

Ookami

Ookami are wolves that Goku fights for food.

Ookane Money

The wife of the world's richest man, Mr. Money, Ookane Money doesn't really have any role other than in DBZ Movie 9.

Oorinji no Senpai

The Oorinji no Senpai, elders of the school that Kuririn attended before training with Roshi, often beat up Kuririn for fun. When they compete against him in the Budoukai, Kuririn beats them all to a pulp.

Oolong

Although he possesses the abili-

DBZ Character BIOs

ty to shape-shift, Oolong, no matter what form he takes, appears weak and cowardly. He spends most of his time collecting women's panties and trying to see Buruma naked.

Oolong's Planned Servant Girl

When visiting a village in search of the Dragon Balls, Goku and Bulma meet a small girl who is being forced to marry the great Oolong. Knowing that this is a horrible thing for her, Goku pretends to be the little girl to discover the true form of Oolong and his hideout. After he finds out that Oolong is nothing more than a small and weak pig, Goku and the villagers force him to release the girl and the other servant girls he has in captivity.

Ooma

A race of worm-like creatures, ki blasts from Goku, Trunks, and Pan won't even crack their exoskeletons. They are finally defeated when Goku learns they are defenseless from behind and the Oomas are thrown into walls and tangled together by Goku and the others.

Oo Tokage

While Gohan trains Videl to fly, Oo Tokage is a small lizard Goten plays with to pass the time.

Oribu

Considered to be the greatest fighter of the northern galaxy, Oribu is from Earth. When matched against Paikuhan, he puts up a good fight but loses in the end.

Orphanage Woman

The head of an orphanage, she attempts to take the children Gohan encounters during his training with Piccolo. After Pigero leaves, she and the police are able to return all of the children to the orphanage.

Otoko Sukii

Participating in the twenty-eighth Tenkaichi Budoukai, Otoko Sukii is delighted to see pretty boy Trunks is his opponent. It is assumed that since Otoko is only human, Trunks is the winner. However, the match isn't shown.

Ox King/Gyuu Mao

The father of Chichi, Gyuu Mao doesn't have much of a role in DBZ. He mainly is seen as the lovable grandfather of Gohan who brings him presents all the time.

Pachinko Boy

A little kid who thinks firing a pachinko ball from a slingshot to Oolong will intimidate Goku.

Pagosu

Pagosu is a member of Penguin Village's police force. He appears in the Dr. Slump/Dragon Ball crossover.

Paikuhan/Pikkon

West Kaio's prize pupil, Paikuhan is the strongest fighter in the afterlife. When first introduced, he is given the task of traveling to hell and taking control by defeating Cell and Furiza. He defeats them both, plus King Cold and the Ginyu Tokusentai. When the afterlife tournament starts, he is expected to win, though no one knows of Gokou's true power.

Pahku

A classmate of Goku Jr. in the Dragon Ball GT TV Special, Pahku is a bully who picks on Goku Jr. Though Goku Jr. could have easily beaten him up, he is a little cowardly and doesn't know his true power. When Goku Jr. sets out to find the Dragon Balls to save his Grandma Pan, Pahku meets up with him and joins the quest. After saving each other from evil witches and monsters, they become good friends.

Palace/Paresu

A girlfriend of Goten's in Dragon Ball GT, Palace is kind of ditzy. Other than Goten, no man but her father has ever touched her.

Pan

The daughter of Gohan and Videl, Pan doesn't have much of a role in Dragonball Z, but she is an essential character in Dragonball GT. She sneaks into the ship that Gokou, Trunks, and Goten are supposed to travel in to search for the black star Dragon Balls. Gokou and Trunks get on, but Goten gets a call from his girl-

Pojo's Unofficial ABSOLUTE Dragon Ball Z

DBZ Character BIOs

friend, so he doesn't enter. Gokou and Trunks see Pan at the controls and she hits the takeoff button, flying into space and leaving Goten behind. She never goes Super Saiyajin, though no female ever does. When Gokou is a Golden Oozaru, a giant ape, it is Pan who gets control of his mind causing him to transform into Super Saiyajin 4.

Pan's boyfriend
A boyfriend of Pan's in the beginning of Dragon Ball GT, he is on a date with her when a bank is robbed. Since the robbery is blocking their way to the movie theatre, Pan beats all the robbers up and saves the day. Frightened by her strength, her boyfriend runs away.

Panbukin

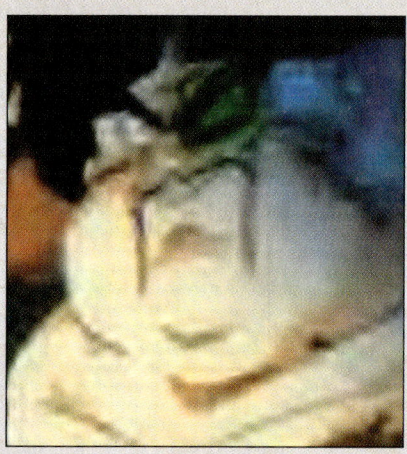

A member of Bardock's team, he is killed by Dodoria's men.

Panda parent and child
The pandas of Giran's village who fearfully witness Tamborine kill Giran.

Panji
Rescued from Oolong by Goku, Panji appears in DB movie 1. She joins Goku and the others and begs for their help in finding Kamesennin.

Panji's dad
Panji's dad stands up for his people against Gurumesu's tyranny, and he is almost killed by Bongo.

Panji's mom
Panji's mom appears in Dragon Ball.

Panputto
Panputto fought Goku in the first round of the 24th Budoukai and lost.

Papaya Man
The identity taken by Uub during the GT Tenkaichi Budoukai, Papaya Man can't fool Goku. Goku screams out that he is really Uub after their match in the semi-finals. After Uub removes his costume, he faces Mr. Satan in the ring.

Papoi
The best student of South Kaio, Papoi dresses like a chef. When Goku is training for his one day visit back to Earth, South Kaio brags about Papoi's strength. When North Kaio suggests that Papoi enter the Earth Budoukai, he accepts. Upon seeing how strong Goku is, Papoi and South Kaio leave and say that the Budoukai is beneath them.

Paragus
The father of the legendary Super Saiyajin, Paragus tries to use Burori's power to get revenge on the Saiyajin's for betraying him. Unable to control his son when he is young, Paragus forcefully places a controller on him to keep him at bay. While trying to escape the planet before a large meteor is to destroy it, Burori catches him in the Saiyajin pod and crushes it over his head, killing his father.

Pasuta
A killer who works for King Gurumesu, Pasuta appears in DB movie 1.

Patrol Car Police Officers
After 18 steals clothes from a store, these police officers attempt to pull her over. Annoyed by the officers, 18 flies out of the van and blasts their car.

Paul/Paoru
A strong fighter in a village located at the bottom of a volcano. Paul likes Krillin.

Piano
An old demon, Piano is most likely a child of Piccolo's before being encased within the Denshi Jar. During Piccolo Daimoa's sec-

DBZ Character BIOs

ond fight with Gokou, Piano is killed when Piccolo falls on top of him.

Piccolo

The offspring of the original Piccolo Daimoa, Piccolo is Gokou's archenemy until the Saiyajin Radditz appears on the Earth. To overcome Radditz's power, he and Gokou team up. After killing Radditz and Gokou, Piccolo takes Gokou's son, Gohan, to train him for the arrival of the other Saiyajin. Gohan's innocence changes Piccolo from a demon into a brave and noble warrior. He even loves Gohan so much that he sacrifices his life to save him. After the arrival of Cell, Piccolo re-merges with Kamisama to became the strongest fighter at that time. In Dragon Ball GT, he decides to die when the Earth explodes because of his love for his home. Though, when Gokou traps him in hell during the Super 17 saga, Piccolo devises a plan to help and requests Lord Enma to send him to hell. Enma refuses since he has already been sent to heaven. Because he has to be sent to hell, Piccolo starts shooting ki attacks and causing destruction in heaven. Since destruction isn't allowed in heaven, Enma sends Piccolo to hell. Piccolo spends the rest of eternity there, helping the demons deal with people who are too strong for them.

Piccolo Daimoa

The evil half of God, Piccolo Daimoa is originally sealed within the mafuba by Muten Roshi's sensei. To conquer the world, he is released by Emperor Pilaf to kill Gokou and collect the Dragon Balls. Because he wants his youth restored, Piccolo Daimoa pretends to help Pilaf gather the balls. So he doesn't repeat his downfall, Piccolo Daimoa creates a son, Tamborine, to kill all participants in the Tenkaichi Budoukai. To prevent him from gathering all seven balls and wishing for his youth, Muten Roshi confronts Piccolo. Since he fails to complete his spell, Muten Roshi dies because the mafuba takes all the energy from the one performing it. This leaves only Tenshinhan to fight, and given that everyone thinks Gokou is dead, Piccolo is able to conquer the world. After Gokou returns powered up, Piccolo is killed when Gokou punches through his gut. Before dying, he gives birth to another child, the Piccolo of DBZ.

Pigero

Pigero protects the orphans from the orphanage. Eventually he realizes the children would be better off at the orphanage and allows them to be taken.

Pinfu

Pinfu is a baby who appears in the Dragon Ball anime.

Piroshiki

A disciple of Mr. Satan, Piroshiki attempts to fight Cell in the Cell Game. He's big, fat and strong for a human, but he is no match for Cell and is easily knocked out of the ring.

DBZ Character BIOs

Pisuke Soramame
Appearing in the Dr. Slump/Dragon Ball crossover, he is the younger brother of Tarou and a good friend of Arale.

Police Officer
Goku meets the Police Officer in Dragon Ball. He helps Goku find Bulma's house.

Police Officers A and B
A pair of Police Officers who chase Lunch after she robs a bank, they fail when Goku and Krillin intervene.

Porunga

The original Shenron, Porunga, like Shenron, grants a wish to the one who gathers the Dragon Balls. His power is much greater than the first Shenron of Earth because he can grant three wishes. Though he cannot revive more than one person at a time. Gohan, Kuririn, and Buruma seek his power after God dies and the Earth's Dragon Balls disappear. Furiza and Vegeta, however, seek his wishes in order to become immortal. Also, like Shenron, his power is limited to the one who created him.

Previous Kami/Gods
These Gods exist in the spirit zone located at the bottom of God's temple. Their job is to keep everyone out. When Kami tries to enter, they attempt to kill him for violating the laws of the Gods.

Priest
The priest of the small village in movie ten, he claims that a sacrifice has to be made to the mountain god in order to rid the village of the monster. Once proven wrong, he is expelled from the village. After the Burori fight, he takes a blood sample of Burori and teams up with Jaga Badda, creating the Burori clone.

Princess Miisa
The Daughter of King Guresu, Princess Miisa is kidnapped by demons. When Goku steps in, she is rescued.

Princess Snake

The halfway point between Hades city and Kaiosama's planet, Gokou thinks Princess Snake is Kaio. After learning that he is wrong, Gokou wants to leave. However, Princess Snake lures him to stay longer with food and bath. When she looks into Gokou's dreams and sees his family, Princess Snake decides to eat him. The palace itself is a mirage so Gokou doesn't know he is within Snake herself. When he escapes, Gokou could have killed her, but since she fed him good food, he just tangles her into a knot.

Pteradon
A large Pteradon who thinks Bulma is his dinner in Dragon Ball. Goku hits him on the head with his Nyobo, killing him instantly.

Puar
Yamucha's best friend, Puar aids him by robbing those who pass through their home. He has the ability to shape-shift, and unlike Oolong, Puar can keep the shape as long as he wants. He can also fly, but he doesn't have any physical strength.

Puipui

The Henchman of Babi-Dee, Puipui is a strong fighter, but he isn't even close to the Saiyajin. He is the first to face off against Gokou and the others, and he has to fight Vegeta. Without even going Super Saiyajin, Vegeta easily kills Puipui.

Pyon Tatto
A fighter in the twenty-fifth Tenkaichi Budoukai kid's division, Pyon Tatto wins his match when his opponent starts crying.

Queen Hi
Queen Hi is the mother of Princess Miisa.

DBZ Character BIOs

Rabbit Gang Members
Working for Boss Rabbit, these members of his gang like to carry guns and are perverts.

Radditz
The brother of Kakarotto, a.k.a. Son Gokou, Radditz comes to Earth to retrieve his brother and return him to destroying planets. When he finds that Gokou hasn't completed his mission of destroying Earth, he steals Gokou's son and orders him to kill one hundred humans by the next day. He is killed when Gokou sacrifices himself and Piccolo fires his makankosappo (special beam cannon).

Raisin
Raisin and his brother – henchmen of Taurus in DBZ movie 3 – attack together to defeat an opponent, but the Z Senshi take them down.

Rakasei
A henchman of Taurus in DBZ movie 3, Rakasei is one of the twins killed by Gohan.

Raspberry
A henchman of Furiza, Raspberry is human-like in appearance. When looking for Bulma and her Dragon Ball, Raspberry and his teammate Blueberry decide to search for the balls instead and take over the galaxy. After being tricked into the ocean, they're killed by a giant crab. This is the same crab Bulma fights off earlier to retrieve the Dragon Ball that fell into the ocean.

Rebels of Galaxy 187
The supposed rebel leaders against Lude, the Rebels of Galaxy 187 are all turned into dolls.

Receptionist Man
The receptionist of the Tenkaichi Budoukai signs in the fighters to allow them to compete.

Recoome/Rikum
A large member of the Ginyu Tokusentai, Rikum is incredibly strong but a little low on intelligence. He fights and defeats Vegeta, and almost kills Gohan and Kuririn. When he faces Gokou, he is defeated with one hit. After the other members of the Ginyu Tokusentai are defeated, he is killed by a ki blast from Vegeta.

Red Ribbon Military Capsule Robot
A robot with a vast knowledge of military tactics and information, he helps Goku pilot a plane. While in flight, he freezes solid and crashes into the snow. A little girl named Suno saves Goku.

Red Shock Organization
The Red Shock Organization appears in the Great Saiyaman saga and is a gang who loves crime. Their leader fights Videl after she learns of the group's existence. Because she has a lot of pride, Videl won't allow the Great Saiyaman to interfere with her battle. She defeats the leader and the rest of the group surrenders.

Revered Scholar
The revered scholar is an old man who spends his life trying to find the bird with feathers of Basho Shen.

Rikishi
A sumo wrestler from the elimination round of the twenty-second Tenkaichi Budoukai, Rikishi is beaten by Tenshinhan.

Rirudo Shogun
Rirudo's mission is to track down Goku and retrieve the Dragon Balls. Giru double-crosses Goku and the others by bringing them to Rirudo. His special technique is to turn common materials into metal. He's eventually killed after a long battle with Goku. However, he later returns when Hell opens up, only to be killed again by Goten and Trunks.

Ritoian/Ritoseijin
A race of people who are almost extinguished by Frieza's army, the Ritoian children are sent aboard a stealth ship to escape. This is the same ship that Bulma, Gohan, and Krillin encounter on their way to Namek.

Romu
Romu finds Gohan unconscious on the beach after he escapes from Piccolo. He brings him back to his home and introduces Gohan to the other orphans.

DBZ Character BIOs

Rou Dai Kaioshin/Old Kai

Imprisoned within the Z Sword, Rou Dai Kaioshin is released when the sword is broken during Gohan's training. He is the ancestor of Kaioshin from fifteen Kaioshin generations past. When released, he powers up Gohan to help him defeat Buu in exchange for being allowed to touch Bulma. Like Muten Roshi, he is a big pervert. When Buu absorbs Piccolo and Gotenks, and is too strong for Gohan to fight, Rou Dai Kaioshin gives up his life so Gokou's will be restored.

Ryan Shenron

A dragon created from the wish to resurrect Bora, Ryan Shenron is the two-star dragon of pollution. The weakest of the evil Shenron, Ryan is easily defeated by Pan. However, the power of his negative energy causes Pan and Goku to weaken quickly in battle, giving Ryan the upper hand. After throwing Pan and Goku in polluted water, he thinks he's the winner. Giru brings Goku and Pan to a clean area of the lake, which allows them to recharge their kis. Learning from their past mistakes, Goku and Pan quickly finish off Ryan, restoring the two-star ball.

Ryuu Shenron

Created from Oolong's wish for a pair of women's panties, Ryuu Shenron is the dragon of hurricanes. Ashamed of this, Ryuu wants nothing more than to kill Goku to avenge this dishonor. Keeping his true form hidden, Ryuu uses hurricane power to make himself appear as a female. He traps Goku on a cliff and showers him with ki attacks. Pan is able to discover Ryuu's weakness with the help of a seagull. His weakness is Ryuu leaves his head unguarded when attacking. Forming a kamehameha, Pan fires and killed Ryuu, restoring the six-star Dragon Ball.

Saber-toothed Tiger

A saber-toothed tiger attacks Goku and Gohan in the first episode of the anime. He later reappears when Gohan trains with Piccolo. He and Gohan eventually become friends.

Saibamen

The Saibamen are little green creatures grown from seeds. Their power level is exactly like Radditz's. Nappa brings them to Earth, and six are grown. They aren't very intelligent and are a little insane. When one is sent to fight Yamucha, he is defeated but locks Yamucha in a hold and self-destructs. Yamucha is killed in the blast. Enraged by the loss of his friend, Kuririn fires a ki blast that kills five of the six Saibamen. The remaining one tries to attack Gohan and is killed by Piccolo's mouth blast.

Saiku Oni

A teenage demon who is responsible for running the evil cleansing machine in Hades, Saiku Oni would rather listen to music than concentrate on his work. When the machine overloads, the evil overtakes him transforming Saiku into Janemba.

Saiyan/Saiyajin

A nation of bloodthirsty warriors, the Saiyans are Goku and Vegeta's race. They are an incredibly strong people compared to most of Frieza's armies, but he fears their combined power. To deal with his concern, Frieza destroys their planet and everyone on it. Only six Saiyans survive the destruction, Kakarotto (Goku), Vegeta, Nappa, Radditz, Paragus, and Brolly.

San Shenron

San Shenron is the dragon of ice and Suu-Shenron's brother. During Gokou's match with Suu Shenron, San Shenron interferes and takes on Gokou himself. After damaging Gokou's eyes, it goes in for the final blow but is punched through the gut. Gokou uses the dragon fist to finish it off. The three star Dragon Ball is restored.

Sansho

A henchman of Garlic Jr., Sansho is large and gray. He is killed by Piccolo as payback for attacking him.

Sauzaa

Sauzaa is Cooler's right hand

DBZ Character BIOs

man, and he is incredibly powerful. He outlives Cooler, and he should have been able to kill Gokou and the others in their weakened state after the Cooler battle. However, Piccolo kills him.

School Teacher
The school teacher introduces Gohan on his first day of school.

Senbe Norimaki
Senbe, the creator of Arale, has the ability to change from an unattractive, kindhearted man into a good-looking, kindhearted man for about three minutes.

Seripa

Seripa is a female Saiyajin and a member of Bardock's team. She is killed by Dodoria's men.

Shamo
Shamo is a small alien in DBZ Movie 8. Brolly captures Shamo and his people and forces them to build a kingdom to fool Vegeta. Like Vegeta, Shamo is named after his world.

Shamoseijin
The Shamoseijin are a small and weak race. Pegasus and Burori enslave and use them to build a kingdom to fool Vegeta. They want Vegeta to think the planet he is on is New Vegeta. The Shamoseijin hope to escape Burori's grasp and return home, but their hopes are shattered when Burori destroys their planet after they join forces with the Z Senshi.

Sharpener
The Sharpener is one of Gohan's classmates at Orange Star High School. He is jealous of Gohan and tries to hit him with a baseball. During the Tenkaichi Budoukai, he also tries to reveal the Great Saiyaman's identity, but he is unsuccessful.

Shen

Shen is a man God possesses so he can compete in the twenty-third Tenkaichi Budoukai without being recognized. Shen is not his real name, but the name given for the Budoukai by God/Shen, short for Shenron. God attempts to use the mafuba to trap Piccolo like he trapped his father. However, Piccolo uses a reverse mafuba and traps God instead. He is eventually released during Piccolo and Gokou's match.

Shen's son
Shen's son is proud of his father's fighting ability in the twenty-third Tenkaichi Budoukai, not realizing that his body is possessed by God.

Shenron

Shenron plays one of the most important roles in DBZGT as he is the entity that emerges when the seven Dragon Balls are gathered. When summoned, he will grant one wish to whomever wakes him. However, this changes when God merges with Piccolo and a new set of Dragon Balls are created by Dende. Dende's Shenron has the ability to grant three wishes. Unfortunately, the power of Shenron is limited to his creator.

Shishi Garyu no Ken Pau Ka
A fighter in the twenty-first Tenkaichi Budoukai, Shishi Garyu no Ken Pau Ka uses the Ken Pau as his fighting technique.

Shou
A henchman to Emperor Pilaf, Shou is a weak fighter. Like his companions, he usually relies on machines to help him fight. Shou is often blamed for farting when Pilaf lets one go, as Pilaf doesn't feel that farting is sophisticated.

Shura
A demon God who spends most of his time terrorizing a kingdom, Shura battles Goku in a tournament. When defeated, Shura ceases his attacks.

DBZ Character BIOs

Shyaoron
The younger brother of Tenron, Shyaoron blames Chinshyou for stealing his wallet in order to fight the boy's father, Chindai.

Skeleton Guard
A dead soldier, the Skeleton Guard protects the home of Uranai Baba.

Slug

A rogue Namekseijin, Lord Slug is evil and is banished from the Planet Namekseijin. Slug wants his full power returned, so he gathers the Earth's Dragon Balls and wishes for his youth. He fights an extremely angry and powered up Gokou, and when losing, unleashes his full power to become a huge monster. To allow Gokou to be freed from Slug's grasp, Piccolo rips off his own ears and calls for Gohan to whistle. Since Namekseijins have much better hearing than humans, the whistling paralyzes Slug in pain and gives Gokou enough time to create a Genki Dama and finish him.

Snow's Daddy
Snow's Daddy is forced to help the Red Ribbon Army search for the Dragon Balls.

Snow's Mommy
Snow's mother assists Goku on his trip to Muscle Tower by giving him food and clothes to survive the arctic temperatures.

South Kaio/South Kai

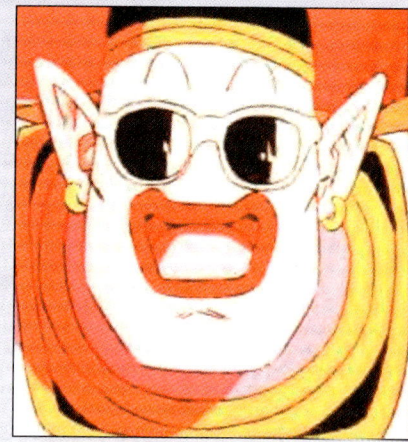

The God of the southern galaxy, South Kaio is a little arrogant. He has many students who compete in the afterlife tournament, but none are even close to Gokou or Paikuhan's strength.

South Kaioshin

The strongest of the Kaioshins, South Kaioshin is the god of the southern universe. He gives Buu a good fight, but Buu absorbs him to gain his power. Once he does this, Buu becomes very large and powerful.

Stock Farmer
Stock Farmer is the farmer who discovers Radditz's space pod in the beginning of Dragon Ball Z. He is killed after he shoots Radditz and Radditz fires the bullet back at him with his fingers.

Stote
A 3500-year-old alien, Stote protected his world from a giant meteor when he was alive. He trains on Dai Kaio's planet in hopes that one day Dai Kaio will train him.

Sugoro
Son Goku meets Sugoroku in Sugaro Space after being dropped by Kaioshin. He forces Goku to compete in a game to learn the way out. Sugoro is easily winning the game, but Goku discovers that Sugoro's son is involved in deciding the winner. Goku screams "Cheat!" and the Sugoro Space collapses. Kaioshin is able to save Sugoro and his son, along with Goku. When Goku's tail has to be pulled out immediately, Sugoro and his son help by shape shifting into a rope and tweezers.

Sugoro's son
Sugaro's son helps his father win games in Sugoro Space by transforming into dice. He and his father's scam is discovered when playing against Goku. After Goku screams, "Cheat!," the Sugoro Space collapses. With all three facing certain death, Kaioshin teleports into the space and brings them to Kaioshin Kai. When Goku's tail needs to be pulled out, he and his father help by turning into a rope and tweezers.

Suno/Snow
Suno is one of the few people who give energy to Goku for the Genki Dama when he is fighting Buu. He lives in Jingle Village.

Pojo's Unofficial ABSOLUTE Dragon Ball Z

This book is not sponsored, endorsed by, or otherwise affiliated with any of the companies or products featured in this book. This is not an official publication.

DBZ Character BIOs

Supa Man

Supa Man, an inhabitant of Penguin Village, is a short and pudgy Clark Kent-like man who changes into Supa Man by putting on his costume in a telephone booth. Instead of an "S" on his chest, he displays the Japanese symbol for "Tsu". He is only a normal human but claims to gain power from pickled plums. Blue orders him to hand over his car when they meet. He refuses and goes into a telephone booth to change. Blue crushes the booth and takes the car while Supa Man is changing.

Super Mega Cannon Sigma

The Super Mega Cannon Sigma is an extremely powerful combination of the EC3. Sigma is powerful because Giru gives him all the data on Goku's movements and techniques. However, after Goku learns Sigma's movements, he destroys him with a kamehameha.

Super One

Super One competes in the GT Tenkaichi Budoukai and makes it to the semi-finals.

Supopo Bitchi/Supopovitch

One of only two humans to become majin, Supopo Bitchi, along with his companion Yamu, is sent to the Tenkaichi Budoukai to gather energy to resurrect Majin Buu. Supopo competes against Videl, and nearly kills her. She would've died if it had not been for the senzu beans. When Gohan is fighting Kibitto, Supopo Bitchi and Yamu interrupt and suck out Gohan's ki with a device provided by Babi-Dee. Gohan would've beaten them, but Kaioshin freezes Gohan in place to allow Supopo ad Yamu to complete their mission.

Suu Shenron

Suu Shenron is created when Piccolo is wished back to life. He is the dragon of the sun and is associated with the four star dragonball. Suu Shenron challenges Gokou to a match and the two fight. When San-Shenron appears, Suu Shenron mocks him for losing honor by interfering with the match. San-Shenron, the dragon of ice, fights Gokou anyway and is killed in battle. Afterward, Gokou and Suu-Shenron continue their match. Gokou admires Suu-Shenron's sense of honor. During the fight with San Shenron, Gokou's eyes are damaged and he can no longer see well. As Suu Shenron is giving Gokou the antidote, he is attacked and nearly killed by Ii Shenron. Later, when Suu Shenron escapes the Dragon Ball, he and Gokou team up against Ii Shenron. However, when he tries to attack Ii Shenron alone, he is killed.

Taada

Taada is a henchman of Garlic Jr. who dies when he angers Gohan.

Taabo Norimaki

Taabo is the genius son of Senbe and Midori in Dr. Slump. He appears in the crossover and builds a dragon radar from scratch.

Tailor A

Tailor is hired to make clothes for General Tao. He works all night to finish the specified outfit for Tao. When he asks for his pay, Tao kills him.

Tailor B

Tailor B makes Goku a new gi after his is torn from all the battles in the twenty-first Tenkaichi Budoukai. Afterwards, he offers Goku some other clothes, but Goku declines because he doesn't like the way the others look. After getting the gi, Goku strips nude and changes in the street.

DBZ Character BIOs

Tamborine
The first child of Piccolo Daimoa after he is released from the mafuba, Tamborine is given the task of killing all the participants in the Tenkaichi Budoukai. When stealing the list, he finds Kuririn and kills him. When he confronts Gokou, he wins the fight. However, once Gokou gets some rest and something to eat, he kills Tamborine.

Tanmen
Tanmen is a little girl Goku encounters on his trip around the world.

Tao Pai Pai/General Tao
A professional assassin and a relative of the crane master, Tao Pai Pai is hired by the Red Ribbon Army to kill Gokou. During the first fight, Gokou is defeated and left for dead. However, after receiving a little training from Karin, Gokou is able to defeat Tao Pai Pai. He later returns as a cyborg, and attempts to kill an old man who is protecting his village during the Cell Game. Once confronted by Gohan, and learning of Gohan's lineage, he runs away.

Tapika
A Fighter of the west galaxy, Tapika fights Torubi in the afterlife Budoukai. He is extremely fast, even Gokou wouldn't have been able to match his speed. However, the ring is rather large, and since Tapika is short, he runs out of energy quickly and forfeits the match.

Tapion
A legendary warrior, Tapion sacrifices his freedom, along with his younger brother Minosha, to imprison the monster Hiredugarn. Once Hiredugarn is cut in half, Tapion and his brother take one half of the monster within themselves and are sealed within an oracle. They are sent to opposite ends of the universe. If Hiredugarn tries to escape, Tapion is armed with a God-made sword and an ocarina that can immobilize Hiredugarn. Once Hiredugarn is defeated, Tapion gives Trunks his sword to thank him for his encouragement and friendship.

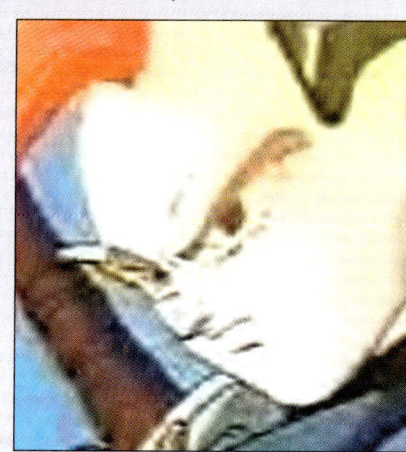

Tarles/Taurus
Physically similar in appearance to Gokou, Taurus is no blood relation to the warrior. However, they are both Saiyajin. Taurus comes to Earth to kill Gokou, believing him to be a traitor to the Saiyajin race. He also hopes to plant the Shinseiju, since Earth contains an abundant amount of life. After seeing the great power that Gohan possesses, he tries to force the boy into joining him. Despite Gokou's strength, his fight with Taurus is a draw until Taurus eats a fruit from the shinseijin. Once eaten, Taurus' power is much greater than the Saiyajin, and he almost kills him. Gokou's saving grace is the powerful Genki Dama.

Taro
Taro is seen for only a minute in the anime. He is the child of Umigame.

Tarou Soramame
Appearing in the Dr. Slump/Dragon Ball crossover, Tarou is the first son of Kurikinton who is very disobedient.

Tenron
Tenron is the martial arts master of Hyoga who intends to kill Chendai.

Tien/Tenshinhan

The bodyguard of Chaozu, Tenshinhan plays a minor role, but an important one, in the three Dragon Ball series. At first, he is Gokou's enemy, like the other characters, and the prize student of the crane master. After realizing his master is evil, Tenshinhan leaves the crane school and joins Muten Roshi. Ten's greatest attacks, and those that have helped the Z Senshi, are the taiyoken and kikoho. He is also the first to perform the multiple forms technique.

Titan's Manager
The manager of the baseball team Yamcha plays on, he tries to bribe Yamcha into hitting a homerun.

Toma
A member of Bardock's team and Bardock's best friend, Toma is nearly killed by Dodoria. He learns of Furiza's plans to double

DBZ Character BIOs

cross the Saiyajin. When Bardock finds him on Planet Meet, Toma is dying. He tells Bardock about Furiza's plans and, with his final words, begs Bardock to gather all the Saiyajin to kill Furiza.

Tooro
The last surviving Kanassan, Tooro curses Bardock with the ability to see the future by hitting him in the neck. When he tells Bardock about the curse and laughs at him, Bardock kills him.

Tooth-Ached Giant
When the giant bites into an apple containing a black star Dragon Ball, the Dragon Ball sticks in his tooth and makes his cavity ache. Goku flies into the giant's mouth and fires a kamehameha, knocking out the tooth and the Dragon Ball. The giant is later seen giving Goku his energy, when Goku creates the mega Genki Dama during his fight with Ii Shenron.

Tori
A white bird that mistakes a Dragon Ball for one of its eggs, Tori and the Dragon Ball are eaten by a Pteradon.

Torubi
A fighter of the south galaxy, Torubi is a bug-like alien who fights against Tapika in the first round and wins. In the finals, his opponent is Paikuhan, and Torubi loses.

Totepo
A member of Bardock's group, Totepo is very large and is constantly eating. Totepo is killed when Dodoria and his men attack him.

Toto Family
The Totos are a family of Pterodactyls that Gohan plays with as a child. When Chibi Toto is kidnapped by a circus owner who wants to display him for money, Mother and Father Toto wreak havoc in Satan City looking for him. Without much choice, Gohan, as the Great Saiyaman, punches the father out. After Gohan threatens the circus owner, he gives up Chibi and promises never to kidnap again.

Tournament Chairman
The Tournament Chairman is the organizer of the twenty-first Tenkaichi Budoukai. He looks like a dog.

Tournament Priest Charter
The Tournament Priest Charter is the Monk of the Tenkaichi Budoukai. He writes the names of each opponent on a board for their specified match.

Troublemaker A and B
The troublemakers force everyone in Chazke Village to make payments to build a safe home to escape from Cell.

Trunks
The son of Vegeta and Bulma, Trunks is best friends with Gokou's second child, Goten. Because he is a year older and a little stronger than Goten, he is able to transform into a Super Saiyajin. This surprises and angers Vegeta, as it did for Gohan with Goten. Determined to avenge his father's death, Trunks attempts to master the fusion technique and defeat Buu. In Dragon Ball GT, Trunks neglects his work and training because he thinks they are too boring. However, when the black star Dragon Balls must be found, he reluctantly joins Gokou in the search.

Trunks' employees
Trunks' employees are a bunch of ditzy girls who work at Capsule Corporation. They stop their work whenever Trunks walks by to grope him and critique his appearance.

Trunks' secretary
In Dragon Ball GT, Trunks' secretary at Capsule Corporation comes into his office and tells him his schedule for the day. Bored by the schedule, Trunks sneaks out the window and flies away.

Tsufurujin
A race of aliens who originally occupy planet Vegeta, the Tsufurujin peacefully coexist with the Saiyans after arriving on the planet. However, the Saiyan's thirst for blood and fighting causes them to start a war that results

Z Character BIOs

in the near extinction of the Tsufurujin race. Only two survive – Dr. Raichii and the DNA of the king, who later becomes Bebi.

Tsuno
A Namekian elder of a village attacked by Vegeta, he and his villagers are killed when they refuse to help Vegeta find the Dragon Balls.

Tsururin Tsun
Appearing in the Dr. Slump/Dragon Ball crossover, Tsururin is Tsukutsun's little sister.

Tsuruten Tsun
She appears in the Dr. Slump/Dragon Ball crossover.

Tsutsutsunodano Teiyuugoutsururin
Appearing in the Dr. Slump/Dragon Ball crossover, she is the mother of Tsukutsun.

TV Announcer

The TV announcer declares the world will be over when Ii Shenron covers it with his negative energy.

Ubu/Uub
The reincarnation of Majin Buu, Uub (pronounced Ubu), is Gokou's first student. Incredibly strong, he tries to defeat Bebi to avenge Gokou's death. After

being defeated, he reemerges with Mr. Buu and fights Bebi again, this time with much more power.

Udo
A giant who fought against Gohan in the movie nine tournament, Udo is defeated with one hit.

Ueberi
A competitor in the Kid's Division of the twenty-fifth Tenkaichi Budoukai, Ueberi loses when he starts crying.

Ugly/Oguri
A fat and ugly pitcher on the opposing team playing Yamcha's Titans, he purposely hits people with the ball.

Ultimate Crab
Searching for the Dragon Ball she lost, Bulma meets a gigantic crab who carries a Dragon Ball on her back. After saving the crab's eggs, the crab rewards Bulma with the Dragon Ball. After making her way to the surface, Blueberry and Raspberry force Bulma to take them to the other Dragon Balls she says are still in the ocean. Bulma tricks them into grabbing the crab's eggs by saying they are Dragon Balls. The crab retaliates and kills Freiza's two henchmen.

Umigame
Muten Roshi's sea turtle, Umigame tries to stop Roshi from girl watching (and touching).

Upa

The son of Bora, Upa helps his father protect Karin Tower and hopes to be as strong as his father when he grows up. Upa also helps defeat one of Uranai Baba's men, when Gokou and the others ask for his help to find the Dragon Balls. When Kuririn first meets Upa, he thinks Upa is a girl and kind of cute. After learning Upa is a boy, Kuririn is disappointed.

Uu Shenron
A dragon of the five-star Dragon Ball, Uu Shenron is the dragon of electricity. Though small, he has the ability to fuse together small jelly-like monsters of his own creation to form a gigantic version of himself. In this form, he beats Goku and Pan, but when it starts to rain, his power is weakened and his fused jelly-like monsters explode. Once defeated, he surrenders and tells Pan she can have the Dragon Ball. He uses this as a trick, and is about to swallow her, when Goku fires a kamehameha. He kills Uu and restores the five-star ball.

DBZ Character BIOs

Vegeta

The proud prince of the planet with the same name, Vegeta travels to Earth after hearing Radditz's message about the Dragon Balls. He is one of the most powerful fighters in the universe and can't stand that a low soldier like Kakarotto (Gokou) challenges him. After losing to Gokou, Vegeta returns to Furiza

planet #79 to recover. After he learns that Furiza has left for Planet Nameksei, Vegeta rushes there to beat Furiza to the Dragon Balls. He spends his time on Nameksei waiting for a chance to steal the Dragon Balls. After being defeated by Zarbon, Vegeta is sent to a healing capsule so Furiza can interrogate him and find where he hid the Dragon Ball. After recovering, Vegeta escapes the ship with five Dragon Balls. However, when the Ginyu Tokusentai arrived, Vegeta is nearly killed, and all the Dragon Balls are taken. Gokou arrives and gives him a senzu bean, and Vegeta kills almost all the Ginyu Tokusentai. Vegeta never gets his wish for immortality, but during the Android/Cell Saga, he has a child with Bulma and begins to behave a lot. During the Buu fight, Vegeta sacrifices his life thinking that the explosion he creates will kill Buu. After Buu becomes too powerful for anyone left alive on Earth to handle, Vegeta is given his day back on Earth by Enma to fight Buu. He agrees, though he knows he doesn't stand a chance. At first he refuses to fuse with Gokou, but concedes when he sees there is no other way of winning. Once on Kaioshin's planet, Vegeta uses the Nameksei Dragon Balls to restore the Earth and all who died after the Tenkaichi Budoukai began, except for the truly evil. As proof that Vegeta is no longer the bloodthirsty Saiyajin, he also is restored to life by Porunga. Vegeta always wanted to face Gokou again to decide who was stronger, even in Dragon Ball GT. He has two children with Bulma: Trunks and Bra.

Vegeta Jr.

Vegeta Jr., who only makes one appearance in the three series, is a third-generation descendant of Vegeta. His grandparents are unknown, though his mother looks exactly like Bulma. He fights Goku Jr. in the Tenkaichi Budoukai that occurs 100 years after DBGT.

Vegetto

A fused warrior, Vegetto is the combination of Gokou and Vegeta. He is believed to be the most powerful character in the Z series. His fusion is made possible using the potera earrings given to Gokou and Vegeta by Rou Dai Kaioshin. The original plan is for Gokou to fuse with Gohan, but after Gohan is absorbed by Buu, it is impossible.

Veku

A fusion of Goku and Vegeta in DBZ Movie 12, it fails because Vegeta's index finger was not extended. Veku is fat and extremely weak. His only attack appears to be a barrage of farts he lets out whenever he's hit. His short battle with Janemba is funny in that he gets punched around like a punching bag, and when he trips, he skids about 100 feet. He un-fuses right before being finished off by Janemba.

Videl

The daughter of Mr. Satan, Videl is an exceptional fighter for a human. She is stronger than her father, but she doesn't know it at first. When she figures out that Gohan is the Great Saiyaman, she gives him an ultimatum to either join the Tenkaichi Boudukai or she will reveal his identity. She also forces Gohan to teach her to fly. She and Gohan eventually marry and have a daughter named Pan.

Character BIOs

Videl's Mom
The only thing known about Videl's mom is that she died shortly after giving birth to Videl. She is never shown in the series.

Vinegar
Vinegar is a henchman of Garlic Jr. Gohan kills him when he attempts to prevent Gohan from saving Kuririn.

Violet Taisa
Violet is the only female to have a high rank in the Red Ribbon Army. She provides Red with the five star Dragon Ball.

Warrior Type Namekian
Appearing only in the anime, these warriors attempt to fight Frieza when Guru's home is attacked. The tyrant kills easily kills them all.

West Kaio/West Kai

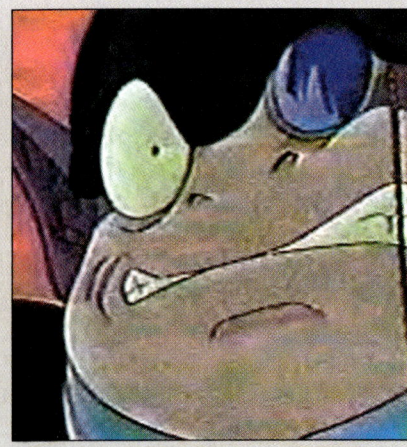

The Kaio of the western galaxy, West Kaiosama is the teacher of Paikuhan, a fighter of heaven who is greater than Cell. He and North Kaio seem to have a rivalry, and it is from his suggestion that the afterlife tournament is staged to commemorate the death of North Kaio.

West Kaioshin

The Kaioshin of the western universe, West Kaioshin is the only female Kaioshin. She is killed by Majin Buu.

Western Capitol Punk
When Goku is looking for Bulma's house, this thief attempts to steal his 100,000 zeni. Goku beats him up.

Western Capitol Woman
When Goku asks the West Capitol Woman where Bulma's house is, she points out a police officer who can help him find Bulma. To thank the Woman for her help, Goku gives her 100,000 zeni.

Woman Newscaster
The anchorwoman who broadcasts Cell's actions.

Yadrottojin
A race of aliens Son Gokou meets after defeating Furiza, the Yadrottojin are weak except they possess unique and powerful techniques. They teach Gokou souki idou (instantaneous movement). They would have been completely destroyed, had the Ginyu Tokusentai not been defeated on Planet Nameksei.

Yajirobe

A fat warrior, Yajirobe is introduced after Tamborine beats Gokou. Originally he dislikes Gokou, because Gokou eats his lunch. He befriends him after Gokou promises him food if he shows him how to get to Karin Tower. Yajirobe doesn't have a large role in Dragon Ball Z, and is usually either the messenger of God or the bearer of Karin's senzu beans. He is quite cowardly, but will pull through if absolutely necessary.

Yakon
Yakon is the second fighter that Gokou and the others face on Babi-Dee's ship. He is from a world of complete darkness. During the fight, he and the others are sent by Babi-Dee's magic to fight on his planet. To cope with

DBZ Character BIOs

the darkness, Gokou goes Super Saiyajin and creates his own light. Unaware that he eats light, Yakon sucks Gokou's Super Saiyajin form away from him. Gokou decides to give Yakon exactly what he wants, and provides plenty of Super Saiyajin light. Yakon's body absorbs so much light that he explodes.

Yamu

One of only two humans to become majin, Yam is more calm and sane than his companion, Supopo Bitchi. He is sent to the Tenkaichi Budoukai to gather energy to resurrect Majin Buu. Once he gets Gohan's ki and brings it to Babi-Dee, he is no longer needed and Puipui kills him.

Yamcha/Yamucha

Originally a bandit, Yamucha, with the help of his friend Puar, rob anyone who passes through his home. When he meets Gokou and the others, he decides to join them in their search for the Dragon Balls. He wants to make a wish of his own. At first, Yamucha is afraid of Buruma and girls in general. Over time, he overcomes his fear and dates Buruma for a while. Yamucha stops training after fighting the androids, but he is still an exceptional fighter.

Yaochyun

Goku meets Yaochyn in the Goro Goro Mountains when he is training with Mr. Popo. Goku mistakes Yaochyun as the man who is supposed to teach him the "Quiet Like the Sky." Once he discovers that Yaochyun isn't right person, he leaves.

Yellow Taisa's Junior Officer

The Junior Officer is one of the officers of Yellow Taisa. He is killed by Bora.

Young Namekians

Appearing only in the anime, the three Namekians protect Muuri and his village by fighting Frieza's men. They are stronger than the henchmen, and are winning, when Dodoria steps in. Without much effort, Dodoria kills all three.

Yuzukaa

As Goku's driving instructor, Yuzukaa deals with trying to teach Goku to drive. It almost kills him. When he witnesses Goku and Piccolo save a school bus from falling off a cliff, he tells Goku he doesn't need a license with all his power.

Zaakuro

Zaakuro is one of the two aliens Bulma, Gohan, and Krillin meet when they crash-land on the false Planet Namek. He disguises himself as a Namekian and attempts to trick Bulma and the others to search for the Dragon Balls. When he thinks Gohan and Krillin are dead, Zaakuro forces Bulma to tell him how to open the ship so he can escape the dead planet. However, Gohan and Krillin survive and knock him out. The Z Warriors escape, and leave Zaakuro behind.

Zangya

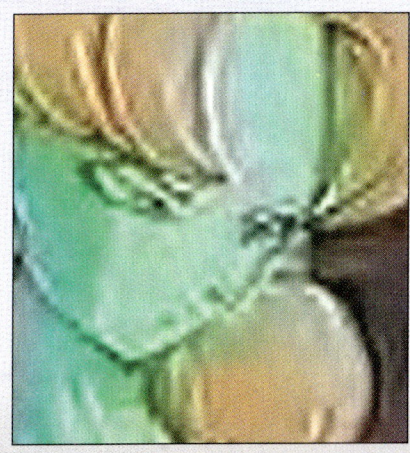

One of Bojack's henchman, Zangya's past is never revealed. She defeats Kuririn and is killed by Bojack after Gohan kills Bido and Bujin.

Zarbon

Zarbon is Freezer's right hand man. He is very strong and has the ability to transform into a

Character BIOs

...deous monster when overpowered. When fighting Vegeta, he is defeated because he doesn't know of Vegeta's ability to gain strength after every battle.

Zeeun
A minion of Slug, Zeeun is killed for calling Slug old.

Zeshin
Zeshin is one of the leaders of the orphans on the stealth-like spaceship that Kuririn and the others accidentally board on their way to Namekssei.

Zod
Zod is a child living in a village being attacked by Ryuu Shenron. He is the only person in the village who sees the evil doings of Ryuu when others praise him as God. Because of Ryuu's hurricanes, the sea gulls are injured and malnourished as all the fish blown ashore are taken by the villagers. Trying to care for the hurt sea gulls, Zod tells Goku and Pan what is happening in his village. Thanks to the sea gull Zod cares for in the episode, Pan is able to discover Ryuu's weakness and defeats the evil dragon.

Zod's father
A fisherman, Zod's father becomes a drunk and lazy after Ryuu Shenron appears. Ryuu's hurricanes allow him to catch fish without work. When Pan and Goku defeat Ryuu Shenron, he realizes the price he was paying by relying on Ryuu. He goes back to work and rekindles his relationship with his son.

Zorudo
Zorudo is a henchman of Garlic Jr. and is fairly weak. He is killed when he angers Gohan.

ZTV's Male Announcer
The only TV reporter who tries to speak to Cell before the Cell Game. He is scared out of his mind the entire time.

Zunama
Zunama, a giant eel-like alien, causes earthquakes when he shakes his antennas. He threatens the people of a small village and tells them if they don't do as he commands, he will create an earthquake. He demands to be married to Lenne. When Goku and the others learn of his existence and foul actions, Trunks pretends to be a girl to replace Lenne. The plan is to cut off Zunama's antennas when he least expects it. They later learn that Zunama only predicts earthquakes with his antennas, not cause them. Apologizing for all the trouble he caused, Zunama ends up helping the people of the planet, predicting earthquakes and warning the villagers.